The New Political Sociology

The New Political Sociology

Power, Ideology and Identity in an Age of Complexity

Graham Taylor
University of the West of England, UK

First published 2010 by
PALGRAVE MACMILLAN

Palgrave Macmillan in the UK is an imprint of Macmillan Publishers Limited, registered in England, company number 785998, of Houndmills, Basingstoke, Hampshire RG21 6XS.

Palgrave Macmillan in the US is a division of St Martin's Press LLC, 175 Fifth Avenue, New York, NY 10010.

Palgrave Macmillan is the global academic imprint of the above companies and has companies and representatives throughout the world.

Palgrave® and Macmillan® are registered trademarks in the United States, the United Kingdom, Europe and other countries.

ISBN-13: 978-0-230-57332-1   hardback
ISBN-13: 978-0-230-57333-8   paperback

This book is printed on paper suitable for recycling and made from fully managed and sustained forest sources. Logging, pulping and manufacturing processes are expected to conform to the environmental regulations of the country of origin.

A catalogue record for this book is available from the British Library.

A catalogue record for this book is available from the Library of Congress.

10   9   8   7   6   5   4   3   2   1
19   18   17   16   15   14   13   12   11   10

Printed and bound in Great Britain by
CPI Antony Rowe, Chippenham and Eastbourne

Contents

Acknowledgements

This book developed as a result of my experience of teaching political sociology at the University of the West of England. I am grateful for the discussions I have had over the years with students taking the modules *States and Societies* and the *Sociology of Power and Social Change*. I acknowledge the assistance of a period of study leave granted by the Department of Sociology and Criminology at the University of the West of England to enable this book to be researched and written. I am also grateful to colleagues for the opportunity to discuss the issues covered in this book, including Andy Mathers, Gunter Walzenbach and in particular Jörg Dürrschmidt whose input on issues around globalization and social change has been invaluable. I am grateful for the enthusiastic support of Philippa Grand at Palgrave Macmillan throughout this project and her patience when other commitments have resulted in missed deadlines. The feedback and comments of an anonymous reviewer on an earlier draft of this book were extremely helpful and constructive and I would like to acknowledge the great help and assistance these have been in the preparation of the final draft. Finally I am indebted to my wife Hilary for her fortitude and forbearance in the year that it has taken to write this book.

Abbreviations

AGM	alternative globalization movement
ANT	actor network theory
APEC	Asia-Pacific Economic Cooperation
ASEAN	Association of Southeast Asian Nations
ATTAC	Action pour la Taxation des Transactions Financières pour l'Aide aux Citoyens
BINGO	business international non-governmental organization
CARICOM	Caribbean Community
CCT	compulsory competitive tendering
CCTV	closed-circuit television
CNN	Cable News Network
ECJ	European Court of Justice
EIF	European industry federation
ETUC	European Trade Union Confederation
EU	European Union
EZLN	Zapatistas National Liberation Army
FIFA	Fédération Internationale de Football Association
FTAA	Free Trade Area of the Americas
GCS	global civil society
GJM	global justice movement
GONGO	government-operated non-governmental organization
GPI	global positioning instrument
GRINGO	government run and initiated NGO
ICT	information and communications technology
IGO	international governmental organization
IMF	International Monetary Fund
INGO	international non-governmental organization
KWS	Keynesian Welfare State
MLG	multi-level governance
MNC	multinational corporation
NAFTA	North American Free Trade Agreement
NATO	North Atlantic Treaty Organization
NGO	non-governmental organization
NSM	new social movement
RMT	resource mobilization theory
TNC	transnational corporation

UN	United Nations
UNESCO	United Nations Educational, Scientific and Cultural Organization
UNICE	Union des Industries de la Communauté européenne (renamed BusinessEurope in 2007)
UNICEF	United Nations Children's Fund
WHO	World Health Organization
WSF	World Social Forum
WTO	World Trade Organization

1
Introduction: The Contours of Social and Political Complexity

Reflecting back to the mid-twentieth century, the social and political world appeared rather uncomplicated. The world was neatly divided into two competing ideological power blocs based on the USA and the USSR. The onward march of modernity seemed inexorable and the dynamic of modernization and the application of scientific and technological rationality seemed ubiquitous throughout the developed and developing world. The nation state had risen like an institutional colossus to dominate the age. Social and political power were neatly bifurcated between the domestic level, where the functions of the state had expanded from the regulation of law and the economy to the administration of welfare and 'public goods', to the international level, where power resided in geopolitical and military force. Social and political identities were aligned through the articulation of Enlightenment ideas in specific national contexts and this provided the basis for a series of fixed socio-political identities based on the categories of the individual, class and nation and institutionalized in the form of liberal democratic, social democratic and state socialist regimes. In the West, the development and expansion of the welfare state had served to expand citizenship beyond the 'civil' and 'political' rights and obligations established in the eighteenth and nineteenth centuries to rights and obligations around social welfare. In the developing world, postcolonial regimes were set firmly on a trajectory of institutional 'modernization' on the basis of blueprints provided by either the USA or USSR. Standing astride these developments was the principal social and political movement of the modern age – the labour or workers' movement. The struggle and mobilization of labour was a key catalyst in the development and form of the nation state, the expansion of citizenship and the social and cultural configuration of civil society or the

1

'public sphere'. The above picture is, of course, a gross oversimplification of what in reality was a far more complex modern world in the post-war era, but it serves to remind us how complex the world is today.

The ideological battle between East and West ended in 1989, with the collapse of the USSR and the fall of the Berlin Wall. In the East, state socialism fractured into a plethora of religious and ethnic nationalisms alongside various forms of IMF-inspired 'turbo-capitalism'. In China, the official Marxist-Leninist state ideology persists in the context of a dynamic export-led market economy. In the West, the euphoric victory cries of neo-liberal ideology proved to be short-lived and it has subsequently been challenged both by a reformist 'third way' that has attempted to develop political programmes beyond the ideologies of socialism and free market capitalism and a range of fundamentalist and revolutionary movements that have challenged the core elements of liberal ideology. The institutional dynamics of modernity remain intact and dominant, but the dominance of scientific rationality has become increasingly questioned and challenged as the negative ecological, economic and social side effects of modern progress and development have become apparent. Social and political power is increasingly located outside and beyond the nation state and the nation state system. Large transnational corporations (TNCs) have developed power as a result of their ability to escape the jurisdiction of nation states. The sovereignty of state power has been 'pooled' at the transnational level in the form of organizations such as the European Union (EU) and 'shared' at the national level with private and third-sector agencies in networked forms of 'governance'. The dynamics of class and nation have become increasingly decentred as markers of identity as a result of the decentring and marginalization of the nation state and the emergence of new forms of identity politics. The crisis of the modern nation state has resulted in the development of a range of cultural and ethnic subnationalisms such as Scottish nationalism in the UK and Québécois nationalism in Canada. The trajectory of development has been interrupted in the developing world. In many cases, nation states have imploded and the resulting 'wild zones' have become breeding grounds for intense political violence, genocide and terrorism. Class identities have been decentred across the developed world as a result of deindustrialization and the numerical decline of the working class and the growing importance of new forms of identity politics based on gender, sexuality, 'race' and the environment. These developments are linked to the growing disarticulation between the nation state and citizenship, as social rights have become decoupled from the enlightenment-inspired universalism associated with the nation state. Groups representing gays and lesbians or indigenous peoples have claimed rights specific to their particular situation, while the growth in international migration has resulted in a range of international treaties that have established social and political rights beyond the nation state. In the context of these developments, deliberation and debate on social and political issues and problems have become increasingly pluralistic and transnational in character and this has transformed the character of civil society or the public sphere.

The social and political world has thus been fundamentally transformed over the past three decades. The processes of transformation have undermined many of the fixed concepts and categories of the modern era, including the nature of social and political power and its connections with the nation state; the form and function of the nation state and its important role in the 'bounding' of power, ideology and identity; the nature of social and political identity and its association with 'class' and 'nation'; the decline of the labour movement and the growing importance of 'new' social movements; the decline of a stable world order and the emergence of new world 'disorder' marked by the threat of political violence and terrorism; the declining importance of national citizenship and the development of social and political rights below and beyond the nation state; and the recomposition of civil society and the public sphere on the basis of a plurality of increasingly transnational social actors. These developments have challenged in a fundamental way the concepts, categories and theories of modern political sociology and constitute the subject matter of the substantive chapters of this book. Over the past three decades the discipline of sociology has taken a number of 'turns' as a result of both the inability of modern sociology to provide adequate explanations for intense processes of social change and social transformation and, partly as a consequence, an increasing sense of disillusionment with the modernist intellectual paradigm. The principal conceptual focus of this book is how these turns can be applied to the sub-discipline of political sociology in order to explore and explain the intense processes of social and political change outlined above. The book explores the impact of what seem to be the three most important 'turns' that sociology has taken over the past three decades: the 'cultural' or 'postmodern' turn, the 'global' turn and the 'complexity' turn.

The 'cultural', 'global' and 'complexity' turns are not coherent and consistent intellectual paradigms, but rather a shorthand way of describing a changing emphasis or set of priorities *vis-à-vis* modern sociology. In each of the substantive chapters that follow, I explore how these 'turns' have transformed the research agenda of political sociology. The 'cultural turn' has focused attention on the social construction of social and political phenomena and the crisis and decomposition of modern social institutions and modes of sociological enquiry. With regard to political sociology, this has been marked by a declining focus on class and social and political structures towards a focus on identity and social action. This has been a necessary corrective to the positivism and objectivism of modern political sociology and has served to highlight the politics of difference and diversity in contemporary society. There remains an ongoing dispute, however, with regard to whether the trends and tendencies highlighted by the 'cultural turn' are occurring within or beyond modernity. Is postmodernism a social movement or cultural aesthetic within modernity or a set of institutions and practices that have developed following the crisis and thorough transformation of modernity? In this book, I take the former position in order to highlight the ambiguous forms of political structure and action which emerge from the development of postmodern political forms within modern society. The 'global turn' has focused attention on the increasing importance of transnational processes and connections in the development and form of socio-political institutions and identities. The 'global turn' has usefully highlighted the limits of 'nation state sociology' at a time when political issues and problems are clearly the result of dynamics and developments beyond the national level. There remains an ongoing dispute, however, regarding the relationship between globalization and modernity. Does globalization result in the globalization of modernity or a more fundamental transformation of modernity that results in the development of a global society with distinctively postmodern dynamics and features? In this book, I reject both positions in favour of an argument that we currently inhabit a society in transition that is between modernity and an undefined and still to be revealed social and political order beyond the nation state. On the basis of this proposition, I highlight the ambiguous and 'liminal' social and political forms that dominate an 'in-between' society. The 'complexity turn' is an attempt to develop tools and concepts that are relevant for the analysis of a post-Newtonian social universe. The 'turn' has usefully questioned many of the assumptions underpinning modern social science, particularly explanations of social and political phenomena premised on linear models of causality. There remains, however, an ongoing dispute as to whether this involves the uncritical application of models developed within theoretical physics and mathematics to social phenomena or the 'complexification' of existing sociological theories and concepts in order to reveal the complex disjunctions of a society in transition. In this book, I take the latter position in order to stress the complex and often asymmetric relationships between ambiguous and hybrid social and political forms in contemporary society.

Power, ideology and identity in an age of complexity

The key objective of this book is to explore how manifestations of power, ideology and identity can be effectively understood and analysed in a world that is increasingly complex and difficult to comprehend. In Chapter 2, I explore the main paradigms and perspectives in modern political sociology and demonstrate how these paradigms and perspectives have been marginalized and, to a large degree, superseded by the theoretical and conceptual developments associated with the 'cultural', 'global' and 'complexity' turns. The principal level of analysis with regard to modern political sociology was at the level of the nation state. While there were enduring disagreements and debates between 'society-centred' and 'state-centred' analyses and between approaches focused on the underlying conflictual or consensual nature of modern state and society, there was, nonetheless, broad agreement that these questions should be explored within the context of the territorially defined boundaries of the nation state. The rapid social change that has marked recent decades and the conceptual and analytical developments associated with the 'cultural', 'global' and 'complexity' turns have served to undermine this assumption. In this chapter, I outline the main developments associated with these 'turns'. The 'cultural turn' was instrumental in deconstructing the apparent universalism of the nation state and the top-down conceptualization of power that dominated modern political sociology. The 'global turn' has served to de-territorialize the analysis of power, ideology and identity and resulted in attempts to explore the extent to which social and political relations have been transposed from the national level to the 'sub-national' and 'transnational' levels. The 'complexity turn' has questioned linear models of social and political change and development, and the asymmetric and often unexpected consequences that result from the unstable and shifting connections between social and political systems in a context of global complexity. The chapter concludes with the argument that while the 'cultural', 'global' and 'complexity' turns have provided valuable insights into the restructuring of social and political life in recent decades, each of these 'turns' overemphasizes the lack of continuity with social and political modernity. In this context,

I argue that social and political relations have only been partially dis-embedded and de-territorialized and highlight how enduring relation-ships of superiority and subordination generate ambiguous and liminal forms of power, ideology and identity.

In Chapter 3, there is analysis of the formulations of social power that marked the paradigm of modern political sociology and a critical review of the ways in which the analysis of power has been transformed by the 'cultural', 'global' and 'complexity' turns. In modern political sociology, the analysis of power was closely related to the authority and legitimacy of the nation state. Power was a top-down, episodic, objective and quan-tifiable phenomenon that enabled social and political actors to engage in either 'negative sum' or 'positive sum' power games. In more radical formulations, power was equated with ideology in order to suggest that the exercise of power involved the distortion of consciousness and that human freedom and autonomy could only be established in a society devoid of power. These assumptions and propositions have been chal-lenged by the 'cultural', 'global' and 'complexity' turns in political socio-logy and, in this chapter, I explore the ways in which these 'turns' have resulted in the reformulation of sociological theories of power. The 'cul-tural turn' is associated above all with the work of Michel Foucault, whose work on the development and nature of power in modern society was instrumental in shifting the analysis of power away from power as an objective and episodic phenomenon towards an understanding of power as a dispositional and bottom-up phenomenon that was insepar-able from individual subjectivity and identity. In this context, power was inescapable and unavoidable owing to the 'panoptical' nature of modern society and could often have a constitutive as well as a negative or dominating presence in society. The 'global turn' has highlighted how the processes of globalization have resulted in the de-territorialization of power and the reconstitution of power in networks and systems beyond the level of the nation state. In the work of theorists such as Manuel Castells this is explored in relation to the development of information and communications technology (ICT) and the ways in which the result-ing informational economy and networked society have dis-embedded power from geographically defined space to a 'space of flows' defined by 'real virtuality'. The 'complexity turn' has taken the metaphor of 'flow' further to suggest that in a context of global complexity, power takes on a 'post-panoptical' form defined by its ability to escape and avoid con-frontation with manifestations of 'anti' or 'counter-power'. I conclude the chapter with the argument that while the 'cultural', 'global' and 'complexity' turns have provided a range of valuable insights that have provided a useful corrective to one-sided, modernist conceptualizations of power, there is nonetheless a tendency to downplay the enduring existence of modern or episodic power alongside the postmodern or dispositional forms of power explored by these various 'turns'. In conclusion, I establish the case for analysing contemporary social power as an ambiguous force. This ambiguity is a product of the contradictory coexistence of modern and postmodern forms of power and the complexity that results from the ways in which these contradictory forms of power are experienced or lived by social actors in their everyday lives.

In Chapter 4, there is an exploration of the development and form of the modern nation state. In modern political sociology, the power of the nation state was analysed either in terms of the monopoly of state institutions over the administrative and physical means of coercion in modern society or in terms of the alignment of state institutions with powerful elite interests in civil society. In both models, the state was socially and culturally 'centred' and territorially 'bounded' in ways that articulated and aligned the relationship between power and identity through the dynamics of class and nation. This model of institutionalized and bounded social and political power has been progressively challenged by developments associated with the 'cultural', 'global' and 'complexity' turns and, in this chapter, I explore critically the main developments and departures established by these 'turns' in political sociology. The nation state was already 'decentred', partially by the analytical shift within political science from a model of public policy formulation based on unitary, centralized government to one based on a process of decentralized, pluralized governance; but this decentring has been taken further by the 'cultural turn' in political sociology. The 'cultural turn' has served to deconstruct the appearance of the state as a centralized institutional power either by exposing its virtual or hyperreal form or by uncovering the everyday forms of domination and subordination underpinning its 'effect'. The 'global turn' has focused on the de-territorialization of state power and the recomposition of the state form in response to the dynamics associated with globalization. The focus here is on the increasingly important role of the state as a key node or hub of an expanding network of global governance. The 'complexity turn' has conceptualized the state as an 'island of order' within a 'sea of disorder' in order to stress the increasingly important 'gamekeeper' role of the state in controlling unpredictable global 'flows' of people, money, information and media images. I conclude the chapter with the argument that while the 'cultural', 'global' and 'complexity' turns usefully highlight an important trend towards the decentring and de-territorialization of state power, the transformation of the modern state remains an incomplete project. In this context, the contemporary world is dominated by ambiguous and liminal forms of institutionalized political power that defy neat categorization as 'modern' or 'postmodern', 'national' or 'global'.

In Chapter 5, there is an exploration of modern political-cultural identity. In modern political sociology, the dominant approach to the question of identity was to consider notions of 'being', 'belonging' and 'becoming' in the context of the relationship between the 'self' and the institutional structures of modernity. The key building blocks of political-cultural identity were the nation state and citizenship, the modern economy and divisions based on social class. The 'cultural', 'global' and 'complexity' turns have resulted in a serious challenge to this model of political-cultural identity. The 'cultural turn' has focused on how the crisis and decomposition of modernity has resulted in the decentring of the fixed and stable identities of the modern era and the development of more fluid, fragmented and multiple sources of social and political identity associated with postmodern culture and society. The 'global turn' has focused on the de-territorialization of political-cultural identity and the ways in which social and political identities are formed in the context of the flows of people, money, technology, media images and political ideas that together constitute the global cultural economy. The focus is on the 'disjunctions' between these flows and the ways in which this results in the generation of complex identities which inhabit the space between the local and the global. This theme has also been explored within the 'complexity turn' which has focused on the complex identities created by the interplay between the dynamics of globalization and localization that together form the complex dynamic of 'glocalization'. The dynamic of 'glocalization' has been presented as a 'strange attractor' that draws diverse systems of meaning and networks of action into its sphere of influence and generates unstable and constantly evolving forms of complex identity. I conclude the chapter with the argument that while the 'cultural', 'global' and 'complexity' turns have provided genuine insights into the changing forms of political-cultural identity in contemporary society, there has been a tendency to downplay important continuities with the era of modernity and the ways in which new forms of political-cultural identity have developed within and against the institutional dynamics of an intensified or 'hyper' modernity. This has resulted in forms of postmodern politics developing within modern society and in the development of the highly ambiguous or liminal forms of social and political identity that mark the contemporary world.

In Chapter 6, there is an exploration of the development and form of social movements in modern society. Modern political sociology focused on social movements as either class-based social actors that mobilized in order to realize social transformation or reform or as an aggregate of individual rational actors who engaged in collective action on the basis of individual cost-benefit decisions. These diverse paradigms shared the perspective that social movements were objective social phenomena that pursued instrumental forms of action through permanent and hierarchical organizations in order to secure material benefits against economic corporations or the nation state. These assumptions have been seriously challenged by the 'cultural', 'global' and 'complexity' turns in political sociology. The 'cultural turn' has focused on how the crisis and decomposition of modernity has resulted in a shift in the orientation and form of social movements. The 'old' social movement represented by the paradigm case of the labour or workers movement has given way to a range of 'new' social movements based on issues such as gender, sexuality, 'race' and the environment that tend to be non-instrumental, non-hierarchical and often hidden or 'latent' in the form of alternative identities and lifestyles. In contrast to the labour movement, new social movements demand cultural autonomy in civil society rather than seeking an institutional engagement with the state. The 'global turn' has focused on how the dynamics of globalization have further decentred the nation state as an arena in which social movements mobilize. The focus has been on how these dynamics shift social movement activity from the national to the local and global levels. With regard to mobilization at the global level, there has been a particular concern to explore how the development and deployment of ICT have enabled oppositional social movements to develop forms of transnational resistance to the networked forms of transnational power associated with neo-liberal globalism. The 'complexity turn' has applied the analytical tools of complexity theory to the analysis of social movements in order to present them as complex networks or 'fluids' that 'swarm' the planet and produce unexpected and often asymmetrical challenges to dominant power networks. While the 'cultural', 'global' and 'complexity' turns have produced a range of useful and insightful observations on the changing form of social movement organization, there is a tendency to downplay important continuities with social and political modernity. I develop the argument that contemporary social movements increasingly take the form of postmodern forms of political mobilization within a hypermodern global system and I demonstrate how this leads to the generation of new social spaces and subjectivities that are highly ambiguous and liminal in form.

In Chapter 7, there is an exploration of political violence and terrorism in modern society. Modern political sociology tended to analyse the phenomena of violence and terror as an objective manifestation of coercive force directed by or against the nation state. This was evident in both the analysis of state violence in classical Marxist accounts of primitive capital accumulation and in Weber's definition of the nation state in terms of an institution with a monopoly over the legitimate exercise of violence. These conceptualizations have been challenged by the 'cultural', 'global' and 'complexity' turns in political sociology. The 'cultural turn' has highlighted the extent to which political violence can often assume a symbolic form, where physical force becomes 'spiritualized' and takes the form of subjective domination. There has also been a concern to explore the extent to which political violence and terror have become simulations in postmodern societies and thus mediated forms of 'hyperreality'. The 'global turn' has focused on how the forces of globalization have generated intense feelings of anxiety and uncertainty with regard to questions of identity and the ways in which these anxieties and uncertainties may become manifest in the form of intense ethnic hatreds, political violence and terrorism. The 'complexity turn' has analysed examples of global terrorism such as al-Qaida as a global 'fluid' that emanates from the 'wild zones' of the global system and poses an asymmetric threat to the centres of global power. This is presented as a manifestation of the chaotic nature of contemporary society where small events and occurrences can have large and potentially devastating effects. The 'cultural', 'global' and 'complexity' turns have provided important insights into the hidden dimensions of political violence and terrorism that were often ignored by modern political sociology and taken the study of political violence and terrorism beyond the territorial confines of the nation state. However, the nation state and the nation state system endure as the principal geopolitical and symbolic theatre in which complex, transnational and mediated forms of political violence and terrorism are played out. I conclude the chapter with the argument that this generates forms of political violence in contemporary society that are highly ambiguous as a result of the liminal forms of political violence generated by the proliferation of postmodern expressions of frustration and anger within the institutional context of modernity.

In Chapter 8, there is an examination of the development of citizenship rights and obligations in modern society. Modern political sociology tended to analyse citizenship as a universal category that described the rights and obligations of political actors within the territorial boundaries of the nation state. In the seminal work of T.H. Marshall, the development of citizenship in the UK was presented as an evolutionary process through which rights and obligations were systematically expanded to the 'civic', 'political' and 'social' realms during the eighteenth, nineteenth and twentieth centuries. The key focus of modern political sociology was a debate concerning the extent to which these developments had overcome social inequalities based on social class. The 'cultural', 'global' and 'complexity' turns have served to question and problematise many of these assumptions. The 'cultural turn' has served to question the universal character of modern citizenship and to highlight the ways in which the formal equality established by modern citizenship is undermined by substantive inequalities based on gender, sexuality, ethnicity and 'race'. In this context, the analytical focus has shifted towards how social justice is more likely to be achieved on the basis of 'group differentiated' citizenship rights. The 'global turn' has highlighted the ways in which the dynamic of political globalization has resulted in the disarticulation of nationality and rights owing to the development of various forms of 'post-national' citizenship. The focus has thus been on the de-territorialization of citizenship owing to the ways in which international treaties and transnational institutions such as the European Union (EU) confer social and political rights and obligations to social actors beyond the nation state. The 'complexity turn' has gone beyond the anthropocentric assumptions of modern political sociology to explore the rights and obligations that attach to the human–technological hybrids that 'flow' across complex global systems. The 'cultural', 'global' and 'complexity' turns have usefully highlighted the emergence of new forms of postmodern citizenship that illustrate an important trend towards increasingly pluralistic, transnational and complex forms of citizenship. I conclude the chapter with the argument that these emergent forms of postmodern citizenship have developed within a global context in which the nation state remains the dominant institutional actor. In this context, I highlight the ambiguous and liminal forms of citizenship that dominate contemporary society.

In Chapter 9, there is an exploration of the development of civil society and the 'public sphere' in modern society. The discourse of civil society has dominated modern political theory and political sociology, but the precise meaning of the term has remained ambiguous and contested. This chapter explores the various ways in which the concept has been used and highlights the extent to which academic disagreements concerning the scope and form of civil society reflect and are linked to the political mobilization of competing social groups in a struggle to define, defend or extend the limits of the 'public' and 'private' spheres in modern society. The development of the 'cultural', 'global' and 'complexity' turns in political sociology have served to question the universal character of civil society and the public sphere and the increasing disarticulation of civil society and the nation state. The 'cultural turn' has attempted to deconstruct civil society in order to highlight the exclusionary practices on which it is constructed and the existence of a plurality of 'subaltern' public spheres that are mobilized in opposition to dominant or hegemonic public spheres. The 'global turn' has focused on the extent to which the processes associated with globalization have resulted in the expansion of civil society beyond the nation state in the form of a 'global civil society' and the potential for the emergent global polity or 'cosmocracy' to spread democracy and civility around the contemporary world. The 'complexity turn' has attempted, somewhat unconvincingly, to apply concepts and categories of complexity theory to analyses of global civil society developed through the 'cultural' and 'global' turns. I conclude the chapter with the argument that the complex nature of global civil society can be captured most adequately through an exploration of the ways in which transnational and postmodern forms of political and social association are articulated through the international system of modern nation states. This results in the development of the increasingly ambiguous or liminal forms of association that dominate the contemporary world.

In the final and concluding chapter, I reiterate the strengths and weaknesses of the 'cultural', 'global' and 'complexity' turns in political sociology. The chapter restates the importance of recognizing the ambiguous and liminal nature of social and political reality in contemporary society and establishes the case for an 'existential turn' in political sociology premised on the ways in which global complexity is lived and experienced.

2
Political Sociology in an Age of Complexity

The core subject matter of political sociology is power, or, more precisely, the origins, form and application of social power. In the modern world, power was articulated in systemic forms of ideation that had a marked impact on patterns of self- and social identification. The core components of political sociology were thus power, ideology and identity. Throughout the twentieth century, these issues were at the heart of the discipline of sociology and, indeed, political sociology was a key and popular sub-discipline. In the twenty-first century, political sociology has become somewhat peripheral and less popular. The reasons for this are not difficult to find. In recent years, the dominant focus within sociology has been on the elision and liquidity of power, the decomposition of ideologies and the decentring of identities. These developments are a reflection of the various 'turns' which the discipline of sociology has taken over the past three decades: the 'cultural' turn, the 'global' turn and the 'complexity' turn. These turns have deconstructed, relativized and complexified the erstwhile solid foundations of modern political sociology and have tended to undermine rather than renew the sub-discipline of political sociology. In this book, I make the case for a renewed political sociology that takes on board the insights of these various sociological turns while retaining what remain useful insights from classical and modern sociology.

The sociological turns alluded to above have developed in response to and helped to shape intense processes of social change. The overall dynamics and parameters of social change remain contested. On the one hand, there have been attempts to analyse social change within the time-oriented narrative of modernity. This involved a focus on the ways in which the institutions and processes of modernity have become intensified or radicalized into 'late' or 'second' modernity. On the other hand, there have been attempts to analyse social change in terms of the temporal and spatial relativization of modernity whereby modernity has been transformed into postmodernity or globality. The resulting confusion or ambiguity is not simply a result of the competing versions of social reality presented by these broad paradigms but reflects the ambiguities of a society in transition or a society that defies definition or categorization and which articulates a sense of disorder or inbetweenness. Dürrschmidt and Taylor have argued that the experience of living in such a society generates a sense of *liminality* and that the most appropriate sociological strategy for exploring this as yet unknown social configuration or 'undefined society' (Melucci, 1996: 485) is a strategy of social complexification that both undermines and complements the competing paradigms of contemporary sociology (Dürrschmidt & Taylor, 2007: 1–6). This is the strategy adopt in this book where I provide an analysis of the ways in which the subject matter of political sociology has been complexified by intense processes of social and political change. However, I reject the argument that the resulting complexity can be captured adequately through a theory of complexity borrowed from the natural sciences and mathematics, and argue, alternatively, for a sociological approach focused on the ways in which we *experience* or *live* the complexity generated by a society in transition.

In this book, I explore in detail seven areas that have been the principal foci of modern political sociology: the nature and form of social power; the development and form of the state; the shifting nature of socio-political cultures and identities; the development and organization of social movements; the nature and significance of socio-political terror and violence; the changing nature of citizenship as a discourse and practice; and the development and changing form of civil society. In each case, I begin by exploring the ways in which these issues were analysed and understood within the paradigm of modern political sociology and proceed to explore the impact of the 'cultural', 'global' and 'complexity' turns on these key areas of political sociology. In each case, I argue that the complexity generated by the 'cultural' and 'global' turns is experienced or lived as liminality and that this is a reflection of the categorical ambiguities and inbetweenness that dominate the contemporary age. This inbetweenness is a result of the ways in which modern political institutions, cultures and practices have declined and decomposed into postmodern forms of politics which increasingly operate in the context of a complex and globalized modernity. In this context, complex socio-political processes generate liminal forms of power. Complex socio-political institutions generate liminal state forms. Complex identities and cultures reflect liminal forms of being and belonging. The complexity of social movement organization and mobilization is reflected in the emergence of liminal socio-political spaces and opportunity structures. The complexity of terrorism and political violence has rendered more ambiguous the boundaries between barbarism and civilization and generated liminal forms of violence and terror that inhabit the spaces between real and simulated reality. The complexity of citizenship has resulted in increasingly liminal rights and obligations between the national and the transnational sphere. Civil society has been transformed into an ambiguous and liminal associational space between the global and the local and the modern and the postmodern. Political sociology in an age of complexity is a study of socio-political liminality. In this chapter, I mark out the key paradigms and perspectives of modern political sociology and proceed to explore the ways in which these have been challenged by the cultural, global and complexity turns.

What is political sociology?

The central task of modern political sociology was both clear and ambitious: to explore and explain the relationship between politics and society, between social and political institutions, and between social and political behaviour (Rush, 1992: 15). Modern political sociology was concerned with power in its social context and the analysis of power was focused at the level of an inclusive society. While there was an acceptance that power suffused all the institutions of society including families, religious institutions and trade unions, the principal focus, according to Bottomore (1993: 1), was the relationship between societies and the social movements, organizations and institutions which were involved directly in the determination of power. In this sphere, power appeared in its purest and most distinctive form and only from this vantage point could its manifestation in other spheres be properly understood (Bottomore, 1993: 1). There were two broad traditions within the paradigm of modern political sociology defined by the purported relationship between the 'social' and the 'political' (Bottomore, 1993: 2–5) that resulted in an important conceptual distinction between society-centred and state-centred approaches to modern political sociology (Pierson, 1996: 70–93).

The 'society-centred' approach was exemplified by the Marxist tradition which was focused on the intimate connections and contradictions between the 'political' realm of the state and 'civil society'. In the Marxist tradition, the state was determined by and dependent on the contradictions of capitalist property relations as manifested in 'bourgeois' or 'civil' society. There is a long-standing debate in the Marxist tradition concerning the degree of autonomy enjoyed by the state from the relations of power and domination in civil society. This debate emerged from the ambiguities in Marx's own writings. The 'instrumentalist' formulation of the state developed in the *Communist Manifesto*, where the state was presented as a direct instrument of capitalist class rule, contradicts the formulation in *The German Ideology* where the state necessarily has a degree of relative autonomy from the contradictory power relations in civil society in order to ensure the long-term survival of capitalist class rule (McLellan, 1980: 206–22). The notion that the state has relative autonomy from the interests of the capitalist class shifted the focus of Marxist state theory away from the notion that the state operates through violent physical repression towards a consideration of the ideological role of the state in maintaining what Antonio Gramsci termed the hegemony of ruling-class ideas in civil society and the active consent of the working class to capitalist domination (Gramsci, 1971; Simon, 1982). The focus on the relative autonomy of the state also tended to take the focus of Marxist state theory away from the centrality of class struggle towards the more functionalist understanding of the state associated with Louis Althusser and Nicos Poulantzas (Althusser, 1971; Poulantzas, 1978). The work of Althusser provided an important impetus to the cultural turn in political sociology owing to the way in which Althusser presented ideology as a material social practice rather than as a product of false consciousness (Nash, 2000: 9). The issue of 'relative autonomy' has remained an important faultline with regard to debates in this paradigm during the past 30 years and, in the context of a marked decline in the influence and popularity of Marxism, there have been a range of attempts to re-establish the centrality of class struggle in the determination and form of the state in capitalist society (see Hay, 2006 for a review of classical and contemporary approaches).

The 'state-centred' tradition was exemplified by the focus of de Tocqueville on the development of democracy and the development of an autonomous political sphere that posed a threat to the liberty of individuals in civil society (Tocqueville, 1945). This approach is also evident in the work of Max Weber on the nation state and rationalization, and in the work of elite theorists such as Gaetano Mosca and Vilfredo Pareto (Pareto, 1963; Mosca, 1939). In the work of Weber, the modern nation state emerged as the most powerful institution in modern society owing to the way it commanded a legitimate monopoly of force within a given territory. The work of Weber was central to the preoccupation of modern political sociology on the ways in which power and force are territorially defined and constrained within and between nation states. According to Weber, the development of the modern state was associated with the increasing domination of society by bureaucratic or legal forms of legitimate authority that resulted in both administrators and the administered becoming trapped in a seamless iron cage. This was presented as inevitable as bureaucratic administration was the only way to manage complex and differentiated societies in a rational way. The political sociology of Weber was essentially pessimistic: human freedom was becoming increasingly constrained by the 'polar night of icy darkness' associated with impersonal administration (Weber, 1948: 128). Weber predicted that socialism would create an even greater nightmare as the countervailing power of the market would be destroyed and bureaucrats would become omniscient. Democracy was also important in challenging the omniscience of bureaucratic elites. Elections enabled charismatic leaders to emerge in order to establish programmatic goals for bureaucrats to realize and provided an opportunity for ineffective and inefficient politicians to be removed from office. For Weber, liberal democracy amounted to a form of elite rule that combined exceptional leaders and bureaucratic experts. These themes were developed further by elite theorists (see Evans [2006] for an overview of the development of classical and modern elite theory). Robert Michels, for example, developed his 'iron law of oligarchy' to argue that democratic political parties and trade unions become inevitably hierarchical and bureaucratic as they grow in size and complexity (Michels, 1962). Joseph Schumpeter conceptualized democratic politics as a competition between political elites for the votes of the people. Political stability required that political and bureaucratic elites had the autonomy to exercise rational judgement free from the capricious whims of popular opinion (Schumpeter, 1943). The themes that emerged from the Weberian tradition were thus the necessary or inevitable autonomy of the state from civil society and the territoriality of power and domination.

Overarching these alternative conceptions of the relationship between the political and the social was a further differentiation between approaches that focused on the functional stability of existing political systems and approaches that focused on political conflict instability and change (Bottomore, 1993: 5–7). The 'consensus' approach included structural functionalists such as Talcott Parsons who presented the political sphere as a subsystem that contributed to the stability of an integrated social system based on shared common goals and values (Parsons, 1969). This approach was also evident in analyses of 'development' or 'modernization'. In the work of Samuel P. Huntington, for example, the political values of consensus, legitimacy and stability were presented as important markers in the modernization of developing societies (Huntington, 1968). While the Weberian tradition tended to focus on the nation state, there were also attempts to explore Weber's argument that power has many sources in modern societies. An attempt to pursue this theme within a paradigm underpinned by social stability and consensus can be found in the pluralist approach that built on the work of Robert Dahl (Dahl, 1956, 1961; Buchanan & Tullock, 1962; Buchanan, 1975; and Smith, 2006 for an overview of this approach). In the pluralist approach, the notion of a monolithic state is replaced by the notion of 'government' comprising a set of competing and conflicting institutions. Public policy emerged in the form of a consensus determined by the struggle between a plurality of competing interest groups to influence government policy. This system of fluid and shifting pressures constituted a 'polyarchic democracy' or the rule of multiple minorities (Dahl, 1971). The pluralist perspective has important parallels with the 'cultural turn' in political sociology with regard to the decentred and fragmented nature of power and political mobilization (Nash, 2000: 17–18; Scott, 2001: 56).

The 'conflict' approach focused on the strains and contradictions underpinning social and political institutions and development, and viewed social stability and social order as short-lived, contingent and subject to constant threat by deep social antagonisms. While this approach was heavily influenced by the Marxist tradition (see Miliband, 1969), it also marked the neo-elite theory approach of Floyd Hunter and C. Wright Mills and more recently Noam Chomsky (Hunter, 1953; Mills, 1956; Chomsky, 1997). Mills highlighted the ways in which military, corporate and political elites formed a 'community of interests' driven by a 'military metaphysic' towards a permanent war economy. The principal paradigms of modern political sociology are set out in Figure 1. These paradigms were cut across by a range of other disputes between positivism and phenomenology and empiricism and structuralism (Bottomore, 1993: 7–9). Modern political sociology was complex and contested prior to its further complexification by the cultural, global and complexity turns. I will now consider the ways in which the paradigm of modern political sociology has been problematized by these 'turns'.

Political sociology and the cultural turn

The 'cultural' or 'postmodern' turn has challenged many of the key concepts and assumptions of modern political sociology. The turn reflected an increasing focus on culture and interpretation, and incorporated the

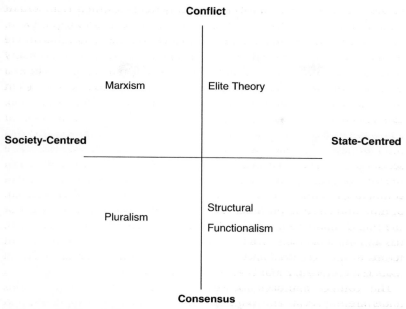

Conflict

Marxism | Elite Theory

Society-Centred | **State-Centred**

Pluralism | Structural Functionalism

Consensus

Figure 1 Modern political sociology: key paradigms

work of many theorists who would reject the label 'postmodernist' on the grounds that important institutional components of modern society remain intact. Nevertheless, there are important elements of post-structuralism, as a mode of thinking about social and political relations, that have important implications for the sub-discipline of political sociology. According to Nash (2000: 33–43), there are five main themes associated with the 'cultural turn' in sociology. First, the 'cultural turn' involves a shift in focus from epistemology and an exploration of the foundations of truth and value towards ontology and the forms of life that lie behind knowledge and truth claims. The 'cultural turn' has introduced a marked anti-epistemological and anti-foundationalist orientation into the discipline and resulted in an increasing focus on the social construction of knowledge and the ways in which this is connected to the exercise of power. Second, the 'cultural turn' involves a focus on the indeterminacy of meaning as a resource for constructing identities and structures. Meanings are seen as fluid and ambiguous, and cultural politics involves a struggle for relative stability and fixity. Third, the 'cultural turn' has stressed the extent to which society is decentred and how social structures are formed as part of an ongoing process in time and space. There is no single institution such as the nation state or a central set of meanings and values around which aspects of social life are organized in a fixed position. This has resulted in the notion that society should be seen in terms of a series of localized structures sustained by face-to-face interaction. Fourth, the 'cultural turn' is premised on an anti-essentialism that stresses the ways in which social and political identities and structures are socially constructed, historically contingent and an object of cultural politics. This has involved a rejection of the 'sovereign individual' associated with enlightenment thought. The attributes of such a subjectivity are seen as the historically and culturally specific constructions of discourse and therefore also a site of cultural politics. Fifth, a rejection of metanarratives that provided universal values and truths to which all members of society subscribed. This involved a rejection of the modern narratives of reason and progress and the argument that such metanarratives were 'terroristic' owing to the way in which they subsume and present everything in their own terms (Lyotard, 1984). This resulted in a relativism in relation to values and the proposition that it is problematic to make value judgements outside one's own 'language game'.

The accusation of relativism and the associated resignation to existing social and political conditions has resulted in many theorists associated with the 'cultural turn' eschewing the label 'postmodernist'. In this context, Best and Kellner (1997) differentiate between 'ludic' and 'oppositional' postmodernism. The former is inherently playful and anti-political and is exemplified by the work of Jean-François Lyotard and Jean Baudrillard. Baudrillard (1983a), for example, has argued that it is no longer worth engaging in politics or taking up a moral position as communication and human interaction have imploded into the masses. As a consequence, individuals were only concerned with the 'hyperreality' presented to them as media spectacle and there is no longer a reality on which to reflect or articulate. In contrast, oppositional postmodernism is associated with the impact of new social movements on sociology and the rejection of 'class' as the central form of oppression in contemporary society. In this context, relativism has been seen in a positive light as it allowed hidden forms of oppression to be explored and the possibility for greater pluralism and equality to develop. The tendency towards relativism and the deconstruction of essential identities and necessary logical connections reflect a 'responsibility to otherness' (White, 1991: 20). However, the result is a suspicion towards notions of 'universal justice' and 'political community' without which resistance to the systematic injustices of the marginalized and oppressed is impossible (White, 1991: 115–16). The result has been an attempt to construct new forms of democracy and new conceptualizations of social justice built on pluralism and a recognition of 'otherness'.

The 'cultural' or 'postmodern' turn in political sociology has resulted in an increasing tendency towards anti-foundationalism, anti-essentialism and the rejection of universal truths or grand narratives. The result has been an increasing focus on the indeterminacy of meaning and the decentring of the nation state and class struggle. In essence, the postmodern or 'cultural turn' represents a rather primitive form of social constructionism that is focused narrowly on the social construction of knowledge: the reflexing of this metanarrative back on the discipline itself so that it too becomes a social construction understood in social terms (Byrne, 1998: 42). 'Modern' sociology, located in the matrix of Western industrial nationhood, became seen as insufficiently 'complex' to capture its own strategic role in the social ordering of multiple forms of resistance, deviance and messiness. In this context, the staple sociological reference points of structures, systems, positions, ideologies and selves were jettisoned in favour of the indeterminacies of movements, mixtures, nomadic and deferred subjectivities (McLennan, 2003: 548). The 'cultural turn' has involved a political attack on Marxism and a rejection of existential philosophy and the existential model of authenticity and inauthenticity, the semiotic opposition between signifier and signified, the Freudian model of latent and manifest, and the Marxist distinction between appearance and essence. These models of depth have been replaced by a conception of practices, discourses and textual play (Sarup, 1993: 181). There are of course glaring inconsistencies in this position; not least that to verify that we do indeed live in a postmodern condition would require the type of metanarrative that is explicitly rejected within the 'cultural turn'. The decentring of the state has resulted in the 'cultural turn' having little to say about the contemporary form and function of the state or the relationship between the state, the economy and everyday life. The 'cultural turn' has also failed to contribute to an understanding of human agency or the self in the constitution of the postmodern order. Indeed, many within the 'cultural turn' have posited the end of the individual self and the end of history, politics and society. While the cultural turn may have much to offer with regard to the 'internal' narrative of postmodern political forms, it has little to say about the complex ambiguities generated by the insertion of these political forms into a context of complex and globalized hypermodernity.

Political sociology and the global turn

The 'global turn' has important implications for political sociology most notably because it brings into question the territorial alignment of power, citizenship and identity with the nation state. Globalization implies a historical process by which the economic, political, cultural and environmental geographies of society are redrawn beyond the territoriality of the nation state. The 'economic' aspects of the global turn focus mainly on the growth of transnational corporations (TNCs) and the development and diffusion of information and communications technology (ICT) (Castells, 2000a). These developments have resulted in the nation state losing control of the economy as increasingly footloose and mobile forms of capital are able to bypass and escape national forms of administration and regulation. In this context, there has been a shift from Keynesian state planning to flexible production and a neo-liberal preoccupation with deregulation, marketization and privatization (Harvey, 1989; 2005: 5–38). This has had important political implications associated not so much with the marginalization of the nation state, but with the consolidation of a liberalized and internationalized state system at the global level (Held, 1995: 130; McGrew, 1997: 10–12; Harvey, 2005: 64–86). New global elites have emerged who share the neo-liberal values associated with the so-called 'Washington Consensus'. These elites inhabit the 'space of flows' of the global informational economy and their activities often elude democratic or popular control. The growth and development of ICT, alongside the growth of migration, tourism and the mobility of global elites, is also responsible for the cultural dimensions of globalization as it has resulted in growing cultural interconnectedness. While this development may or may not lead to manifestations of global consciousness, the development of the global cultural economy through the movement of people, finance, media images and ideologies impacts on the meaning and understandings of established forms of self- and collective identity, citizenship and political engagement (Appadurai, 1990). Globalization also has an environmental component in the form of transboundary pollution and the degradation of environmental commons such as oceans and the icecaps (Goldblatt, 1997) and proliferation of human-generated risks and hazards such as Avian Flu (Davis, 2005).

The 'global turn' in sociology is, however, differentiated internally on the basis of whether these developments mark a continuation or intensification of modernity or the transcendence of modernity. Axford (2000) differentiates between a 'weak' and a 'strong' version of the globalization model. The 'strong' version of globalization theory takes as its starting point the claim that the world has become a single place with its own systemic properties (Axford, 2000: 239; Robertson, 1992: 135; Albrow, 1996). An important example of this can be found in the work of Castells on the 'information society' (1997, 2000a, 2000b). According to Castells, the proliferation of ICT has resulted in the emergence of new global spaces and temporalities that have their own logic and systemic qualities. The 'space of flows' confirms the logic of the network and stands in contrast to the ineluctably grounded 'space of place'. This has important cultural implications insomuch as globalization is often equated with postmodernization. In this context, globalization involves the development of cultural forms marked by ephemerality, fluidity, fragmentation, hybridity and pluralism. The globalization of culture involves the relativization and pluralization of the Western values of liberal humanism and nationalism (Smith, 1990). The global turn thus highlights the ways in which power, ideology and identity have taken on new temporalities and spatialities as a result of globalization.

The weak version is premised on the notion that globalization involves an increasing connectedness between places and people across distance and within the economic, political and cultural sub-spheres of society. This approach focuses on the historicity and novelty of the interdependencies generated by the world market and new technology. In many ways, this approach constitutes a further elaboration of modernization theory: globalization as a narrative plot that more or less continues the linear story of modernity (see, for example, Hirst & Thompson, 1999; Therborn, 1995; and Hannerz, 1998). The most important examples of attempts to reformulate political sociology from this perspective can be found in the work on globalization and reflexive politics by Anthony Giddens and Ulrich Beck (Giddens, 1990, 1991, 1994; Beck, 1992, 1994, 1995). Giddens has argued that the intensification of globalized modernity marked by the disembedding of social relations by a process of time-space distanciation and the reflexive appropriation of knowledge has resulted in a shift from 'emancipatory politics' to 'life politics'. The latter is essentially the politics of lifestyle and is intimately connected to globalization owing to the ways in which globalizing influences intrude deeply into the reflexive project of the self (Giddens, 1991: 214). Beck has argued that the proliferation of human-made hazards that transcend nationally defined boundaries results in forms of 'sub-politics' that bypasses the institutions of formal government. In the context of 'reflexive' or 'second' modernity, individuals and groups develop the capacity to question the objectivity and necessity of government and corporate policies.

The 'weak' and 'strong' positions of the globalization debate represent two contradictory but overlapping positions. While both positions are underpinned by the claim that an understanding of contemporary society has to go beyond the established categories of nation state sociology, one position continues within the time-oriented narrative project of modernity, while the contrary position seeks to frame contemporary social change through the spatial frame of 'globality'. Both accounts fail to recognize sufficiently the essential ambiguity of contemporary social change and transition. The idea of 'late', 'radical' or 'second' modernity, no matter how radicalized, conceals the ambiguities generated by the conceptual continuity between subsequent stages of modernity. On the other hand, 'globality' opens up a new perspective that is sensitive to novelty and discontinuity, but in so doing serves to sideline important instances of continuity within radical processes of transition. The resulting tension has been addressed by what Holton (2005: 5) has termed the 'post-scepticism' phase of the globalization debate. Hay and Marsh (2000) have argued that globalization is a trend generated by an array of cross-border interconnections and interdependences which are reversible by counter-trends. In this context, globalization is the *explanundum* which needs to be explained rather than the *explanans* which provides the explanation of social change. There is an acceptance that the nation state system and international relations continue to predominate in the world system but that 'global transformations' have emerged because the nation state is increasingly unable to contain or structure significant elements of social life including the ordering of territory (Held *et al.*, 1999; Held & McGrew, 2002, 2003). The limits to globalization have been stressed in terms of both the non-global preconditions in the form of legal, political and social infrastructure on which globalization processes depend and the counter-trends and resistances to globalization in the form of nationalism and localism (Scott, 1997; Rieger & Leibfried, 2003). There has also been a move away from the conceptualization of globalization as an unstoppable Juggernaut towards a more detailed consideration of the role of human agency in the processes of global transformation. This has included a consideration of the agency of executives in multinational corporations (Sklair, 2001), the labour movement (Munck, 2004; Munck & Waterman, 1998) and social movements (Cohen & Rai, 2000). In other words, there has been a recognition that there exists an array of alternative competing and contradictory globalizations including the competing conceptions of 'elite globalization' and 'globalization from below' (Geyer & Paulmann, 2001; Hopkins, 2001).

Political sociology and the complexity turn

The development and application of complexity approaches to political sociology reflect a wider interest in exploring the relevance of complexity and chaos theory to the analysis of social and political phenomena. Complexity approaches embody a new 'structure of feeling' premised on a greater sense of contingent openness to people, corporations and societies, the unpredictability of outcomes in time-space, a charity towards objects and nature, the non-linear nature of changes in relationships and a recognition of the increasing hypercomplexity of technologies and socialities (Capra, 1996, 2003; Urry, 2006; Byrne, 1998: 14–34). The complexity turn in sociology has developed on the basis of attempts to apply mathematic models of complexity and chaos to the analysis of social and political phenomena. This has been premised on the 'discovery' that the natural and social worlds are remarkably similar and that 'nature' and 'human nature' share the attributes of being unpredictable, sensitive to surroundings and influenced by small fluctuations. The 'complexity turn' in sociology has developed through a critical engagement with the 'global turn' and an increasing concern amongst commentators on globalization that the conceptual tools and techniques associated with the 'global turn' are incapable of grasping adequately the 'intractably disorderliness' (Gray, 2001) of global complexity. This is combined with a rejection of the perceived relativism underpinning the cultural turn. There is an imputed convergence between the social sciences and theoretical physics and mathematics around the analysis of complex, non-linear adaptive systems (Byrne, 1998; Capra, 2003). According to Urry (2005), many of the key analysts of modernity and globalization draw implicitly on 'complexity' ideas and concepts (Giddens, 1990; Harvey, 1989; Hardt & Negri, 2000; Castells, 2000a; Beck & Willms, 2003; Urry, 2003) and indeed, in the context of his analysis of the crisis and contradictions of capitalism, Marx constituted a complexity theorist *avant la lettre*.

The focus of the 'complexity turn' has been on systems that adapt and evolve as they self-organize in time and space and thus on systems that are emergent, dynamic and self-organizing that interact in ways that influence the probability of future events. This is a world of avalanches, founder effects, self-restoring patterns, punctuated equilibria, butterfly effects and tipping-point thresholds (Urry, 2005: 237). The complexity turn articulates the end of certainty, a rejection of both determination and arbitrariness and the coexistence of order and chaos as components of a system that are locked on the 'edge of chaos'. The interactions between elements in a system are seen as non-linear and consequently elements at one location can have disproportionate and significant time-space effects elsewhere through multiple connections and trajectories, and there is, therefore, no consistent relationship between cause and effect. There is a stress on negative feedback mechanisms and positive feedback loops that produce long-term emergent or vitalist patterns through the coevolution and mutual adaption of elements within a system. The emergent patterning of a system is related to the effects of 'attractors' that determine the direction of dynamic systems through multiple iterations and feedbacks. Complex systems may reach a point of bifurcation or a 'tipping point' when minor changes in the controlling variable take the system beyond a threshold and emergent properties turn over.

The 'complexity turn' involves a rejection of the argument that globalization involves a shift from bounded national systems towards a similar configuration at the global level. The model of a global system constituted by systems of linear scales stretching from the local to the global whereby the global dominates the local, national and the regional is rejected. In contrast, global complexity is presented as 'multiple systems of mobile connections' with 'connections or circulations that effect relationality at multiple and varied materialities and distances ... systems of networked or circulating relationships implicated within different overlapping and increasingly convergent mobile material worlds or hybrids' (Urry, 2005: 244–5). Hybrid systems are understood to be neither natural nor social, neither ordered nor anarchic and underpinned by extreme forms of complexity (Urry, 2006: 112). According to Urry (2005: 245–9), these systems are manifested in the form of global networks and global fluids. The analysis of the former builds on the insights of 'actor network theory' (ANT) to present global networks as enduring and predictable connections between people, objects and technologies that stretch across multiple and distant space and times (Law, 1994: 24; Murdoch, 1995: 745). These networks are comprised by multinational companies that deliver predictable and routinized products and services across national and regional boundaries. Global fluids travel along global route ways or scapes according to irregular shapes and temporalities and have unpredictable consequences. These phenomena have an autopoietic, non-hierarchical and rhizomatic character and include global money (Eatwell & Taylor, 2000) the internet (Plant, 1997) and the anti-globalization movement (Aingers *et al.*, 2003; Chesters & Welsh, 2006). The world is thus constituted as multiple 'islands of order' within a sea of increasing disorder as diverse systems swarm across the world, each constituting the environment in which others adapt and coevolve (Urry, 2005: 247–8).

This has important implications for political sociology. Commentators within the 'complexity turn' have stressed how the nation state is increasingly constituted as an 'island of order' that coevolves alongside a complexity of global networks and fluids that transform space beyond its boundaries. The regulatory role of the state has been intensified in order to develop the productive powers of territory and produce new spatial configurations. This suggests a 'post-panoptical' conception of power in which the primary technique of power is 'escape, slippage, elision and avoidance' and the 'end of the the era of mutual engagement' (Bauman, 2000: 11). Power is about speed, lightness, distance and weightlessness. Power is technologized, hybridized and runs in and jumps across global networks and fluids and is detached from territory and space and increasingly non-contiguous (Urry, 2005: 248). Power functions like an attractor, and the trajectories of systems are drawn to attractors that exert a gravity-like effect. Power is mobile, performed and unbounded, and attempts to order power can have complex and unintended effects. In this complex universe, the individual self is totally decentred. Large-scale societal patterning emerges from but is not reducible to micro-dynamics. Urry quotes an example from the discipline of physics:

> The laws governing gases derive not from the behaviour of each individual atom but from their statistical relational patterning ... it is the dance and not the dancers that are key. (Urry, 2005: 238)

Complexity theory highlights serious limitations with regard to the globalization paradigm (Urry, 2002: 58–60). The globalization paradigm has explored many of the material worlds implicated in the globalization of social, political, economic and environmental relationships. However, the 'complexity turn' has highlighted its failure to explore how emergent properties develop at the system level which are neither well ordered nor in a state of perpetual anarchy. In other words, it is argued that the globalization paradigm has taken the global level for granted in order to demonstrate how localities, regions, national states, environments and cultures are the new 'agents' shaped and transformed in a linear fashion by the all-powerful global 'structure'. In contrast, from the viewpoint of the 'complexity turn', the global is seen as disordered, paradoxical and marked by irreversible and juxtaposed complexity (Urry, 2002: 58). Urry has argued that the linear metaphor of scales stretching from the micro to the macro or the local to the global should be replaced by the metaphor of complex mobile connections. These connections comprise those aspects of the social that are produced neither by structure nor agency but comprise a circulating entity (Latour, 1999: 17) that are neither micro nor macro phenomena but circulate between each. Connections effect relationality through performance at multiple and varied distances, and relationality is effected by the wide array of circulating and networked relationships implicated within overlapping and convergent mobile, material worlds. The global system is constituted by a large number of elements and as a consequence is unpredictable and lacks a finalized order: 'there is only order is on the edge of chaos' (Urry, 2002: 59). Order and disorder inhere in all physical and social entities. Global systems lack, what Talcott Parsons and the functionalist tradition called, the 'steering mechanisms' required to achieve equilibrium and, in complex systems, any attempt to achieve equilibrium will tend to generate unforeseen consequences that take the system away from equilibrium. In complex systems, ordering is achieved 'on the move' and the social becomes materially heterogeneous: texts, bodies, machines, architectures, etc. are implicated in and perform the social (Law, 1994: 2). According to Urry (2002: 60), this type of thinking enables the transcendence of the determinism versus free will dilemma through a conceptualization of the world as unpredictable, unstable, sensitive to initiate conditions, irreversible and rarely socially organized. In general, it could be argued that the 'complexity turn' attempts to complexify the insights of the 'cultural' and 'global' turns while rejecting the relativism of the former and the linearity of the latter.

The application of complexity theory to sociology results in an essentially post-societal conceptualization of the world. As McLennan (2003: 554) has argued, Urry (2000) fails to demonstrate either that the contemporary world is any more complex than earlier social formations or that the mobilities of the contemporary world render the concept of 'society' redundant. The complexity approach is unable to consider the extent to which the 'social' has been recast in complex and non-linear ways beyond the nation state. McLennan (2003: 554–5) is also critical of the argument that the post-panoptical or 'gamekeeper' state is restricted to the regulation of mobilities in contrast to the 'gardening regime' of the modern nation state that involved a concern with patterning, order and regularity. Alternatively, the two can be seen as operating simultaneously, and historically 'gardening' regimes were involved intimately in the mobilities of immigration, urbanization and markets. Mobilities and their regulation are not unique to the contemporary era. There is also a sense in which the application of complexity theory to the social realm is reductionist owing to the way in which it applies a metatheory – built on theories and concepts with which social scientists have little knowledge and expertise – to the analysis of social phenomena that have always been recognized as intrinsically complex. As Stewart (2001: 330) has argued:

> This reductionism is not because human society does not display innumerable signs of non-linearity, high complexity, emergence and autopoietic systems: it does. The reductionism is because we already know quite a lot about the autopoietic system known as a woman or a man – and we know immediately that the 'nature' of this system involves knowns and unknowns of history, language, family, personality, ideology and education.

The starting point for the analysis of non-linear complexity should therefore be the *existence* of social actors in complex global networks. The complexity turn has the capacity to generate interesting and illuminating analogies and metaphors but these analogies and metaphors are meaningless unless related to a deeper and revelatory level of analysis. As McLennan (2003: 556) argues convincingly, when Urry (2000: 194) describes 'global fluids' as displaying distinctive 'viscosities', speeds, directions and temporalities, how does he know? The statement is meaningless unless 'flows' are used as a metaphor for flows of social actors or 'things' set in motion by social actors.

Towards a sociology of sociological 'turns'

It is widely accepted that the discipline of sociology has taken a series of 'turns' in recent decades. The immediate problem that we confront in our journey through these sociological turns, however, is how to make sense of the changing relationship between social reality and the discipline of sociology that these 'turns' seem to be describing. On one level, the notion of a sociological turn reflects the end of linear causality as unexpected events and discoveries disrupt the smooth and linear unfolding of the modern sociological narrative. We can trace the emergence of the 'cultural turn' to the eruption of counter-cultural politics during the 1960s and 1970s which disrupted the smooth unfolding of the politics of class and nation and resulted in the discovery of an array of subterranean identities based on hidden and obscure sources of power. We can trace the development of the 'global turn' to the collapse of the USSR and the development of microchip technology which disrupted the established boundaries of capitalist modernity and resulted in the discovery of new spatialities and hybridities. We can trace the emergence of the 'complexity turn' to developments in genetic and nanotechnology and theoretical physics which have disrupted the established boundaries between human beings and their natural and synthetic environment and resulted in the discovery of new patterns of causality and relationality. On another level, however, these 'turns' reflect a deep ambiguity about the type of society we inhabit. The twists and turns of contemporary sociology stand in stark contrast to the bold and universalizing 'paradigms' that dominated modern sociology. In the modern age, the coordinates of past, present and future were clearly set out in a range of competing *Weltanschauungen* that maintained relatively stable and solid patterns of power relations and systems of meaning and identity.

We have left this world behind but the coordinates of the new social world(s) we are entering remain unclear. The attempt to overcome the resulting ambiguity through the development of new totalizing paradigms, whether based on late/postmodernity, globality or complexity, obscures as much it reveals. We inhabit an age of transition between a decomposing modern order and an emerging order whose parameters and coordinates are undeveloped and unclear. It is this state of 'liminality' or 'inbetweenness' that defines the complexity of contemporary society (Dürrschmidt & Taylor, 2007: 1–4). A political sociology for the twenty-first century must attempt to grasp this complexity rather than avoid it through the application of simplifying and totalizing frameworks associated with the cultural, global and complexity turns. For example, in a recent text on political sociology, Nash (2000: 30–46) outlines *the* new political sociology that has emerged as a result of the 'cultural' or 'postmodern turn'. In his work on the 'information age', Castells (1997, 2000a, 2000b) defines new forms of power and identity politics in terms of the spatial restructuring and dislocation associated with the 'global turn'. In his work on global complexity, Urry (2003) defines power, citizenship, social movement politics and terrorism through a simplifying neo-systems approach borrowed somewhat ironically from complexity theory. There have been attempts to combine the insights of all three 'turns' as evidenced in Bauman's conception of 'post-panoptical' power (Bauman, 2000). This serves to highlight the dominant themes running through all three turns: escape, avoidance, movement, dissolving and slippage. These concepts provide rich and valuable insights into the intense processes of social change that are decomposing political modernity without engaging adequately with the important continuities between political modernity and the contemporary era and hence the ways in which social actors live with and make sense of the dissolving and disruptive processes described by the 'cultural', global' and 'complexity' turns.

What is required is a phenomenological approach to social and political complexity that brings the human subject back to the centre stage of sociological enquiry. The human subject has been systematically decentred by the 'cultural', 'global' and 'complexity' turns and, it is my argument in this book, an 'existential turn' is required to overcome the anti-humanism of the dominant theoretical approaches in contemporary sociology. I will illustrate this proposition through a systematic exploration of the key substantive and theoretical developments in the sub-discipline of political sociology. A good place to start with this endeavour is an important and enduring insight to be found in the work of Georg Simmel on the phenomenology of social power. Simmel (1896: 169) argued that the relationship between superiority and inferiority is manifested in every human association and is one of the forms in which 'society' comes into being. The task of sociology is to interpret historical examples in order to demonstrate the material or formal conditions underpinning the development of this form of society and to discover the material and formal consequences associated with the resulting social relations. Simmel (1896: 170) reminds us that relationships of superiority and inferiority are almost always reciprocal and exhibit a degree of spontaneity on the part of both the superior and the inferior. In other words, power relations are neither subjective nor objective but dialectical, complex and ultimately contradictory phenomena. This complex relationship can be analysed through a focus on 'being in the world': the way in which our being exists within a matrix of power relations. In the contemporary world, we can see this matrix shifting constantly owing to temporal (modernity) and spatial (globality) restructuring and the over-determined and non-linear interaction between temporal and spatial restructuring (complexity). We exist in a shifting matrix of power. The matrix is multidimensional with many levels and dimensions. The dimensions of power relate to the experience and the effects of the superior and the inferior and the mediation, avoidance and negation of power. The important point is that even the post-panoptical model of power conceptualized by Bauman can be subjected to a phenomenological analysis. The 'other' is not absent but the presence of the other is increasingly difficult to comprehend as a result of temporal intensity, spatial dislocation and technological mediation. The post-panoptical model of power over-emphasizes the degree of disembedding without re-embedding (Bauman & Tester, 2001). Even spaces of intense liminality require forms of social attachment and forms of social presence somewhere albeit in ephemeral and fragmented ways (Dürrschmidt & Taylor, 2007: 161).

Social power that is abstracted totally from social relations of superiority and inferiority is neither power nor social. In the contemporary world, decisions are made and actions are taken that start wars, move millions of dollars to off-shore tax havens, open or close hospitals and schools, build motorways or expand airports. The individuals affected by these decisions and actions may be unaware that a decision or action has been taken, be ambivalent or confused as to the consequences or may be opposed vehemently to what is taking place. Technological software and hardware are designed and developed, and social relations of inferiority and superiority are embedded within the design process. In this context, social relations are mediated rather than dissolved. The resulting forms of power are simultaneously an intensification of modern power and a rupture from modern power owing to the ways in which they are reordered and intensified through time-space restructuring. Liminal power has liminal effects and contributes to the generation of liminal or ambiguous ideological discourses, ambiguous social and political identities and liminal forms of citizenship based on complex and contradictory opportunity structures and networks of obligation. In essence, the insight of Simmel remains valid: we continue to live in a world marked by reciprocal relations of inferiority and superiority. The developments outlined by the 'cultural', 'global' and 'complexity' turns provide important insights into the ways in which this relationship has been transformed by intense processes of social change, but this should not be allowed to obscure the enduring importance of reciprocal relational power to the constitution of contemporary society.

Summary and conclusion

In this chapter, I have explored how the key concepts and substantive foci of modern political sociology have been transformed by the 'cultural', 'global' and 'complexity' turns in sociology and have argued for the reformulation of contemporary political sociology on the basis of an 'existential turn' that recognizes the complex ambiguities of a society in transition. I began by outlining the key paradigms of modern political sociology and constructed an ideal type schema which differentiated between society-centred and state-centred approaches and between approaches based on societal consensus and societal conflict. The competing paradigms of modern political sociology, however, shared the assumption that the analysis of power and its social forms should be focused at the level of an inclusive society and the organizations, institutions and movements through which power was determined. This assumption has been subjected to sustained critique by commentators and theorists associated with the 'cultural', 'global' and 'complexity' turns. The 'cultural' turn has 'decentred' the socio-political institutions of modern society through a thorough deconstruction of universal models of power, knowledge and identity. The 'global' turn has served to redraw the geography of power, knowledge and identity beyond the territoriality of the nation state and a corresponding 'inclusive society'. The 'complexity turn' has highlighted the unpredictable and non-linear relationship between social and political phenomena in a context of 'global complexity'. In the final section, I argued that while these sociological 'turns' have usefully highlighted important trends and tendencies in the social and political world, they have tended to over-exaggerate fundamental or epochal social change and downplay important continuities between modern and contemporary society. In contrast, I argued that it is important to recognize the ambiguities generated by a society in transition and the analytical promise of an 'existential turn' in political sociology that has the potential to uncover and explain the social and political forms of liminality that increasingly dominate the contemporary world.

3
Complex Powers: Beyond the Panopticon?

Throughout the modern era the nation state was central to the analysis of the origins and form of social and political power. The dominant paradigms of modern political sociology tended to analyse power within the framework of the sovereignty and legitimacy of the nation state and shared a conceptualization of power as an objective category. 'Episodic' power was connected to agency and the capacity to act and could be combined, concentrated and applied or rejected and challenged through the concentration and application of counter-power. The reality of the ways in which power was lived and experienced was always more complex and this was reflected in the 'subterranean' tradition of analysing power associated with Nietzsche and Foucault (Clegg, 1989, 2000) which challenged the universalism and essentialism of Enlightenment thought. This tradition focused on forms of 'dispositional' power whereby power is constituted as a system of social meaning, and 'being-in-the-world' is connected to the modes of subjectification associated with particular and specific ontologies. The metaphor of the panopticon was central to the model of power developed by Michel Foucault and provided an apt model for the configuration of power in modern society. The object of social power was the control or coordination of populations or bodies of people under the gaze of bureaucratically organized governments, corporations and institutions. The cultural, global and complexity turns have rendered the 'panoptical' model of power increasingly problematic. In an age of global complexity, power is presented as exterritorial or unbound and unconstrained by space. The new global elites rule as 'absentee landlords' unencumbered by the costly and inconvenient problems of surveillance and discipline and deriving power from the techniques of escape, elision, slippage and avoidance (Bauman, 2000: 10–11).

The key objective of this chapter is to engage critically with the argument that the complex configurations of power operating within contemporary society mark the end of the era of mutual engagement and the emergence of a 'post-panoptical' configuration of social power. In the following section, 'Power in modern society', I outline the principal contributions to the analysis of power from within the paradigm of modern political sociology. I outline and contrast 'negative sum' and 'positive sum' conceptualizations of power in modern society and the ways in which critical and radical approaches to the analysis of power often conflated these conceptions of power in confusing and contradictory ways. In the section 'Power, discourse and subjectivity', I explore how the modern conceptualization of power was challenged and transformed by the cultural turn in political sociology, focusing in particular on the seminal work of Foucault on power and subjectivity. The section 'Power and the global turn' discusses how the 'global turn' has impacted on the analysis of power with a particular focus on how the de-territorialization of power has resulted in neo-medieval configurations of power. The work of Manuel Castells is explored in order to consider the role of ICT in the disembedding of power relations from local places and the reconstitution of power within the informational networks of the global economy. The section 'Complex powers' provides an exploration of the ways in which power has been conceptualized through the 'complexity turn'. This is focused on the model of post-panoptical power developed by Zygmunt Bauman and the analysis of unstable forms of hybrid power that have developed as a result of the application of complexity theory to the analysis of social power. On the basis of Simmel's work on power and social form, I argue that despite the insights and developments outlined by the 'cultural', 'global' and 'complexity' turns that power remains an existential category. I argue that 'episodic' and 'dispositional' forms of power have been counterposed in a false dichotomy within sociological debates on the nature of power and should be thought of as the two sides in a relational, reciprocal and reflexive power relation which, in the contemporary context, is generating ambiguous and liminal social forms of being.

Power in modern society: liberal, reformist and critical perspectives

The debate on power within modern social and political theory was concerned principally with issues of sovereignty and legitimacy. The focus on power as sovereign or legitimate provided the basis for two competing conceptions of power. The focus on sovereignty suggested that power existed as a generalized capacity to act or a quantitative phenomenon linked to human agency. The tradition of conceptualizing power as a capacity to act can be traced back to Thomas Hobbes. Hobbes presented power as a condition of human agency or the mastery of man over his environment. Power was a quantitative, cumulative phenomenon that could be combined to produce a power greater than any individual: the *Leviathan*, necessary to prevent the war of all against all. The focus of this approach has been the individual and institutional exercise of power and counter-power. In this context, power can be either symmetrical or unsymmetrical and may be manifested either directly or indirectly through behavioural expectations (Goehler, 2000: 44). Max Weber described this as the probability for one man to prevail over another in a social relationship despite resistance and regardless of the basis on which this probability rests (Weber, 1978: 53). This could also be achieved through violence, according to Weber, which suggested that power operated as an instrument of domination and involved a 'negative sum' power game.

The focus on legitimacy suggested that power existed as a qualitative phenomenon that was dependent on the consent of those over whom it was exercised. The tradition of analysing power as legitimacy can be traced to John Locke. In the work of Locke, there is the notion that the sovereign has a series of obligations to his or her subjects. Legitimate power rests upon both the capacity to act and the right to act and can only be used for the public good as defined by the people. Power can thus be usurped and exercised by those with no right to act. The 'social contract' between sovereign and subjects and the legitimacy of the sovereign emerge from civil society on the basis of civil law and the law of reputation. The focus on power as legitimacy produced analyses that focused on the ways in which power underpins social order and social stability. In the work of Parsons (1986), for example, there was a rejection of the quantitative 'zero-sum' conception of power in favour of a 'positive sum' account focused on how power was produced. Power engaged with counter-power and resulted in an increase in power for both sides. The amount of power in a society reflected the ability of a social system to realize its goals which were related to the maintenance of social order and social stability. Power was the political equivalent of money, and the separation of power and coercion was analogous to the separation of money from its metallic base and reflected a generalized increase in the legitimate authority of societal leaders. Power was thus the 'generalized medium of mobilizing resources for effective collective action' (Parsons, 1986: 108). A more radical conception of this model of power can be found in the work of Hannah Arendt, who contrasted power with violence and conceptualized the former as the self-empowerment of a community through political engagement in the public sphere (Arendt, 1958, 1970). This essentially normative model of power was based on a conflation of fact and value and implied the existence of a 'positive sum' power game.

These two approaches can be contrasted as 'transitive' and 'intransitive' models of power. Power is transitive when it refers to others and intransitive when it refers back to itself (Goehler, 2000: 43). Corresponding to transitive and intransitive forms of power are the two basic functions of politics: regulation and integration (Goehler, 2000: 52).

The dominant approaches to the analysis of power within modern sociology have combined 'transitive' and 'intransitive' models of power in ways that were often inconsistent and contradictory. For example, the debate between pluralists and elite theorists in the so-called 'community power debate' that emerged in the USA during the 1950s concerned both an attempt to quantify the power held by individuals and groups and the extent to which such a distribution of power was legitimate and based on democratic consent. Contemporary pluralism developed in response to elite theory in an attempt to argue that the state was not dominated by a single interest or elite group, but comprised a plurality of competing groups and interests. The most important advocate of pluralism in the post-war period was Robert A. Dahl. Dahl was critical of community power theorists such as Floyd Hunter who had developed a 'reputational' model of power in order to demonstrate the unequal distribution of power in local communities (Hunter, 1953) and elite theorists such as C. Wright Mills who had described the existence of economic, military and political elites at the national level alongside the existence of an elite culture (Mills, 1956). In *Who Governs* (1961) Dahl explored the outcomes of political decisions in New Haven, USA in the areas of urban renewal, public education and political nominations. Through this study, Dahl argued that decisions were based on a 'plurality of interests' and that rather than being dominated by a single group or elite, the policy-making process was comprised of a range of competing groups (or elites) corresponding to each policy area. Dahl labelled this form of government a 'polyarchy' or rule of the many. The state takes the form of an arena within which diverse (though not necessarily equal) groups and interests compete and bargain for influence in the policy-making process. Democracy is presented as a set of institutional procedures designed to ensure equality in decision-making: power prevails in the decision-making process rather than in power resources which exist only as potential power.

Critics of Dahl questioned the methodological assumptions underpinning his study: methodological individualism and empiricism. Dahl restricted his analysis to observable decisions on issues that appeared on the political agenda and this led critics such as Bachrach and Baratz to highlight the problem of institutional bias and the issues that fail to make the political agenda and thus on the power of non-decision-making and the decision not to make a decision (Bachrach & Baratz, 1963, 1970, see also the study by Crenson, 1972 on the politics of non-decision-making in relation to air-pollution regulation in two US cities). A more radical critique of pluralism was developed by Lukes (2004), who argued that it was possible to isolate three dimensions of power. The *first* dimension of power related to observable decisions and conflict and formed the basis of Dahl's conceptualization of power. The *second* dimension of power related to observable but covert non-decisions and conflict and formed the basis of the non-decision-making power isolated by Bachrach and Baratz. The *third* dimension of power was conceptualized as a form of insidious power based on 'latent conflict' over 'real issues'. The *third* dimension of power was a realm of 'false consciousness' where individuals were unaware of their real interests because the values dominant in society led them to misconstrue reality. The analysis of power developed by Lukes rested on three key assumptions and these assumptions also underpinned the models of power developed by the Frankfurt School tradition exemplified by Herbert Marcuse and, more recently, Jürgen Habermas. First, the individual is presented as a creation of social conditions as determined by the configuration of power in society. Second, the autonomous individual capable of determining his or her own interests is presented as an ideal. Third, it is argued that this ideal could be realized in the absence of the illegitimate effects of power in the form of an idealized, utopian civil society (Hindess, 1996: 95). Hindess (1996: 84) suggests that Lukes conflated two conflicting conceptions of the human individual in this formulation of power. On the one hand, the individual was conceptualized as a malleable creature of social conditions and, on the other hand, the individual was conceptualized as an autonomous rational agent. This resulted in a conception of civil society constituted as both a sphere of social interaction and as an arena for contending social forces. Within this arena, the power of dominant groups prevented subordinate groups from recognizing their true interests.

In the radical view of power, the community of autonomous persons exists as both a model against which to measure the impact of power and a utopian form of civil society where such autonomy could be found in the absence of power. In the work of Marcuse (1972), this sphere was constituted by those 'outcasts and outsiders' unaffected by the rationalization of private space. In this approach, an autonomous civil society provided the moral foundation for a critique of political power. In the work of Habermas, we find a less ambiguous commitment to the enlightenment project in comparison with earlier critical theorists (Flyvbjerg, 1998a). For Habermas, the negative consequences of rationalization were a result of the intersubjective conditions in which it took place. The intrusion of power into the 'lifeworld' undermined the rationality of communicative action owing to the way in which agreement was secured for non-rational motivations. Counterpoised to the colonization of the 'lifeworld' was the 'ideal speech situation' premised on the decolonization of the lifeworld (Habermas, 1983). Habermas (1979: 97) defined human beings as democratic beings or as *homo democraticus*. Validity and truth emerged intersubjectively on the basis of the 'universalization principle' (U) of discourse ethics (Habermas, 1990: 120–1): the only force in civil society is the 'force of better argument' (Habermas, 1990: 198). Habermas was thus concerned with procedural rather than substantive rationality and the forms of legal institutionalization necessary for political will formation. Hence, for Habermas, 'the authorization of power by law and the sanctioning of law by power must occur *uno acto*' (quoted in Flyvbjerg, 1998a: 214): sovereignty was a prerequisite for the regulation of power by law. As Flyvbjerg (1998a: 215) has noted, the conceptualization of power developed by Habermas was insufficient owing to the way in which he outlined the utopia of communicative rationality, but had little to say about the barriers inscribed by existing relations of power, abuse and degradation that stood in the way of its realization. Hence, the conviction of Habermas in ideal speech situations and universal validity claims rested ultimately on what Kirkegaard termed a 'leap of faith'. The notion that it is possible for communication to be uncorrupted by power is contested by the intellectual tradition represented by Nietzsche and Foucault which suggested that power is always present (Foucault, 1988b: 11, 18). The ensuing debate between Habermas and Foucault constituted the faultline between modern conceptions of power and the application of the 'cultural turn' to the analysis of social and political power.

Power, discourse and subjectivity: Foucault and the cultural turn

In the work of Foucault, the relationship between power and knowledge is mutually constitutive rather than oppositional. This position involved a rejection of Cartesian epistemology premised on a separation of the self and the external world in favour of a self-constituting ontology in which our being in the world is inseparable from our perception of it. This being-in-the-world is not self-creational, but the product of a historically specific set of social relations. Habermas accused Foucault of being a 'cynic' and a 'relativist', but as Flyvbjerg (1998a: 221) has argued, Foucault overcame the foundationalism–relativism dualism through a situational ethics premised upon context. For Foucault (1984: 247), nothing was fundamental, and socially and historically conditioned context constituted the most effective bulwark against relativism and nihilism and the most effective basis for political action. Foucault was oriented towards *phronesis* in contrast to Habermas who was oriented to *episteme* (Flyvbjerg, 1998a: 223). For Foucault, freedom was a practice and its ideal was not a utopian absence of power: resistance and struggle were the most solid basis for the practice of freedom. The focus of Foucault was on substantive micro-politics and the struggle against domination. In contrast to Habermas, where freedom in civil society was premised on consensus and agreement, Foucault highlighted the intimate connection between conflict and freedom. The ability to engage in conflict was presented as an integral component of freedom and this resulted in a conceptualization of civil society as a public sphere in which obstinate differences in power, material status and interests could find expression (Ryan, 1992: 286). Civil society does not imply 'civilized' as in 'well-mannered'. Distrust and criticism of authoritative action are omnipresent as a result of political conflict (Flyvbjerg (1998a: 229) and civil society only guarantees a public and not a public consensus (Alexander, 1991). Foucault was thus interested in what holds society together in its heterogeneity. This involved a combination of force relations, extending from indirect domination and discursive forms of knowledge to relations of direct repression (Goehler, 2000: 46).

Foucault on power

Foucault's work on power can be divided into three phases, each of which throws light onto different aspects of social power: the 'archaeology', the 'genealogy' and the 'care of the self'. The 'archaeology' includes *Madness and Civilization* (1977a) and *The Order of Things* (1973). In these works, Foucault was concerned with the forms of tacit knowledge which constituted the conditions of possibility and the ways in which systems of meaning related to particular ways of being. The transition to the modern period involved the constitution of man as an object of knowledge and, following Kant, an epistemology in which knowledge was not reducible to an order which existed prior to our perception of it. The ordering of the world according to *a priori* categories resulted in the 'death of God': Man constituted as the source of all truth. Foucault was concerned with the subsequent 'death of man' which resulted from a situation in which being-in-the-world was determined by local systems of thought or historical *a prioris* that are not *a priori* to all experience, but only to particular experiences in particular historical epochs. There is, therefore, no universal truth, but particular ontologies that are constituted by and constitute variable social relations. The 'genealogy' included *Discipline and Punish* (1977b), *Power/Knowledge* (1980) and *The History of Sexuality* volume 1 (1979). In these works, Foucault supplemented his archaeological description of systems of thought with an analysis of the ways in which these are simultaneously constituted by and constitute power relations. This is presented in terms of an inescapable struggle between systems of thought and different forms of knowledge that reflected competing claims to truth and different modes of being. While there was no escape from knowledge saturated by power, each era was marked by a particular relationship between power and knowledge. In the modern era, the constitution of man as the source of knowledge resulted in the development of social and human sciences that classified particular modes of being as deviant, delinquent and abnormal on the basis of discourses of power and truth. Deviants and delinquents were objects to be classified, judged and resocialized on the basis of discursive technologies of power. Truth was thus a mechanism of pacification and subjection that operated to privilege certain ways of interpreting the world while disqualifying others. The 'care of the self' included volumes 2 and 3 of *The History of Sexuality* (1979, 1987, 1988a). In these works, Foucault explored the possibilities for self-constituted resistance to dominant forms of knowledge as a project of emancipation. The care of the self, however, did not imply the possibility of emancipation in terms of an escape into undistorted truth or true consciousness but rather the experimentation with subversive forms of knowledge as alternative forms of being.

   The work of Foucault effectively cuts off the King's head and moves the analysis of power away from issues of sovereignty and legitimacy. The development of Foucault's thought amounted to a shift from an extremist denunciation of power in his earlier writings to an engagement with questions of government in the later works. Foucault suggested that there is an intimate relationship between power and liberty. Power is exercised only on those in a position to choose, and where there is no possibility of resistance there is no relation of power. Power is everywhere and available to everyone and consists of instruments, techniques and procedures that are brought to bear on others.

Power is unstable, ambiguous and reversible. Foucault described domination as an asymmetrical power relation where the margin of liberty is limited. In his earlier writings, Foucault failed to distinguish adequately between power in general and domination as a particular form of power relation. In his later work, however, power was not evil *per se* and the objective was to allow the game of power to be played with minimum domination. Foucault described 'government' in terms of those forms of self-regulation between domination and reversible power connected to discourses on how to conduct state and population. Hence, there was an intimate connection between the principles of political action and personal conduct: outside relations of domination the governed regulated their own conduct and the government created the conditions which made this possible. In the 'genealogy', Foucault presented government as the technologies that regulated conduct and argued that during the modern period these technologies had expanded. Government was premised on the 'reason of state' and this was distinct from both religion and the power of the sovereign. There had been a marked governmentalization of the state during the modern period and the activities of the state were increasingly premised on rational calculation and took the form of 'government' as a distinctive institutional structure. The Prince was replaced by the 'art of government' premised on population and the regularities of births, deaths and diseases. The state does not, however, exhaust the notion of government and Foucault also explores the importance of discipline, pastoral power and liberalism.

In *Discipline and Punish* Foucault (1977b) explored the forms of productive power that are exercised over an individual in order to develop the skills and capacities required for self-control. The expansion of discipline developed alongside the invention of the human subject and claims to knowledge about the character of the human subject. A relationship developed between disciplinary power and fields of knowledge, particularly the social and human sciences in which disciplinary techniques led to the generation of knowledge which then led to the further enhancement of disciplinary techniques. While Foucault explored the development of discipline in closed institutions and prisons, it is nevertheless clear that he considered discipline to be a ubiquitous process of surveillance, regimentation and classification. We live in a world of cross-cutting disciplinary projects whose effects go beyond the effects of any particular case (Hindess, 1996: 118). Foucault explored pastoral power through the metaphor of the shepherd-flock game in order to develop the theory of police and cameralism. In this context, police had a broader meaning than in its contemporary usage and related to the

comprehensive regulation of social life in the interests of the development of society. The shepherd was in charge of the flock and each
member of the flock existed only through the activity of the shepherd.
This form of power emerged in the confessional states during the nineteenth century based on confession, self-examination and guidance,
but in the twentieth century this had expanded into secular forms such
as counselling, social work and the welfare state. The power of liberalism is embedded in the training of individuals to develop responsible
autonomy and, therefore, the liberal rationality of government regarded
the liberty of subjects as an indispensable element of government. Liberal
rationality was thus an indirect form of regulation through institutions
such as the education system. For Foucault, therefore, government is
performed by both state and non-state agencies, and government is intimately involved in the moulding of the boundary between the public
and the private and hence the nature of citizenship. The welfare state
involved both political power over legal subjects and pastoral power over
live individuals. Political power extended far beyond the state.

The focus of Foucault on concrete genealogies and resistance to domination has made his approach attractive to feminists and other minorities
and pivotal to the cultural turn and the exploration of pluralistic cultural
politics in civil society. The elaboration of genealogies of gender, race,
sexuality and disability has provided a basis for determining strategies
of social change that enable relations of domination between different
people to be challenged and overcome (McNay, 1992; Bordo & Jagger,
1990; Fraser, 1989a; Benhabib & Cornell, 1987; Snyder & Mitchell, 2006;
Tremain, 2005; Weeks, 1991). In contrast to Lukes, Foucault does not
introduce power in order to explain the non-existence of a utopian world
that is devoid of power. Power is an inescapable feature of human interaction. Foucault did not develop a normative model of the ideal human
person. Indeed, the existence of such a person would be seen as a consequence of domination and the individualizing effects of rationality.
Human personalities cannot develop independently of power, and power
is often creative and inscribed in the personalities of those that are subject
to it. Power presupposed an element of freedom as resistance and evasion
are inescapable elements of human interaction: part of what Nietzsche
called the 'celebration of life'. The 'care of the self' also presupposed a
degree of freedom as it presumed a process of self-cultivation in the
context of power. There was, therefore, no universal project of human
emancipation. There is, however, an enduring tension in the work of
Foucault with regard to the counterpoising of domination and liberty.
The 'care of the self' clearly involved avoiding the necessary evil of

domination as far as possible and not abusing your own power over others. This was clearly based on a normative judgement and suggested a global or radical project of emancipation that Foucault rejected explicitly. Following Nietzsche, Foucault presented domination as an indispensable condition of liberty or the liberty we learn to desire. As Hindess (1996: 158) has argued, Foucault's critique of sovereignty is incomplete and requires a genealogy of the concept of community to complement the genealogy of the individual. In the following section, I explore the work of commentators who have attempted to demonstrate how forms of discursive power link the individual to wider communities of power and anti-power.

Communities of power: the framing of hegemony

The work of Stewart Clegg (1989) is an interesting example of an attempt to synthesize Foucault's model of power with some of the enduring insights developed within the modern perspective in order to explore the ways in which power is framed within political communities. Clegg is critical of analyses of power that focus one-sidedly on either legitimate power or resistance to coercive power and suggests that both dynamics are contingent and conditional rather than necessary (Clegg, 2000: 78). According to Clegg, the 'cultural turn' had transformed the key theoretical concepts of the radical tradition, particularly the concept of 'hegemony' which provided the principal theoretical underpinning for the 'third dimension' of power outlined by Lukes. In the work of Gramsci (1971), hegemony was constituted by a form of ideological control manufactured from the contents of knowledge in the socio-cultural sphere of civil society. Hegemony facilitated active consent to capitalist domination through the generation of 'false consciousnesses'. During the 1980s, the concept was deconstructed and reconstructed through the work of Ernesto Laclau and Chantal Mouffe in a way that built implicitly on Foucault and took the concept of power through the 'cultural turn'. Laclau and Mouffe (1985) rejected the argument that hegemony was built on the content of ideas and suggested that hegemony exists wherever there is 'discursive fixity'. This implied a rejection of the causal model of power inherited from modern theories of power and a reappraisal of the argument that language provided an ideological 'mask' in order to obscure the 'real interests' of individuals and classes. The relationship between language and consciousness was no longer to be seen as being premised on falsehood. Reality could only be known through its representation in language and language was the medium through which the possibilities of existence become known and which determined these possibilities in relation to one another. Hence, our sense of self as a distinct subjectivity was constituted through 'discursive practices' and the meaning and membership of categories had become a principal site for struggles over power. Identity was thus contingent, provisional, achieved and relational rather than given or intrinsic to a particular type of person or life-experience. This shifted the focus away from the relationship between class and power that had marked the work of theorists such as Lukes towards a focus on how power was linked to identity and inhered in a plurality of categories based on gender, ethnicity, 'race' and sexuality. In this context, identity was defined by difference, and signifiers of the self were shifting, ambiguous and contradictory. Hegemonic power resided neither in specific individuals or elites nor in particular concrete practices, but rather in the ways in which agents and practices articulated a fixed ensemble of representations. Power was thus textual, semiotic and inherent in the very textuality, meaning and signification of the social world: power fixed the terrain of its own expression (Clegg, 2000: 80).

Clegg (2000: 82) has argued that Foucault's concept of government is able to capture the relationship between organizers and organized or the organization and the individual through a focus on the ways in which liberal forms of governance link the two levels together. Governance is underpinned by free human agency, and Van Krieken (1996) has developed the concept of proto-governmentalization to highlight the ways in which the initiatives, projects and strategies of individuals and groups become mutually aligned with those of elites. Government works on and through knowledge and the forms of social relations that embed and constitute such knowledge. Clegg (2000: 83–5) has suggested that forms of social relations can be conceptualized in terms of an ever-widening circle from the self or self-organization, through to significant others and face-to-face relations, to solidaristic others and solidaristic organization, to generalized others and generalized organization. Knowledge may be more or less subject to 'social framing' and produce variable opportunities for resistance or organizational outflanking. At the level of the self, reflexive self-organization or isolation can be the result of high or low levels of social framing. Reflexive self-organization is an important precondition for effective resistance. Time and space may be ordered and reordered in ways that prevent the social framing of knowledge with significant others leading to confusion. However, where divisions can be overcome, the sharing of self-consciousness may lead to cultural organizations of resistance. Resistance through solidaristic action may lead to coordinated action or divisions depending on the organization of framed bodies of knowledge. Finally, the building of alliances with generalized others requires framing within news or media values otherwise it remains as unframed defiance that is easily surmounted and overcome. Neither resistance nor legitimacy are endemic, but occur through the discursive expressions of existing conditions of existence that are socially framed. This is ultimately dependent on the relationship between the practical consciousness of everyday life and the discursive consciousness delivered by representational media. The emergence of a unified narrative or historical subject is rare owing to the plurality and diversity of media representations. The emergence of such an identity requires the generation of capacities capable of overcoming individual isolation, the divisions between putative subjects, the knowledge that frames the practical consciousness of these putative subjects and the objective conditions that sustain that knowledge (Clegg, 2000: 90). The focus of Clegg on the spatial organization and reorganization of episodic and dispositional power provides a useful linkage with analyses of power that have been developed within the 'global turn'.

Power and the global turn: exploring the coordinates of de-territorialized and disarticulated power

During the past 300 years, world politics has been subject to the structural domination of the nation state and the international system of nation states. The 'global turn' in the analysis of power has involved an exploration of the extent to which the power matrix of the modern nation state system is undergoing a process of disordering or disarticulation. At this point, it is useful to differentiate between globality, globalism and globalization. The condition of globality has been generated by an amalgam of forces, many of which are technological and irreversible, that are breaking down barriers of time, space and nation and fashioning the planet into a coherent global community (Beck, 2000: 10). This is distinct from 'globalism' which constitutes a contestable political discourse that promotes a transnational world-view, a philosophy of governance and a particular set of institutional structures (Beck, 2000: 9). Globalization comprises the processes through which sovereign nation states are crisscrossed and undermined by transnational actors with varying prospects of power, orientations, identities and networks (Beck, 2000: 11). The power relations underpinning the process of globalization include the global articulation of the economic and military strength of the USA and the maintenance of important security and coordination functions within nation states (Lentner, 2000: 200–1). Globalism has developed in the form of a neo-liberal discourse or a Foucauldian 'technology of power' which simultaneously individualizes (through the global diffusion of market relations) and totalizes (through the legitimation of this diffusion on the basis of the discipline imposed by the forces of globalization) (Penttinen, 2000). On the basis of these geopolitical and economic dynamics, the distinction between the national and international level has become increasingly undermined. On the one hand, the domestic nation state has become more permeable and vulnerable to international and transnational dynamics and this has undermined the ability of domestic politicians to develop 'national' policies in a coherent or strategic way. On the other hand, globalization has undermined and transformed international relations as a system constituted by unitary nation states and this has resulted in the proliferation of complex multi-layered webs of governance and public–private networks (Cerny, 2000: 171–2). This process has increasingly resulted in the breakdown of existing bulwarks of order without their being replaced by new institutional mechanisms of order, and the result has been a self-perpetuating expansion of endemic, low-level conflict and expanding violence resulting in the emergence of a new world *disorder* (Cerny, 2000: 173). A generalized state of insecurity has emerged marked by a generalized threat of uncontrollable nuclear annihilation compounded by a series of threats from below, including an increasing number of civil wars, tribal and religious conflict, terrorism and international criminality. The global–local dialectic has produced a dynamic of 'fragmegration' (Rosenau, 1997) through which the nation state is simultaneously undergoing transnationalization and internationalization from above and micro- and meso-level fragmentation from below. The result is a 'durable disorder' that has been conceptualized as neo-medievalism (Cerny, 1998). In this context, the nation state is undergoing a process of 'disarticulation' (Lake, 1999) and this has resulted in an increasingly serious 'governance gap' (Cerny, 2000: 177).

The nation state has become less effective in delivering those functions that were important for its development in the modern era, including redistribution, structural regulation and the delivery of public services. However, the nation state has become an increasingly important mechanism through which decisions made at the international and transnational level through public or public–private networks are translated into domestic legislation and public policy. In this context, the overall scale of state intervention has increased rather than declined as a result of globalization. Indeed, the state remains essential with regard to the effective operation of the global liberal economy. These developments amount to the triumph of the liberal state and its institutionalization at the international level in the form of the WTO, IMF and World Bank (Lentner, 2000). Beck (2005) argues that globalization is a narrative about power and has developed an analysis of 'transnational metapower politics' in which the key actors are states, capital and global civil society. Following Strange (1996), Beck argues that states are engaged in a competitive power game in which they compete in world markets for world market share and foreign capital in order to realize their national interest. In this process, the power of the state is undermined, not through imperialist conquest, but through non-imperialist withdrawal in which the retreat of investors constitutes the core of global economic power. The nation state is threatened by non-conquest and the supply-side state longs for nothing more than invasion by multinationals. In the context of globalization, therefore, power is increasingly associated with the capacity to escape or take flight and the power of the nation state transformed into a capacity to attract and contain forces that flow within, between and beyond its territorial borders.

The de-territorialization of power is also explored by Castells (2000a) in his analysis of the 'networked society'. Castells (2000a) explores how the process of globalization has resulted in the de-territorialization of power and the reconstitution of power within and between the hubs and nodes of the networked informational economy. In the networked society, power migrates from the 'space of place' to the 'space of flows'. Castells (2000a: 442) defines the space of flows as the material organization of time-sharing social practices that work through flows. Flows are defined as 'purposeful, repetitive and programmable sequences of exchange and interaction between physically disjointed positions held by social actors in the economic, political and symbolic structures of society'. Dominant social practices are embedded in dominant social structures which are constituted by those organizations and institutions which play a strategic role in shaping social practices and social consciousness. It is clear from Castell's analysis that power has become hybridized. The space of flows comprises three layers of material supports. The first layer is constituted by a circuit of electronic exchanges comprising telecommunication networks, computer-processing devices, broadcasting systems and high-speed transportation systems. The spatial articulation of dominant functions takes place in the network of interactions made possible by information technology. The second layer is constituted by nodes and hubs which are organized hierarchically according to their relative weight in the network. The third layer is constituted by the spatial organization of the dominant managerial elites. The twin mechanisms of domination in the networked society are the spatial articulation of elites and the spatial segmentation and disorganization of the masses. Elites are cosmopolitan while people are local: power and wealth are projected around the world while everyday life and experience are rooted in places, culture and history.

Castells rejects the impression that he has developed a contemporary version of elite theory in the tradition of C. Wright Mills. Rather, social domination results from the ways in which cultural codes are embedded in the social structure in ways that open up access to the power structure without the elite needing to bar access to its networks. This involves the construction of secluded communities behind the real barrier of real-estate pricing that leads to the constitution of a series of symbolic socio-spatial hierarchies and the unification of a symbolic elite lifestyle and environment that supersede the historical specificity of locale. This is a world of international hotel chains, airport VIP lounges and the postmodern monumentality of corporate headquarters. In the networked society, social domination takes on a temporal as well as a spatial dimension owing to the increasing dominance of what Castells (2000a: 461–99) calls 'timeless time'. The development of the network society shatters the linear, irreversible, measurable and predictable forms of time associated with modern industrial society. These are replaced by a 'forever universe' of self-maintaining, random incursive time that, using technology to escape the contexts of its existence, appropriates the value of any context or tense that could contribute to the ever-present. In other words, timeless time dominates the space of flows while places are time-bounded. The 'global turn' has thus highlighted the tendency for power to become dis-embedded and de-territorialized and the tendency for it to flow in non-regular and non-linear ways through the networks of the emergent global system. In the work of Castells there is a focus on both episodic and dispositional power, but these have been detached from 'placed' individuals and become attributes of the system. This tendency has been exacerbated by the approach to power developed within the 'complexity turn'.

Complex powers: the limits of the 'complexity turn'

An important linkage between the 'cultural', 'global' and 'complexity' turns can be found in Bauman's conception of post-panoptical power (Bauman, 2000: 8–15). According to Bauman, post-panoptical power has emerged as a result of the transition from 'solid' to 'liquid' modernity. During the era of 'solid' modernity, time was the principal tool of power and domination: space was solid and inert while time was active and dynamic; always on the offensive as an invading, conquering and invading force. This was reflected in Foucault's panoptical metaphor for modern power, where the inmates were fixed in space not knowing whether they were being watched or able to perceive the movement of their guards who were free to move at will. The source of power was embedded in the mastery of time and institutionalized in the routinization of time-rhythms. The pyramid of power was built on velocity and freedom of movement. The panopticon implied a relationship of mutual engagement and confrontation between two sides in a power relationship in which managers attempted to simultaneously guard their own freedom of movement while constraining the movement of subordinates. The latter impinged seriously on the former and the potential for 'absentee landlords' was seriously limited within the panoptical model of power. The strategy was, moreover, expensive as it involved administrative costs and burdens. Contemporary patterns of social change are marked by the emergence of social conditions in which attempts to accelerate speed of movement have reached its natural limits. According to Bauman (2000: 10–11), power can now move at the speed of an electronic signal and is essentially instantaneous. Power has become exterritorial – unbound and independent of space – and the awkward, expensive and irritating aspects of panoptical power can be abandoned. The age of post-panoptical power marks the end of mutual engagement, and the prime technique of power is escape, slippage, elision and avoidance and the rejection of territorial confinement (Bauman, 2000: 11). The contemporary global elite rule as 'absentee landlords' unburdened by the pressures of administration, management and welfare or the virtues of enacting moral or enlightened reform.

The most explicit attempt to explore the nature of power after the complexity turn can be found in the recent work of John Urry (Urry, 2003: 111–13; 2002: 60–1). According to Urry, complexity subverts the distinction between structure and agency and thereby renders problematic the dominant sociological accounts of power that have posited power as an aspect of human agency. In the age of complexity, power is no longer a thing or a possession, but something that flows or runs and may be detached from territory or space (Urry, 2003: 112). Urry essentially adopts Bauman's model of post-panoptical power that no longer involves actual or imagined co-presence, but rather the end of the era of mutual engagement in which power is subject to escape, slippage, elision and avoidance. The essence of power is travelling light: power defined by its speed, lightness, weightlessness and globality. This form of power is a capacity of both the global elites and civil society movements that challenge global elites. Power is hybridized in the way it combines social and material forms (cf. Latour, 1999) and unpredictable owing to its capacity to change form and to be simultaneously everywhere and nowhere. In the twenty-first century, the mutual visual reflexivity between public authorities and citizens has become increasingly complex. The planet is criss-crossed by complex forms of mediated informational power in the form of a web of satellites, CCTV, GPI devices, mobile communication devices, the internet, etc. However, everyday mobilities involve speed, lightness, distance and a capacity to move unnoticed between transmuting identities such as student, tourist and terrorist. Informational and mediated power is mobile, performed and unbounded. This is a source of both strength and weakness: complex ordering can lead to unintended consequences that can result in unintended and unpredictable transformations. Complex power is like sand which may stay in place forming clear bounded shapes, or avalanche and race away sweeping all before it. In the modern period, citizenship and social order depended on mutual visibility between the citizen and the state. In a world of global complexity, there has been a shift towards informational and mediated forms of power. Power is technologized through informational technology. Resistance to power is also mediated and fluid in form. Mediated power functions like an 'attractor' to which the trajectories of systems are drawn and which exert a gravitational effect on relations which come within their ambit. The global media exert such a gravitational effect as the whole world is both watching and seduced into being watched – like the reality show *Big Brother* written onto the global screen (Urry, 2002: 61).

The 'complexity turn' has usefully highlighted the changing characteristics of power in contemporary society and the tendency for power to be increasingly mobile, fluid and mediated. Complexity theory can, however, contribute little to an understanding of the social dynamics that rendered the articulation of social and political power more complex. The systematic decentring of the human subject by the 'cultural', 'global' and 'complexity' turns has systematically undermined any attempt to develop a sociological account of how and why social and political power have been complexified. These 'turns' have usefully highlighted the crisis, decomposition and de-territorialization of modern institutionalized forms of power. However, in order to uncover the dynamics underpinning the emergence of new complex configurations of power we need to explore how the articulation of social power has been 'complexified' by the intense, complex and contradictory processes of social transformation that have accelerated over recent decades and the ways in which these new configurations of power are lived or experienced. In an article first published in 1896, Georg Simmel argued that superiority and sub-ordination were the subject matter of sociology (Simmel, 1896). Simmel argued that superiority and inferiority were to be found in every human association and that in order to generate insights into particular social formations it was necessary to examine the particular and distinctive forms of superiority that exist in particular social formations (Simmel, 1896: 169). A key component of my argument in this book is that this remains the case even in our own age of global complexity. The analysis of power explored in this chapter highlights the extent to which power has always been complex. Modern forms of power emerged in both episodic and dispositional forms. The dominance of the nation state in the modern era ensured the dominance of episodic power and either rel-egated dispositional power to a subterranean status or successfully aligned the episodic power of the nation state with the subjective identities and dispositions of social subjects. This was reflected in the apparent solidity of the meta-ideologies and political identities of the modern era. The developments associated with the cultural and global turns have de-constructed and relativized the dominant institutions and processes of political modernity and shifted the balance of importance from episodic to dispositional power. This is reflected in the increasing dominance of postmodern forms of identity politics in contemporary society. The relationship between episodic and dispositional power is, however, con-tingent and conditional as it reflects ultimately the *form* in which the relationship between superiority and inferiority develops. These develop-ments do not imply an end to the era of mutual engagement. Power con-tinues to be channelled along the circuits of political modernity even if the dominant institutions and categories of political modernity are zombified relics (Beck & Beck-Gernsheim, 2002: 27) of those that existed in the period of 'high', 'first' or 'solid' modernity. The nation state con-stitutes an important hub in the informational matrix of the network society. The nation state also remains the most important player in the neo-medieval world of the new global disorder.

Modern forms of power are not yet totally exhausted and post-modern and global forms of power are not yet totally dominant. Power is ambiguous in form and experienced as liminality or a state of inbetweenness that is difficult to categorize. The world of superiority and inferiority outlined by Simmel remains intact even if these relationships are increasingly mediatized and mediated. The key challenge for polit-ical sociology in the twenty-first century is not to deny the enduring existence of mutual relations of power, but to uncover the mediations and reveal the patterns of superiority and inferiority that mark the contemporary world. Postmodern forms of power are generated within modernity and constitute a serious challenge to modern institutions and processes. In the following chapters, I will uncover the ambiguous forms of power underpinning the contemporary state, the determination of contemporary political cultures and identities, the mobilization of new social movements, the organization of global terror networks, contemporary citizenship rights and obligations, and the constitution of global civil society. The shifting balance between episodic and dispositional power can be seen in the transition from the modern to the postmodern state *form*. It can be witnessed in the growth of identity politics and the development of postmodern social movement politics. It is evident from the growth and changing form of terrorism and political violence. It can be seen in the transition from nationally determined to globally emergent forms of citizenship. The processes combine to create an unstable and ambiguous global (dis)order. The institutional architecture of modernity was based on the episodic power of the nation state and this was the form taken by its discontents. The current phase of transition is marked by the shift towards the increasing dominance of dispositional forms of power and anti-power within the decomposing institutional architecture of modern, episodic forms of power and anti-power. This is the genesis of the ambiguous and liminal social forms explored in the following chapters.

Summary and conclusion

In this chapter, I have explored the ways in which social and political power were conceptualized within the sub-discipline of modern political sociology and the ways in which this conceptualization has been challenged by the development of the 'cultural', 'global' and 'complexity' turns in political sociology. Within the modern paradigm, power was conceptualized as an objective and quantifiable phenomenon that was mobilized in 'episodic' fashion through or against the modern nation state. In more radical formulations, power was equated with ideology and was the mechanism through which powerful or dominant groups in society were able to generate distorted or 'false' consciousness amongst dominated or subservient groups. In this context, human freedom and autonomy were only possible in forms of human association where power was absent. The 'cultural' turn has built on the work of Michel Foucault to challenge the objective and 'episodic' model of power and to highlight the ways in which power is linked to knowledge and can take subjective and 'dispositional' forms. In this model, power is inescapable and can often have a constitutive as well as a dominating function *vis-à-vis* individual subjectivity and identity. The relationship between this conceptualization of power, the individual and the community has been explored through an analysis of the ways in which hegemonic 'discursive practices' fix patterns of meaning and belonging through postmodern forms of identity politics. The 'global' turn has explored the ways in which the dynamics of globalization have resulted in the de-territorialization of power and the disarticulation of power and the nation state. In the global 'networked' society power is increasingly located in the 'space of flows' which link together or bypass and ignore the specificities of place. The notion of 'post-panoptical power' links the 'global' and 'complexity' turns. The 'complexity turn' has highlighted the fluid and hybrid nature of power in a world system marked by global complexity. I concluded the chapter with the argument that the complexity of social and political power in contemporary society can only be understood adequately through an approach that explores how the ambiguous forms of social power that are generated by processes of social transformation are lived and experienced.

4
The End of the Nation State?
The Disarticulation of Power
and Identity

The nation state was the institutional colossus of the modern age. The power of the nation state was the prized possession of ruling classes and the target for hungry revolutionaries. The nation state institutionalized the universalizing Enlightenment values of liberalism and democracy on the basis of territorially defined nationhood. In the modern era, ideologies were *state* ideologies. The nation state provided a universalizing and internally consistent set of ideas about the role of the state in the process of human development, an essentialist view of human nature or the human condition and a utopian vision of the future. The nation state played a central role in the maintenance of fixed and stable political cultures and stable identities around universal and essentialist categories. This was achieved through either the repression of insurrectionary cultures and identities emerging from the dispositional power of the marginalized and oppressed or the co-option of oppositional movements into the dominant culture through the power of dominant ideologies and the 'imagined community' of national citizenship. The nation state thus articulated power and identity through the institutionalization of modern ideologies. In the previous chapter, I highlighted how intense processes of social and political change in recent decades have resulted in the increasing disarticulation of power and the nation state and the ways in which the 'cultural', 'global' and 'complexity' turns have conceptualized this as the decentring, decomposition and de-territorialization of the nation state and the emergence of new forms of power that are increasingly dispositional, fluid and non-linear. This has tended to disarticulate state and nation and thus power and identity and accentuate the 'global' orientation and functions of state institutions *vis-à-vis* national and domestic orientations and functions. However, I also noted how these complex and emergent forms of power continue to move primarily within and between the networks and hubs of political modernity and consequently the ways in which power exists as an increasingly ambiguous social form. The nation state played a central role in the development of modern social power and continues to provide the institutional architecture that supports the existence and movement of fluid and emergent forms of power. Consequently, the state has become an increasingly complex and ambiguous social form.

In this chapter, I explore the decomposition of the modern state and the disarticulation of 'state' and 'nation' in order to highlight the increasingly complex and ambiguous nature of the state in contemporary society. The chapter begins with an outline of the key sociological debates and perspectives on the modern state and the ways in which the focus on the governmental role of the state has become increasingly challenged by a focus on 'governance' and the importance of non-state actors in the development and implementation of public policy. The focus on governance has resulted in a focus on the ways in which the state has become 'hollowed out' as a result of policy 'overload' and the dynamics of privatization and deregulation. The section 'The nation state and the cultural turn' explores the impact of the 'cultural turn' on the analysis of the modern state which has challenged both the material existence and universality of state institutions. This has involved an increasing focus on the importance of discursive practices and symbolic rituals in the legitimation and reproduction of the state. The cultural turn also involved a deconstruction of the modern state by feminist commentators concerned to demonstrate the patriarchal dynamics underpinning the origins and form of the modern state and hence the non-universal and essentially 'fractured' nature of the modern state. The section 'The nation state and the global turn' explores the impact of the 'global turn' on the analysis of the modern state which has focused on the ways in which the dynamics of globalization have transformed the state into an important node in the global cultural economy. The consequences of these developments include the increasing disarticulation of 'state' and 'nation', the crisis and decomposition of national forms of citizenship and the emergence of new forms of transnational governance such as the European Union which highlight the shift towards an increasingly polycentric and multi-level global (dis)order. The next section, 'Political complexity and the state', investigates the ways in which the 'complexity turn' has explored the transformation of the state in terms of a shift from a nationally bounded 'gardener' function concerned with maintaining order and stability to a 'gamekeeper' function premised on the control of complex and non-linear global flows. The final section, 'The liminal state', highlights the essential ambiguities of contemporary political forms in the context of the transition from the 'modern' to the 'postmodern' state. I highlight the importance of understanding the state as an existential category and the ways in which this contributes to a clearer understanding of contemporary forms of power, ideology and identity.

The modern state: key paradigms and debates

While there were fundamental disagreements between the main paradigms of modern sociology with regard to the development and form of the modern state, the dominant approaches all articulated an 'episodic' or 'transitive' understanding of social power. The modern nation state was understood as an ensemble of institutions that performed the key regulatory functions of social reproduction including the mediation of competing or conflicting interests in civil society. The power of the nation state was analysed as a product of either the monopoly of the state over instruments of administrative and physical coercion or the alignment of state institutions with the interests of elite social forces in civil society or often a combination of the two. This was reflected in the sociological analysis of the modern state which followed three main avenues of enquiry. First, there were a variety of attempts to present the state as an institutional aggregate of competing interests. Important examples of this approach were pluralism and corporatism. Second, there were attempts to present the state as determined by societal relationships and interests. This approach took on both Marxist and non-Marxist variants. Third, there was a variety of state-centred approaches which presented the state as an independent, purposeful actor. I will present a brief overview of each of these modern approaches (see Hay *et al.*, 2006 and Pierson, 1996 for recent overviews of modern state theory).

The dominant approach within the conceptualization of the state as an aggregate of competing interests was pluralism. In essence, pluralism is a non-theory of the state. It is a theory of how power is fragmented in society across a plurality of competing interests and a theory of democracy focused on how liberal democratic systems adjudicate between competing interests. Early examples of the pluralist approach can be found in the work of H.J. Laski in the UK and David Truman in the USA (Laski, 1967; Truman, 1951), but it was the work of Robert Dahl that established pluralism as a leading paradigm in the interpretation of the modern state. In the context of a critique of elite theory,

Dahl (1956) developed a theory of 'polyarchal democracy' premised on the notion that the state had limited authority owing to the 'separation of powers' between a plurality of policy-based pressure groups. The role of the state was to oversee the competition between these groups as an impartial umpire in order to ensure that competition was fair and resulted in the public interest being maintained. In his later work, Dahl (1985) became more pessimistic with regard to the possibility for the pluralist model to overcome entrenched socio-economic inequality and inspired the formation of a critical pluralist approach that highlighted the excessive weight of corporate interests within the public sphere (Lindblom, 1977). There are close parallels between critical pluralism and corporatist and neo-corporatist approaches to the analysis of the modern state. Corporatism is premised on the notion that the articulation of sectional interests is integral to the smooth running of state machinery and the maintenance of social stability. Corporatism was closely aligned with fascist ideology and practice in the early twentieth century, but in the post-war period it emerged as a variant of neo-elite theory premised on interest-group agreement and compromise between capital, labour and the state as the basis for societal stability (Aron, 1950). In the neo-corporatist paradigm, the state is tied into a dependent bargaining relationship with key socio-economic groups in which favourable policies are traded for cooperation and expertise (Cawson, 1982). The focus is thus on elite inclusivity, intermediation, incorporation and reciprocity between key socio-economic actors. In Europe, corporatism tended to focus on state intermediation between the organized interests of employers and workers in bipartite or tripartite bargaining relationships (Baglioni, 1987; Therborn, 1992; Crouch, 1993). In the USA, the focus was on the ways in which the Federal Government encouraged corporatism in order to augment the micromanagement of policy (Milward & Francisco, 1983).

The notion that the form of the state is determined by societal relationships and interests was developed in both non-Marxist and Marxist forms. One of the most important non-Marxist contributions to this approach can be found in the work of Gianfranco Poggi. In *The Development of the Modern State*, Poggi (1978) explored the decreasing institutional autonomy of the state in the context of the shift from the nineteenth-century constitutional state to the modern liberal democratic state. The former had unrivalled power in relation to corporate interests in civil society and was able to maintain a marked degree of institutional separation between state and society. The growing power and influence of bourgeois interests in civil society resulted in the liberal state granting concessions in response to bourgeois demands and this compromised the autonomy of the state. The breakdown of the division between state and society impinged on the autonomy of the state leaving it with diminishing room for manoeuvre. Poggi highlighted the internal and external constraints on state action and the extent to which, in the context of extensive state involvement in civil society, state action is mostly *ad hoc* and reactive rather than an effective steering mechanism for the delivery of goal-oriented public policy. The Marxist approach to the analysis of the modern state has focused on how relations of exploitation and domination between capital and labour in civil society shape the form and function of the state. Two competing approaches emerged from the somewhat ambivalent position of Marx and Engels on the form and function of the state in capitalist society. On the one hand, following the position of Marx and Engels in the *Communist Manifesto*, the state was presented as a direct instrument of class rule. This position was later articulated further by Lenin in *State and Revolution* and can be found in the neo-Marxist approach of Miliband (1969) which developed an analysis based on an instrumentalist alignment between the state and the ruling economic elite. On the other hand, following the position of Marx and Engels in the *German Ideology*, the state was presented as being relatively autonomous from the interests of the bourgeoisie in order to overcome divisions within the ruling class and ensure the long-run maintenance of bourgeois domination. The debate within Marxism reflected both this underlying inconsistency in the political writings of Marx and attempts to overcome this inconsistency by efforts to 'derive' the form of the capitalist state from its logical or historical role in the reproduction of capitalist relations of production (see Frankel 1982 for an overview of the development of Marxist state theory in the twentieth century and Clarke, 1991; Hay, 2006; Jessop, 1990, 2008; and Bonefeld & Holloway, 1991 for more recent debates).

The approach within Marxism that has had the most enduring influence on contemporary state theory has built on the insights of Antonio Gramsci. In *The Prison Notebooks* (1971), Gramsci presented the state as a complex of practical and theoretical activities that maintained the hegemony of the capitalist or ruling class through the dissemination of ideas, language and moral codes in civil society. In the context of the resulting ideological hegemony, the working class submitted or consented to its own domination. This process required the state to be relatively autonomous from the economic power of the bourgeoisie. This position was developed further by Poulantzas (1978), who developed Gramsci's concept of hegemony and the arguments of Althusser (1971) concerning the differentiation of political and ideological structures from economic power, to argue that the key function of the state was to unify the interests of capital while disorganizing the working class. In order to fulfil this role, the state required autonomy from the class it sought to protect. Hence, the autonomy of the state was real. Poulantzas (1978) argued that struggle was inscribed within the state and that its development and form were determined through struggle. In the final analysis, however, the economic interests of capital were always decisive and the advances made by the working class within the state reproduced its ultimate domination. More recently, there has been an attempt to escape this teleological position by Jessop (1990, 2008), who combined the work of Poulantzas with insights from discourse analysis, regulation theory and systems theory to develop a strategic-relational account of the modern capitalist state. In this approach, Jessop posits a structural coupling between the state and the economy but with no necessary causal priority between the two. This approach overcomes successfully the determinism and teleology of Poulantzas, but the extent to which this approach remains in any way 'Marxist', however, is seriously open to question (Hay, 2006: 76).

In contrast to Marxist approaches, Weberian analyses of the modern state focused on the institutional autonomy of state organizations. The re-emergence of state-centred approaches in the 1970s marked a renewed theoretical interest in the Weberian tradition at a time of growing disillusionment with Marxist approaches. This approach presented the state as an independent rational authority determined by either the individual actions and intensions of state decision-makers or the objective organizational and administrative machinery of state structures. A series of new approaches were developed that built on an earlier tradition of 'institutionalism' that had been eclipsed by holistic approaches such as structural functionalism and Marxism and individualist approaches such as behaviourism. This 'new institutionalism' was marked by a unified belief that political action, beliefs and behaviour could only be adequately understood in their institutional context. The 'new institutionalism' took three main forms: rational-choice institutionalism; historical institutionalism; and sociological institutionalism (Schmidt, 2006: 102–9). Rational-choice institutionalism explored the interests and motivations behind the behaviour of rational actors in particular institutional settings. This approach was particularly concerned with the ways in which rational behaviour could lead to sub-optimal outcomes in particular institutional settings (Elster & Hylland, 1986; Ostrom, 1990) and the dynamics of principal–agent relationships in bureaucratic and regulatory institutions (McCubbins & Sullivan, 1987) and in multi-level institutions such as the EU (Moravcsik, 1998; Pollack, 1997). Historical institutionalism focused on the ways the state structures political action and the ways in which state capacity and policy legacies structure policy outcomes (Schmidt, 2006: 104). Through a range of historical case studies, analysts highlighted the 'path-dependencies' and the unintended consequences of historical development that emerge when institutions diverge from the intentional designs of social actors (Skocpol, 1979; Katzenstein, 1978; Hall & Taylor, 1996). Sociological institutionalism departs from Weberian assumptions to explore how political institutions are constituted by the norms, cognitive frames and meaning systems that guide human action and the cultural scripts diffused through organizational environments that serve symbolic and ceremonial purposes as well as utilitarian ones (Schmidt, 2006: 107). In this context, rationality is socially constructed and culturally and historically contingent, and goal-oriented action is guided by a 'logic of appropriateness' (DiMaggio & Powell, 1983, 1991; March & Olsen, 1989). The 'cultural turn' has impacted on new institutionalism through the ways in which a 'discursive institutionalism' has been applied to the forms of institutionalism outlined above. This is reflected in an increasing interest in ideas and the ways in which they are communicated through discourse within institutions and the ways in which this contributes to institutional change (Schmidt, 2002; Hall & Soskice, 2001; Blyth, 2002). Communication is achieved in the form of either 'coordinative' discourses which are disseminated through 'epistemic communities' (Haas, 1991), 'advocacy coalitions' (Sabatier & Jenkins-Smith, 1993) and 'institutional entrepreneurs' (Fligstein & Mara-Drita, 1996) within institutions, or 'communicative' discourses between political institutions and the public. The institutions explored by the 'new institutionalism' are not confined to state institutions and this approach has played a key role in articulating the shift of focus from centralized 'government' to increasingly decentralized forms of governance.

From government to governance: the hollowing out of the modern state?

An important bridge between the analysis of the modern state and the 'cultural' and 'global' turns in state theory is provided by the increasingly important and influential debate on governance. The focus on governance reflected a paradigm shift in the discipline of political science as the notion that state power was located in the central executive and parliament was increasingly questioned by an approach focused on the importance of non-state actors in the policy-making process and the 'hollowing out' of the state. The origins of the governance approach can be traced to the 1970s and the emergence of two approaches that highlighted an emerging challenge to the sovereignty and effectiveness of the centralized state. First, in the context of the growing crisis of the Keynesian Welfare State (KWS), a number of commentators highlighted the problem of an 'overloaded state' which had become overburdened by the demands of and obligations to the electorate and locked into a vicious circle of increasing scale and complexity, and, as a consequence, the state was increasingly unable to deliver policy outputs in an effective way (King, 1975). This was complemented by the work of 'post-Marxist' commentators, who highlighted how the contradictory role of the state in delivering both economic efficiency and social welfare was resulting in increasingly serious 'rationality' and 'legitimation' crises in advanced capitalist societies (Habermas, 1976; Offe, 1984). Second, there was a focus on the inter-organizational or intergovernmental nature of policy-making that highlighted the ways in which policy emerged from the interaction of a plurality of state and non-state actors with a plurality of separate goals and strategies (Scharpf, 1978). This approach was influenced by developments in the Federal Republic of Germany (FRG), where commentators highlighted the existence of a system of multi-level governance marked by fragmented decision-making and delivering suboptimal policy outcomes (Scharpf *et al.*, 1978), but which nonetheless achieved a degree of order through voluntary coordination (Hanf, 1978).

The more recent contributions to the governance approach have focused on the operation of policy networks in the development of government policy (Rhodes, 1997). Governance involves self-organizing, inter-organizational networks of actors who are interdependent although not harmonious. Central government is one actor amongst many and policy networks are presented as having significant autonomy from the state. In this model, governments are dependent on governance as a result of the way in which the state has been 'hollowed out'. The hollowing out of the state is a result of both external dynamics, such as the internationalization of finance and production, and internal dynamics, associated with policies of marketization, privatization and contracting out (Smith, 1999). In the UK context, commentators have highlighted the fragmentation of the core executive and its increasing dependence on complex policy networks (Hay & Richards, 2000). Similar tendencies have been isolated in Central and Eastern Europe (Goetz & Margetts, 1999). This hollowing out of the state is associated with a marked decline in state power (Peters, 1993: 47–50) and, in the UK context, is presented as a product of European integration, new forms of managerial accountability (Rhodes, 1994: 149), the growth of CCT (compulsory competitive tendering) and contracting out in local government (Patterson & Pinch, 1995), the centralization of budgetary control (Wanna, 1997) and the increasing employment of 'think tanks' and consultants by the state executive (Bakvis, 1997). The governance approach has become the new orthodoxy (Jessop, 1997: 574), reflecting the impact of Thatcherism or neo-liberalism (Holliday, 2000) and changes in the conceptual focus of social scientific analysis around Foucauldian theories of governmentability, new institutionalism and the neo-systems approach of Luhman.

While the state has been 'decentred', there is a general agreement within the governance approach that it has not disappeared. The state has disproportionate authority, finance and control *vis-à-vis* other policy actors (Smith, 1999: 253), and public agencies and institutions are dependent on central government for resources (see Holliday, 2000; Taylor, 1997; Skelcher, 2000; Morgan *et al.*, 1999 for UK case studies). The argument that the position of the state as 'first among equals' is unlikely to have the capacity to steer complex networks (Rhodes, 1997) is therefore contested. Müller and Wright (1994: 10) have argued that the new public management of the 1980s did not mark a reduction in central government authority, but a return to an earlier traditional form of state regulation that intensified political and administrative control within the central state. Indeed, Lowe and Rollings (2000) argue that there is nothing particularly new about governance and that there was a tension between governance and government throughout the twentieth century. Fragmentation and powerlessness proceeded the Thatcher years and resulted from the impact of external interest groups and departmental factionalism. With this in mind, it is perhaps useful to conceptualize the current situation in terms of a 'congested state' constituted by fragmented and plural forms of governance (Skelcher, 2000). While 'new institutionalism' and governance approaches have embraced the cultural turn to some degree, these approaches remain anchored firmly within the modern paradigm. Nevertheless, there are powerful arguments premised on the notion that the modern state has been decentred and dematerialized as part of the shift from modernity to postmodernity. In the following section I focus on these arguments in more detail.

The nation state and the cultural turn: the ritual or hyperreal state

The main impact of the cultural turn has been to question the existence of the state as a centralized, hierarchical sovereign body. There has been a concern to explore the state as a cultural form or at least to explore the mutual interdependence between the state and the cultural realm. Despite the importance of the 'cultural turn' in the social sciences, state theory has remained relatively aloof from discussions of culture (Steinmetz, 1999). It is, however, possible to discern an increasing concern to explore the state in the context of ideas or ideology or as a site of ritual and the symbolic. Early explorations of the ideational determination of the state were influenced by Talcott Parsons (1951) and the conceptualization of culture in cognitive terms as a set of ideas and beliefs that form the basis for social action and moral integration. This tended to produce behaviourist accounts of the state that attempted to explore how culture, in the form of popular attitudes towards government, shaped political systems and institutions (see, for example, Almond & Verba, 1963). More recent approaches have given considerably more autonomy to culture and have focused on how ideas, as expressions of culture, are responsible for creating and sustaining the state. There have been a number of attempts from within the Weberian tradition to demonstrate the importance of ideas in the development of the state and state policy. This has downplayed, but not ignored totally, the importance of material interests and institutional and socio-economic context to suggest that without ideas states are hollow, meaningless entities. A series of historical and contemporary case studies have attempted to demonstrate how autonomous cultural forms play a pivotal role in the generation of divergent policy styles (Hall, 1986; Carruthers, 1994; Scott, 1998; Hood, 2000). Within the Marxist paradigm, the cultural turn in state theory became manifest with the increasing popularity of neo-Gramscian approaches. This approach highlighted the importance of ideology in maintaining and legitimating the role of the state through the mutually reinforcing dialectical relationship between the state and culture. This approach was pioneered by Hall *et al.* (1978), who highlighted the ways in which the coercive practices of the state are extended and augmented by the close ties between ideological strategies and the forces of law and order. Critics of Gramscian Marxism have highlighted the way in which culture remains subservient to the state (Sullivan, 2000: 115–16) and Steinmetz (1999: 22–3) has argued that both Gramscian Marxism and neo-Weberian approaches maintain a conceptual distance and distinction between ideas and the state.

The cultural turn in state theory has resulted in a renewed interest in the work of Durkheim and an increasing focus on the state as a site of drama and ritual. The importance of ritual was explored by Geertz (1993) in his cultural anthropology of the Balinese state. In this analysis, the symbolic expression of political power is an end in itself rather than a means to an end. Power exists only in and through its expression in ritual: highlighting the enduring insight of the Roman poet Juvenal that statecraft requires 'bread and circuses'. Power not only intoxicates but it exalts (Geertz, 1993: 143). Pomp and ceremony are central to the successful execution of statecraft and have an instrumental payback as the state derives its powers from its imaginative energies and its semiotic capacity to make inequality enchanting (Geertz, 1980: 123). An attempt to explore the importance of ritual with regard to the modern British state is presented by Corrigan and Sayer (1985). Their cultural and historical analysis is an attempt to delve behind the 'idea' of the state in order to reveal its constructedness and its message of domination. State institutions are revealed as self-regulating cultural forms whose ability to regulate society rests upon the moral authority of cultural symbols and bourgeois-influenced rituals. Symbolic activities create moral boundaries, and the demarcation of acceptable images and behaviour by the state serves to normalize social divisions. Corrigan and Sayer highlight the important continuity of ritualized and theatrical forms of government alongside the development of more rational state machinery in eighteenth-century Britain. Indeed, core areas of the central state, such as the courts of law, remained unbureaucratized and these enduring theatrical forms of government obscured and facilitated the fundamental economic changes that were taking place during the period. The state was thus an important site of what Durkheim termed 'collective representation': the generation of symbols of collective meaning which provide a moral order that gives meaning to individual existence. Hence, the rituals of the eighteenth-century state unified emergent industrial elites through a set of rituals that safeguarded and strengthened their power. In order to be effective, symbolic forms of domination have to be both generated and transmitted through society. One of the most influential attempts to explore this process is provided by Pierre Bourdieu in his political sociology of symbolic forms. Bourdieu (1996) highlighted the way in which the state legitimates social advantage and disadvantage through its recognition of the qualifications and credentials of elite schools. The state is constituted as an autonomous 'field': an objective structure of power relations that provides a context for purposeful individual action. The state generates cultural capital and concentrates coercive, informational, symbolic and economic capital (Bourdieu, 1994). Struggle is inscribed within culture in the form of a competition for cultural capital in local 'fields' within and outside the state.

This position has been rejected by social constructionist approaches which are premised on the notion that the distinction between the state and ideas is artificial and that the state has no existence outside the texts and discourses through which the meaning or 'idea' of the state is communicated. The notion of the 'hyperreal' state has developed from the work of Jean Baudrillard, who presented the state as a simulation or real illusion. This notion has developed the work of Abrams (1988), who argued that the state as a free-standing superordinate entity is an illusion and that the 'idea' of the state is a reification built from the array of institutions that constitute the state system. In the work of Abrams, the idea of the state contributes to the ideological distortion of reality to the extent that it allows the perception of civil society as a sphere of fairness and equality and legitimates state violence. The social constructionist position has also been developed by Foucauldian analysts concerned with explaining the 'state effect' through which the state appears as an external power separated and divided from society. Mitchell (1999) has argued that the state is grounded in mundane material practices that involve discipline and regulation through supervision, surveillance and temporal and spatial arrangements. The state is intertwined deeply in everyday life which 'normalizes' its 'effect'. From this perspective, the power of the state is essentially a chimera and the state is implicated in chimerical forms of domination and control.

The feminist critique of the modern state

An important component of the cultural turn was the feminist critique of the universalism of the modern state. The early feminist contributions to the debate on the form and function of the modern state reflected a wider concern to theorize the interrelationship between the inequalities of class and gender (Eisenstein, 1979). Hence, feminist theory explored how the operation of the welfare state contributed to the structural dependence of women on men (Wilson, 1977). The early development of feminism involved a close, although often uneasy, marriage with Marxism. The divorce of these paradigms resulted from an increasing concern amongst feminist commentators to establish gender as an analytically distinct category. This involved the argument that Marxism conflated class and gender inequalities by giving causal priority to the former (Barrett, 1986) and thereby obscuring the operation of male power (Burstyn, 1983). This resulted initially in the 'dual systems' approach which attempted to explore capitalism and patriarchy as separate but interrelated dynamics (Eisenstein, 1979; Walby, 1990) and then a more radical agenda to explore patriarchy as a system of domination and oppression with its own independent dynamics. In relation to state theory, radical feminism involved a fundamental rejection of the conceptualization of power within 'malestream' political analysis. While the latter located power relations within the administrative structure of the nation state, the former located power within the private sphere of personal relations. Hence, Pateman (1979) contrasts the 'vertical state' of 'malestream' political analysis which is located in the public sphere and where political concepts relate exclusively to men with the 'horizontal state' which was rooted in the 'private' sphere and comprised a set of institutions that were integral to everyday life and which reinforced gender inequalities.

The feminist paradigm resulted in the conceptualization of the patriarchal state: the state reflecting and institutionalizing patriarchal social relations. While male domination existed outside the orbit of the state, the state was nevertheless presented as a fundamental and significant source of social power that expressed the interests of men over women. The state maintained patriarchal power as a result of the ways in which laws are formulated and enacted. Mackinnon (1989) contrasted the 'positive state', where legislation is enacted to either protect male authority or curb the worst excesses of patriarchal domination in order to legitimate male authority, and the 'negative state' which is exemplified by the US Constitution and where the oppression of women is not overcome because civil society is subject to legal safeguards. This focus on legally constituted patriarchy has often been extended to a consideration of the role of state force and violence in the control of the private sphere of everyday life. For radical feminists, violence is inherent to patriarchy as evidenced by the prevalence of domestic violence, rape and sexual abuse. The state utilizes its monopoly of legitimate force and violence to maintain existing forms of domination and oppression and thus male force over women is institutionalized by the state (Daly, 1987). In this context, war constitutes the institutionalization of sexual violence as it naturalizes gender oppression and sexual violence (Hoffman, 2001: 119–20). The state has also been presented as an agency of symbolic force and violence. In her analysis of the state censorship of pornography, Butler (1997) has argued that this state activity constitutes an extension of state power which seeks to produce subjects according to explicit or implicit norms. Through its definition of 'hate speech' the state threatens the cultural operation of certain forms of sexual politics, and through the intervention to censor hate speech, the state ends up supporting and reproducing the language of hate. The analysis of the patriarchal state has, however, been criticized owing to the instrumental conceptualization of state power within the radical feminist paradigm and the way this tends to produce an account of the state as monolithic, one-dimensional and homogeneous (Jessop, 2001a: 155; Mills, 2003: 206).

In the context of these conceptual problems, feminist theory has either retreated somewhat from a monolithic or homogeneous model of the patriarchal state in order to highlight the 'relative patriarchy' of the state (Marinetto, 2007: 83–4) or has embraced the post-structuralist approach and deconstructed the 'essentialist' categories of 'gender' and the 'state'. The former approach has focused on the 'constitutive' role of the state in both the reproduction of gender inequalities and the historical possibilities for their abolition (Franzway *et al.*, 1989). There has been a focus on 'femocracy' or the ways in which the state is able to transform the social and political circumstances of women in the context of the growth of female political representation (Hernes, 1987), the 'mainstreaming' of an integrated approach to gender inequality across governing institutions and policy areas (Mazur & Stetson, 1995) and the progressive role of transnational governance structures such as the EU (Walby, 1999). Post-structural feminism has developed the Foucauldian model of power as defuse, fragmented and elusive in order to construct a model of the postmodern state as an arena of conflict where unequal gender relations are institutionalized but challenged (Pringle & Watson, 1992). In this approach, the state is presented as a fractured structure comprising practices and discourses. Struggle is inscribed in the state form and is thus an important site of resistance to unequal gender relations. In an analysis of sexual politics in the UK local state, Cooper (1995) highlighted how the ambiguities of the state and the lack of fixed boundaries enabled state power to be challenged and feminist groups to gain access to the power of the local state. The state is thus presented as constitutive as it has the power to establish gender boundaries and operate as a site of multiple resistances where gendered identities are shaped and defined. However, the notion that women have a common interest has been challenged by analyses focused on the deconstruction of gendered identities and the argument that gendered identities are not fixed but subject to constant renegotiation. This has resulted in the argument that there are many versions of masculinity and femininity (Connell, 1990) and the question as to whether women have a common interest or a divergent range of interests, agendas, tactics and strategies (Jessop, 2001b). The 'cultural turn' in state theory has thus served to deconstruct the universalism of the state and highlight the ways in which both material and symbolic forms of domination are inscribed within state discourses and practices. I now turn to a discussion of the 'global turn' in state theory which has tended to highlight how the institutional power of the state has been de-territorialized resulting in the disarticulation of 'nation' and 'state'.

The nation state and the global turn: the end of the nation state?

It is something of a paradox that the global turn has witnessed a renewed interest in the state. The resulting debate has tended to mirror earlier debates on the relationship between state and society although the focus has been transposed to the transnational level. The debate has focused on the sovereignty of the state in the face of globalizing forces and the extent to which the process of political globalization has resulted in the emergence of transnational modes of governance. The former focus has tended to explore the extent to which the dynamics of the global economy associated with developments such as the growth in international trade and the liberalization of financial markets have undermined the sovereignty of the nation state. The argument that the sovereignty of the nation state has been undermined by global processes has been developed from a hyperglobalist or transformationalist perspective that encompasses both supporters of neo-liberal globalism and neo-Marxist critics. These approaches share a concern to explore the denationalization of the world economy and the ways in which economic forces beyond the nation state associated with international agreements such as WTO and NAFTA have undermined the ability of the nation state to subject economic actors to democratic accountability. To supporters of neo-liberal globalism such as Japanese business consultant Kenichi Ohmae, these developments are an inevitable and welcome by-product of globalized markets. The state is presented as an unnatural business unit that should cede control to agents of the global market in order to ensure global peace and prosperity (Ohmae, 1995). A similar correlation between globalized markets and global peace and prosperity has been made by Friedman (2000), who developed his, subsequently discredited, 'golden arches' theory of conflict prevention to argue that no two countries containing a branch of fast-food outlet McDonald's have ever been engaged in warfare. The opposite case is made by Ritzer (2004), who has argued that the dynamics of global capitalism have undermined the sovereignty of the state and in the process have destroyed locally controlled patterns of social life and economic activity. Strange (1996) has argued that globalization has resulted in a fundamental shift in the balance of power between nation states and the global market linked to the production structure of the world economy and the denationalization of the market. There is something of a paradox here as the decreasing power of the state has apparently coincided with the increasing involvement of the state in the micromanagement of socio-economic life.

There are, however, critics of the hyperglobalist position who, while accepting that the nation state has lost a degree of independence and control, nevertheless argue that the nation state has maintained an important regulatory role within the international economy. According to this perspective, the state has played an important role in facilitating the expansion and liberalization of global markets and remains the key institutional form of legal regulation and social and political integration (Hirst & Thompson, 1999). Hirst and Thompson have questioned the assumptions of the hyperglobalist position with regard to the extent of global economic integration and the decline of state sovereignty in the contemporary period. The current globalization of the economy, they suggest, is less marked than it was during the era of the Gold Standard (1879–1914), and nation states had less autonomy during this period than during the contemporary era. Hirst and Thompson suggest that the current period is marked by a highly internationalized economy with high levels of cross-border trade between companies that remain largely rooted within national boundaries. This international economic configuration remains subject to the governance of effective and viable nation states. Indeed, Weiss has argued that the state has expanded its functions into the global era in order to ensure the alignment of domestic and global economic forces and can be seen as facilitator rather than victim of globalization (Weiss, 1998). There are, however, less narrowly economic accounts that highlight how globalization has intensified the importance of the nation state owing to the cultural imperatives of a stateless but increasingly important global society.

The end of the nation state thesis is rejected by the so-called 'Stanford School' who have developed a sociological variant of the 'new institutionalism' to argue that globalization strengthens rather than weakens the importance of the nation state (Meyer, 1997, 2000; Meyer *et al.*, 1997a, 1997b). The growth, development and operation of the world system is dependent on its 'statelessness', and the cultural and associational properties of world society have a determining effect on many features of the contemporary nation state. The form of the contemporary nation state is determined by worldwide models that are constructed and propagated through global cultural and associational processes which define and legitimate national agendas and determine the shape of nation state structures and policies. This accounts for the 'structural isomorphism' of diverse nation states with divergent traditions, histories and organizational forms. The world level of social reality is thus seen as culturally transcendent and causally important in three important ways (Meyer *et al.*, 1997a: 148). First, nation states routinely organize and legitimate themselves in terms of universalistic (world) models based on citizenship, socio-economic development and rationalized justice. Second, these models are quite pervasive at the world level and there is a great deal of consensus on the nature and value of issues such as human rights, citizenship, the environment, development and education. Third, the models rest on claims to universal world applicability rather than having local or regional relevance. The world level is thus seen as providing the cognitive and ontological models of reality that specify the nature, purposes, technologies and resources of nation states. Nation states are more or less exogenously constituted entities and this has three important implications with regard to the nature of the contemporary nation state (Meyer *et al.*, 1997a: 151–2). First, nation states exhibit a marked degree of isomorphism with regard to their structure and policies. Second, nation states strive to become rational actors and as a consequence often exhibit considerable decoupling between purposes and structure and intentions and results. Third, nation states often undergo expansive structuration in largely standardized ways. Hence, the argument that globalization diminishes the sovereignty of the nation state is rejected in favour of the argument that globalization strengthens the world-cultural principle according to which national state structures are designed and operated. Nation states are the principal agents responsible for identifying and managing the problems and dilemmas generated by globalization. The expansion of the authority of the nation state may result in unwieldy and fragmented structures but this does not imply that the nation state has become weaker.

Global governance and the recomposition of the nation state

In the context of globalization, the role of the nation state in maintaining the productive power of a particular territory is widely seen as having increased in importance. The administrative apparatus of the nation state is expanding to cope with the complex demands of global systems. The power of the nation state has thus been recomposed into a polycentric and coordinated form of networked global governance. While state regulation involved the nation state mediating between the competing interest groups of civil society on issues of resource allocation, governance is premised on the multi-level coordination of networks of institutional actors, including nation states, on issues of broad value and goal consensus (Rosenau, 1999). The resulting transnational spaces are populated by the autonomous actions of a range of trans- national actors including a range of intergovernmental organizations (IGOs) and international non-governmental organizations (INGOs). The main IGOs include the United Nations and its subordinate agencies such as UNESCO, UNICEF, WHO and the IMF, and organizations such as the World Bank, WTO and NATO. IGOs have become more important at the regional level as evidenced by the development of the European Union, the North American Free Trade Agreement (NAFTA) and the Association of Southeast Asian Nations (ASEAN). The number of INGOs has pro- liferated since the 1960s and includes environmental pressure groups such as Greenpeace and Friends of the Earth, religious forums, sports' organizations such as FIFA and welfare organizations such as the Red Cross. Global governance networks include IGOs, INGOs, MNCs and BINGOs (Business INGOs) such as international trade and employers' organizations. The notion of neo-liberal globalism highlights the extent to which the global elite wedded to the liberalizing agenda of the 'Wash- ington Consensus' have been able to dominate the emerging trans- national public sphere. This is reflected in the liberalizing agenda of organizations such as the World Trade Organization (WTO) and the International Monetary Fund (IMF) and a policy emphasis on the liberal- ization of trade in goods and services, and the reform of social welfare and social protection systems by organizations such as the European Union (EU).

The increasing importance of multinational agreements and trans- national and intergovernmental institutions has resulted in a shift from state-centric analyses of the international political system to a focus on the dynamics underpinning an emergent system of multi- level governance (MLG). Global governance is constituted by an array of formal supra-state bodies, regional organizations and transnational policy networks that involve, *inter alia*, government officials, tech- nocrats, corporate representatives and NGOs (Held & McGrew, 2002: 59). MLG is a process whereby key regulatory activities have shifted from nation states to a complex network of supranational, national and sub-national bodies and institutions (Sørensen, 2004: 65). The EU is an example of 'deep integration' that involves the voluntary cession of sovereignty by nation states. The debate on MLG has focused on the extent to which this form of governance involves a diminution of nation state sovereignty. On the one hand, there is an argument that political globalization has rendered the state less powerful and more dependent on sharing sovereignty and so the development of MLG involves a shift from a state-centric international order towards an autonomous multicentric world (Rosenau, 1990). On the other hand, Marks *et al.* (1996) argue that MLG involves the pooling of sovereignty which also has the effect of strengthening the domestic powers and capacities of nation states. The global polity approach sidesteps this debate to some extent through the argument that, while the development of worldwide government is unlikely under present circumstances, the current situation is marked by a situation of governance with many governments rather than governance without governments (Ougaard, 2004). Hence, the global polity is not constituted by hermetically sealed nation states but entities (including states but increasingly non state actors) which occasionally reach agreements and cooperate on specific policy issues (McGrew, 2002; Keck & Sikkink, 1998). This is presented as part of a global associational revolution and the beginnings of a global system of democratic global governance (McGrew, 2002: 210–25).

There are serious problems with both the globalist and anti-globalist analyses of the state and political globalization. The globalists have tended to over-exaggerate the earlier autonomy of the state while the anti-globalists fail to differentiate or recognize the difference between qualitative and quantitative shifts in the global economy and hold to an overly economistic conception of globalization (Held *et al.*, 1999: 11–12). However, the analysis of the social, political and economic spaces between the local and the global is more than the search for a compromise (cf. Marinetto, 2007: 126), but is essential in order to overcome the limits of the global turn and embrace global complexity. An important contribution to this project is the work of Sørensen (2004), who suggests that economic globalization has resulted in the nation state undergoing a process of complex flux or transformation. The alternative analyses presented by state-centric or realist, liberal and critical analyses each focus on a different aspect of a complex reality. With regard to sovereignty, the state is both a winner and a loser in the face of economic globalization. The principal focus of state activity has shifted from intervening to prevent market failure in the domestic economy to the role of maximizing the competitive advantage of nationally based economic activity in the global economy. This reflects the crisis of the Keynesian Welfare State (KWS) and the transformation of the state into a 'competition state' (Cerny, 1990) or 'Schumpeterian workfare state' (Jessop, 2002). Hence, the functions of the state have been transformed by the dynamics of global competition but the nation state remains a significant albeit transformed global actor. This insight is developed further by commentators within the 'complexity turn' who stress the increasingly important role of the state with regard to the regulation of complex global networks and flows.

Political complexity and the state: from gardener to gamekeeper?

The 'complexity turn' has analysed the form and function of the state in the age of global complexity in the context of the post-panoptical model of power. The principal role of the state, it is argued, has shifted from 'gardener' to 'gamekeeper'. The principal function of the modern nation state was to act as a 'gardener' in order to produce order and affect governmentability within a relatively fixed territory which contained a relatively unchanging 'community of fate' (Lash & Urry, 1994). However, post-panoptical power is not premised on the imagined co-presence of others, but is defined by 'escape, slippage, elision and avoidance' and 'the end of the era of mutual engagement' (Bauman, 2000: 11). The new global elite rules 'without burdening itself with the chores of administration, management [and] welfare' (Bauman, 2000: 13). This does not result in the marginalization of the nation state, but a transformation in its form and function: from 'gardener' to 'gamekeeper'. As John Urry has argued:

> The fluid and turbulent nature of global complexity means that states have to adapt and co-evolve in relation to enormously different sets of global networks and fluids that transform the space beyond each state. States thus co-evolve as the legal, economic and social regulators, or *gamekeepers*, of systems of networks generated through the often-unpredictable consequences of many other systems. (Urry, 2005: 248; my emphasis)

The nation state takes the form of an 'island of order' within a sea of disorder. The nation state coexists alongside other 'islands of order' which include complex hybrid diasporas, supranational state institutions, transnational religions, international organizations and NGOs (Urry, 2003: 108).

In the age of global complexity, the state has developed the important functions of developing the productive powers of territory and producing new spatial configurations (Swyngedouw, 1992: 431). The emergence of global fluids has precipitated the development of an increasingly diverse range of 'new' nation state structures designed to regulate the flow of information, people, terrorism and health and environmental risks which move across borders in dizzying and transmuting form (Meyer *et al.*,

1997a: 157). The EU, for example, has played a key role in encouraging the mobility of capital, labour, goods and services within Europe and, through European legislation and directives, has played a key role in aligning the public policy of European nation states around a commitment to competition and the elimination of barriers to competition (Urry, 2003: 110). The EU has played the role of 'midwife' in encouraging the development and growth of global networks and fluids and, in this context, states are increasingly important agencies in an unpredictable system of global complexity. States are 'networked' through international treaties and conventions and play the important role of promoting and performing the global (Castells, 2000b). States are not developing in a uniform direction, but are becoming more diverse, as can be seen through the comparison of the EU, USA and states such as Afghanistan and Iran. In each case the state adapts and coevolves in a relationship with the systems it seeks to orchestrate (Weiss, 1998).

In the context of global complexity, states have become increasingly detached from 'nation'. Urry (2003: 87) argues that the interaction between the nation state and the 'strange attractor' of glocalization has resulted in the 'nation' becoming a free-floating signifier within the swirling contours of the new global order (see also Harvey, 1996; Delanty, 2000). This is a result of the increasing permeability of national borders and the decreasing importance of territory in the process of national self-definition (Maier, 1994: 149; see also McCrone, 1998). In this context, nationality is increasingly constituted through specific local places, landscapes and symbols: national icons within the contours of global business, tourism and branding (Urry, 2003: 87). States have emerged as the legal, social and economic regulators of practices and mobilities that are generated by the unpredictable consequences of many other entities (Urry, 2003: 109). The modern nation state strove to striate the space over which it reigned in order to vanquish nomadism and control flows of population, commodities and money (Deleuze and Guattari, 1986: 59–60). In contrast, global networks and global fluids transform the space beyond which each state has to striate and, therefore, states have emerged as the legal, social and economic regulators of practices and mobilities that are generated by the unpredictable consequences of many other entities (Urry, 2003: 109).

The liminal state: from global governance to the 'scream' of anti-power!

The past three decades have witnessed the decentring, de-territorialization and complexification of the nation state and this has transformed the socio-political landscape of modern society. The 'cultural', 'global' and 'complexity' turns in political sociology have provided valuable insights into the dynamics underpinning these processes, but have contributed little to an understanding of the changing ways in which the state is 'lived'. The disarticulation of 'state' and 'nation' has decentred the state as a central component in the process of identity construction. However, the increasing focus on the symbolic power of the state has intensified the idea of the nation, and ideologies of nationalism have become increasingly de-bound from the material territoriality of the nation state. The power of the state has been de-territorialized into a power matrix which spans multiple levels and sites in an expanding system of global governance that has imposed the neo-liberal doctrine of globalism across the planet. However, the state remains 'placed' and also remains the only political institution imbued with democratic legitimacy. The state system coexists alongside an array of other complex systems in an increasingly chaotic and unstable global system of complexity. Yet the nation state system is the only 'attractor' capable of imposing a measure of 'ordered chaos' on the global system.

As Sørensen (2006) has argued, we know the time of the modern state is past but we do not know for sure what is developing in its place. The transformation of the state is complex and it involves fundamental changes in global configurations of power and identity. In the face of economic globalization, the role of the state has been neither strengthened nor weakened but transformed from an agency of economic management towards a procedural-regulatory agency which takes an increasingly polymorphous form within transnational and multi-level networks of other state and non-state actors. The development of multi-level governance has raised fundamental questions with regard to established models of democracy, legitimacy and sovereignty. There are, however, no clear-cut answers to these questions. While MLG undermines the democratic legitimacy of the nation state, it has the potential through transnational cooperation to bring under political control economic and environmental forces which escape national boundaries and evade national regulation. In relation to sovereignty, the development of MLG has transgressed the basic regulatory rules of national sovereignty: non-intervention and reciprocity (Sørensen, 2006: 199). The example of the EU highlights the extent to which states intervene in the affairs of others as a matter of routine and develop non-reciprocal relations in order to achieve policy outcomes such as social cohesion. The development of MLG is also contributing to the emergence of complex and ambiguous political identities. While there are few signs that 'national identity' is being marginalized as the principal location for communities of 'citizenship' and 'sentiment', the content of 'nationhood' is being transformed by sub-national and supranational networks of obligation and political opportunity structures. The crisis of the modern state is thus producing increasingly ambiguous political cultures and identities.

This ambiguity is particularly apparent with regard to what Castells (1997: 8) terms the 'resistance identitities' of those groups of social actors whose position is devalued by the dynamics of globalization and the increasing dominance of transnational networks. An interesting expression of this ambiguity has been explored by Holloway (2002) in his reformulation of 'revolution' following the experience of the Zapatista uprising in Mexico (see also Holloway & Peláez, 1998). The established definition of revolution was an 'extra-legal takeover of the central state apparatus' (Trimberger, 1978: 12) leading to a fundamental trans-formation in the state and class structure of society (Skocpol, 1979; see Kimmel, 1990: 4–7 for an expanded definition). In the modern era, therefore, the aim of a revolution was to seize and transform the state. The Zapatista uprising highlighted an emerging ambivalence to the state amongst those movements and groups struggling against oppression. Holloway (2002: 1) presents this as the 'scream': an expression of collec-tive rage in recognition of a world of oppression articulated as opposition, negativity and struggle. In the context of the failed 'Marxist' revolutions of the twentieth century, the meaning of revolution today is not to secure 'power over' the state but to articulate a form of 'anti-power' that can deliver an autonomous 'power-to' that results in the dissolution of 'power-over'. However, as McNaughton (2008: 3–4) notes, responses to oppression are significantly more complex than Holloway suggests and involve resistance and despair, self-destructive behaviour and forms of both conscious and unconscious identification with the oppressor. Indeed, the relationship between the Zapatistas and the Mexican Govern-ment is highly ambiguous and the Zapatistas' demands included both recognition and autonomy from the state.

As Sørensen (2006: 204–5) has argued, the state is between the 'modern' and the 'postmodern'. I wish to extend this insight to a sociological inter-pretation of the liminality or inbetweenness of the state. The contem-porary nation state articulates the ambiguities of a political order that is undergoing transition. As I demonstrated in Chapter 3, an important component of this transition is a shift in the balance of importance between 'episodic' and 'dispositional' power. The 'cultural', 'global' and 'complexity' turns have all highlighted the ways in which this shift has impacted on the universality, territoriality and linearity of the territorially defined nation state as a system of rule and a form of power. The problem with these approaches is the tendency to present the shift from modern to postmodern political forms in transformational terms rather than part of an ongoing process that is partial, incomplete and institutionally 'messy'. Postmodern political forms are developing within a framework in which the institutions and ideologies of modernity remain dominant. While it is true that these institutional and ideological forms increasingly constitute 'zombie categories' that have died but live on in a new context (Beck & Beck-Gernsheim, 2002: 27), postmodern political forms are nonetheless developing within the decomposing structure of political modernity. The state is not simply a 'thing' but a social relation that is 'lived'. We need to consider the changing and ambiguous form of the state in existential terms. In contemporary society, we 'live' the state as a liminal social form: a liminal state in a state of liminality. In Chapter 5, I develop this insight further through an analysis of the ways in which the crisis and decomposition of the modern state is resulting in the emergence of ambiguous and liminal forms of political culture and identity, and in Chapter 6, I explore in more detail how the ambiguities of the contemporary state are associated with the emergence of ambiguous and liminal social and political movements in contemporary society.

Summary and conclusion

In this chapter, I have explored the development of the modern nation state and the ways in which it has been decentred, decomposed, recomposed and restructured in the context of the intense social change that has marked recent decades. The chapter highlighted how the 'cultural', 'global' and 'complexity' turns in political sociology have attempted to make sense of the changing form and function of the nation state. Modern political sociology analysed the nation state as a unitary, legitimate and sovereign institution within an international order of sovereign nation states. The 'cultural turn' was presaged by the recognition that the crises and contradictions of state regulation were resulting in the decentring or 'hollowing out' of the nation state and the emergence of decentred and networked forms of governance. The 'cultural turn' took this analysis further through the deconstruction of the universal and sovereign form of the nation state and a concern to explore the symbolic and discursive power of the 'state effect' rather than the reified institutions and structures of the nation state. The 'global turn' has focused on the ways in which the dynamics of globalization have resulted in the further decentring and decomposition of the nation state and the integration of the nation state as an important node or hub in the global political system. The state is increasingly structured at the global level and plays a pivotal role in an emerging system of transnational multi-level governance. The complexity turn highlighted the increasing disarticulation of 'nation' and 'state' and the increasingly important 'gamekeeper' role of the state in the regulation of complex global networks and global fluids. I concluded the chapter with the argument that in the context of the intense social change of recent decades, the power of the nation state has been neither reduced nor enhanced but transformed into a complex and ambiguous socio-political form that is increasingly 'lived' or experienced as a liminal state or a state of liminality.

5
Glocalized Identities: Political Culture between Place and Space

A central concern of modern political sociology was a consideration of the ways in which political beliefs and political action were related to the generation of symbolic meanings or 'culture' and the patterns of 'being', 'belonging' and 'becoming' associated with individual and collective identity. In modern society, culture and identity were determined by the spatial and temporal dynamics of modernization: political-cultural identity was both 'placed' and inexorably bound up with the temporal unfolding of the modernist project. Modern political-cultural identities were forged as individuals and groups in diverse localities responded to and resisted the structural changes unleashed by the universalizing dynamics of capitalist modernity. The dynamics of modern development had a corrosive effect on pre-modern identities, and modern identities have been unable to solidify owing to the dissolving and corrosive effects of (de)industrialization, urbanization and migration. The institutions of modernity simultaneously fragmented modern cultural identities and provided the institutional glue which attempted to impose coherence and stability on the fragments. The constant tendency towards fragmentation was only ever partially and temporarily overcome by cultures of resistance within communities and workplaces that challenged the abstract dynamics underpinning the money economy and the power of the nation state to construct and maintain patterns of being, belonging and becoming through the 'imagined community' of nationhood (Anderson, 1991). The decomposition of modernity has resulted in the decentring of the nation state as centralized state regulation has morphed into decentralized forms of governance. States are increasingly constituted as 'nodes' or 'hubs' in the network that constitutes the global cultural economy with the principal function of capturing, controlling or containing global flows of capital, labour and information. In this context, the role of the state as an 'imagined community of fate' (Lash & Urry, 1994: 280) has been increasingly marginalized as national forms of citizenship have been undermined by transnational dynamics and nationhood has become increasingly decentred as a source of self- and social identity. In this context, modern cultures and identities have become increasingly fragmented, fluid, mobile and de-territorialized.

In this chapter, I explore how the disarticulation of 'state' and 'nation' has impacted on modern forms of political-cultural identity. In the following section, 'Political-cultural identity and modernity', I outline the way in which political-cultural identity was conceptualized within the paradigm of modern political sociology and the ways in which the modern paradigm has been adapted by theorists such as Anthony Giddens to take account of the globalization and intensification of modernity. The analysis of self-identity in late modernity has resulted in a concern to explore the individualizing tendencies of globalized modernity in terms of a search for ontological security in an increasingly risky 'runaway' world. This provides a link to the section 'Identity and the cultural turn', which is concerned with how the 'cultural turn' has transformed the analysis of political-cultural identity. The focus of the cultural turn has included a consideration of the ways in which the ambiguity generated by the postmodern condition has resulted in the development of new forms of identity politics based on shifting and unstable collectivities and fractured and fluid identities. This is widely held to have degraded democracy and resulted in the emergence of new forms of medieval tribalism. The section 'Globalization and the de-territorialization of culture and identity' explores the impact of the 'global turn' on the analysis of political-cultural identity with a particular focus on the work of Argun Appadurai (1990), whose work has highlighted the ways in which culture and identity have become increasingly de-territorialized by the flows of the global cultural economy. The section 'Complex cultures and identities' explores the impact of the 'complexity turn' on the analysis of cultural-political identity and the ways in which complex identities are presented as having emerged from the effects of the 'strange attractor' of 'glocalization'. In the final section, 'The postmodern political condition', I argue that while the 'cultural', 'global' and 'complexity' turns have usefully highlighted important changes in the constitution and composition of socio-political culture and identity, these approaches fail to consider adequately important continuities with socio-political modernity. I suggest that this can be understood through the notion that liminal cultural-political identities have developed through the ways in which postmodern forms of politics continue to be articulated in and through modern political categories and institutions.

Political-cultural identity and modernity: between collectivism and individualism

Modern political sociology was concerned with a particular aspect of identity through which private self-understandings are expressed within the public sphere. This notion of political-cultural identity (Preston, 1997) was concerned with the question as to how we come to think of ourselves as members of a political community. Within the classical sociological tradition, the issue of political-cultural identity focused on the role of political-economic, social and institutional factors in the construction of the self, where the self was ethically engaged and bound up in the modernist project. In this model, the political-cultural self is socially constructed in the context of locale, networks and memories and involves the self-conscious location of the self in the social world. While there were approaches which attempted to reduce the self to an 'essence' based on language, 'race' or gender (Smith, 1986), the dominant approach was to see the self as learned and relearned or acquired and involving multiple readings or presentations (Giddens, 1991). Political-cultural identity was thus defined by the creative response of groups to both necessary and contingent changes in their structural circumstances (Winch, 1958). These changes involved costs in terms of responding to new locales, the building of new social networks and the reordering of memory. An important source of political-cultural identity in modern society was the locale where 'person-centred' understandings of individualities and collectivities were constructed on the basis of folk knowledge and folk ideologies. In the locale, political-cultural identity was formed partly on the basis of biographical accident and, on this basis, patterns of power and authority tended to be informal and practical while engagement with formal politics tended to be episodic. Radiating out from diverse local contexts were networks of groups forming the wider collectivity. Overarching these locales and networks were patterns of memory through which individuals, groups and collectivities secured understandings and legitimations of the power underpinning social relationships. Memory was constituted by common sense, folk traditions, institutional truths and official histories.

The central components of political-cultural memory in the modern era were notions of nation, nationalism and nation statehood. The 'nation' emerged as an 'imagined community' during the nineteenth

century on the basis of the proliferation and consolidation of v
print languages (Anderson, 1991). The development of the na
involved the construction of modern citizenship defined by
ship of a community of political equals and associated with the notion
of nation statehood. During the nineteenth century distinctive state
regimes with distinctive state projects developed and these were con-
solidated further during the first half of the twentieth century. The nation
state was an institutionalized form of political authority through which
state elites were able to pursue political opportunities within an international state system, while simultaneously organizing their domestic
populations on the basis of formal and informal ideologies and agencies
of social control. The development of democracy highlighted the extent
to which state projects were based on the exercise of rational debate in
the public sphere. In the context of industrialization and the development and consolidation of the nation state system, therefore, nationalism
emerged as a historically contingent response to changing circumstances
and the dynamics of class struggle (Nairn, 1988; Gellner, 1983; Hobsbawm,
1992).

During the post-war period, patterns of political-cultural identity formation were relatively solid and stable. In the developed world, the
notion of the 'free West' provided the overarching legitimating framework for the nation state, while 'socialism' and 'development' played
this role in the second and third worlds respectively (Preston, 1997:
12–13). The structural changes that have taken place since the mid-
1970s, however, have provided the context for important changes in
the dominant forms of political-cultural identity. There have been a
range of important structural changes associated with the crisis of
the USSR and the end of the Cold War, the global integration of the
world economy, particularly through the globalization of finance and the
increasing importance of transnational and multinational corporations,
the emergence of new global divisions and inequalities and a marked
process of regionalization. The necessary and contingent responses made
by social actors to these important structural changes provide a focus on
how social agents themselves 'read' social change. In the context of
global regionalization, structural change has broadly confirmed the
bipolar character of the new global (dis)order. In Europe, the crisis of the
Keynesian Welfare State (KWS) and the resulting process of economic and
political integration combined with the existing ideological currents of
Christian and social democracy to produce a new political-cultural identity of European-ness. In Pacific Asia, the end of the Cold War resulted in
the emergence of political-cultural identities premised on state-directed

capitalist development underpinned by existing ideological currents of family and community. In the USA, political-cultural identities have continued to express an ongoing commitment to free market individualism within the context of the new tri-polar global order. In the undeveloped world, however, the development of political-cultural identity has proved far more problematic. While there are examples of economic growth and development, particularly in nations with reserves of oil, the generation of Westernized political-cultural identity has proved problematical owing to political instability, environmental degradation and deepening social inequalities. The shift from 'high' to 'late' modernity has intensified the process of social dis-embedding and time-space distanciation which underpinned the development of modernity, and this has undermined the importance of locale and face-to-face interaction in the formation of political-cultural identity. The nature of these changes has been explored by Anthony Giddens in his work on self-identity in late modernity.

Self-identity in late modernity

The precise relationship between globalization and the transformation of self-identity is highly contested. The main faultline is between accounts that present globalization as the further development or intensification of modernity and those accounts where globalization is understood as a central component of postmodernization. An important contribution to the former position and an important attempt to develop a political sociology of 'late' modern identity can be found in the work of Anthony Giddens. The work of Giddens on self-identity builds on his theory of structuration: an important attempt to overcome the dualism between structure and action in modern social theory. According to Giddens, structure and action do not exist in opposition to one another, but form a duality whereby social structures are both constituted by human agency and at the same time the medium of this constitution (Giddens, 1976: 121). Social practices have a socially constitutive role in social reproduction as shared practical knowledge underpins the orderliness of everyday encounters. In more recent work, Giddens (1990, 1991) has explored the relationship between globalization and modernity in order to develop an ontology of the self and a theory of identity. Identity is presented as a reflexive project of the self grounded in relations of trust and security and risk and anxiety. The development of globalized or 'late' modernity has further dis-embedded social relations from fixed localities and this has undermined the importance of the traditional parameters of place, kinship and locale for the fixing of self-identity. Trust is increasingly embedded in global networks and institutions. Individuals are confronted by a range of ambiguous institutions and networks and face an almost unlimited number of personal choices concerning 'lifestyle'. In this context, 'life politics' increasingly takes over from 'emancipatory' politics as the dominant expression of radical or progressive politics. The late-modern self is an uncertain personal relationship and is faced by an indeterminate world that is full of clever people (Giddens, 1994: 7): skilled and knowledgeable individuals moving between social contexts and using social institutions in order to achieve security and stability in their everyday lives.

The ontology of the self developed by Giddens is premised on the notion that the modern world is ontologically unique. This uniqueness lies in its reflexivity, the internality of its referential systems and its transformational character whereby all individuals in society attempt to 'bend' the future. The modern world is, following Durkheim, marked by the plasticity of its traditions and, in late modernity, the property of plasticity also marks institutions, identities, sexualities and subjectivities. The uniqueness of modernity is not the product of reflexivity *per se* but a specific post-traditional form of reflexivity linked to the increasing scale of knowledge and information associated with the historical changes that have impacted on institutional and everyday contexts. These changes involve the 'end of nature' as nature is dissolved into the social resulting in a fully humanized or plastic nature (Giddens, 1994: 101). The resulting relations with nature generate the 'manufactured uncertainties' of late modernity as individuals exist in created environments and are forced to make practical and ethical decisions (Beck *et al.*, 1994: 29). Environmental risks become high-consequence risks precisely because the environment as both an external ecosystem and an internal bio-anatomical system is the medium and outcome of human activity. These manifestations of 'second nature' are the source of intense epistemological uncertainty and ontological angst. The objective world appears as an out-of-control Juggernaut as the objectivity of the object is obscured by social relations of trust and risk.

The increasing importance of reflexivity and risk provides the context for the model of identity developed by Giddens. Identity links feelings and emotions with institutional and social change. Identity and the self are both grounded in reflexivity. While the latter is grounded in mundane or practical reflexivity, the former is grounded in the proliferation of knowledge and information in global modernity and, in this context, 'trust' forms the bridge between self and identity. The body is integral to modern self-identity as it forms the embodiment of modern personhood. Modern bodies instantiate the absent properties of the self anew on each occasion of their social use (O'Brian, 1999: 33). The body constitutes a practical mode for handling the world in the service of psycho-social coherence and its failure can lead to personality disorders and pathologies. The modern world is a world seething with feelings and emotions; every action and decision constitute an emotional investment of the self. The linking of the public and the private, and the personal and the political, by Giddens in this way results in the model of 'utopian realism' as the politics of late modernity. Utopian realism links autonomy and solidarity in the modern world through the pursuit of 'dialogic democracy' in the personal and public spheres. Realism is linked to actual social processes while utopian relates to the 'will to dialogue'. Dialogue is facilitated by globalization and rooted in the emergence of the 'pure relationship'. The 'pure relationship' originates in the realms of sexuality, marriage and friendship and is based on commitment, trust, exploration and intimacy outside the constraints of traditional relationships based on kinship, family and locale. In this context, there is no shared tradition and any tradition becomes an option amongst many. Dialogic democracy amounts to the 'democratization of democracy' and emerges at the micro level in the form of the negotiation of intimate relations and at the macro level in the form of the cosmopolitan confusion of competing traditions and normative frameworks and the globalization of shared risks and uncertainties. In globalized modernity, there are, therefore, countervailing pressures towards dialogue on the one hand and fundamentalism and violence on the other. The normative agenda of utopian realism involves fostering the conditions under which dialogue is able to prevail over fundamentalism and violence. This involves a commitment to 'generative politics' premised on an active trust in government, the regeneration of civic culture and the encouragement of individual responsibility. According to Giddens (1994: 180–94), this has three important implications for the reorientation of radical politics: the redefinition of welfare in the direction of 'positive welfare'; the development of a generative model of equality; and the development of the 'autotelic self'.

Critics of Giddens, however, have questioned the radical credentials of the utopian realist project. The model of self-identity developed by Giddens rests upon an acceptance or indeed a celebration of philosophical conservatism. As O'Brian (1999: 36–7) notes, in the context of enduring problems of poverty and social exclusion, it is difficult to assess the extent to which the emergence of the autotelic self is part of the problem or part of the solution. The confrontation of risk and the translation of threats into challenges can have both positive and negative consequences as it involves the successful or unsuccessful management of stress. The management of stress, however, involves the management of an inner core of feelings and emotions that form a key part of the social fabric through which individual selves are formed, maintained and changed. Moreover, the social institutions of globalized modernity constitute emotional regimes or matrices where feelings and emotions are organized in the service of instrumental goals (Hochschild, 2003). For O'Brian (1999: 37), this raises a further question with regard to whether the autotelic self is a product of social change or a normative goal to promote individuation over sociation. It could, therefore, be argued that generative politics amounts to the subordination of the 'hetrotelic self' to the autotelic self associated with the individualization of threats, risk and stress. While Giddens rejects the label of 'postmodernism', the focus on the fragmentation of culture and the individualization of political identities in his approach provides an important contribution to the 'cultural turn' in the sociological analysis of self- and social identity. I will now focus on the implications of the 'cultural turn' for the analysis of political-cultural identity in more detail.

Identity and the cultural turn: being and becoming in a fragmented world

The key argument underpinning the 'cultural turn' is the notion that the 'postmodern condition' undermines the coherence of modern ideologies. The postmodern condition involves epistemological uncertainty as foundationalism has given way to the notion that knowledge is context bound and therefore undependable and ambiguous. This leads to ontological pluralism and the recognition of a multiplicity of different realities all with equal significance and importance. Hence, the postmodern condition undermines foundational knowledge and 'decentres' fixed and stable sources of meaning and identity. Zygmunt Bauman has argued that this creates a state of *ambivalence* amongst individuals which results in a loss of faith in science, scientific rationality and 'metanarratives' such as liberalism, socialism and Marxism (Bauman, 1991: 244–5). The 'dissolving of the social' and the bonds that bind people together in communities has resulted in the emergence of a new social order based on the random activities of individual people attempting to make sense of the world and their place within it. In modern society, social solidarity was achieved by the state administering universal policies that overcame the differences between individuals. The distinction between 'purity' and 'dirt' or order and dis-order within modernity created the distinction between 'insiders' and 'outsiders', and the nation state attempted to deal with the latter either through assimilation (the imposition of uniform beliefs and language), expulsion (through ethnic or social cleansing) or through destruction (the Holocaust) (Bauman, 1997). The 'social' had economic, political and geographic boundaries that needed to be policed, and state inter-vention in the personal sphere was rendered natural, normal and, there-fore, legitimate. The postmodern condition involves a rejection of uniform truths and universal moral codes. The postmodern condition is a world without certainty in which individuals have to formulate their own sense of social solidarity. In the postmodern world, class, race and gender have become increasingly immaterial and 'decentred' as the principal loci of self-identity. The process of identity formation has become a skilled activity through which individuals actively organ-ize the fragments of their existence in order to maintain ontological security. In contrast to the hierarchical organization of knowledge in modern society, knowledge increasingly takes the form of the rhizome. Deleuze and Guattari (2002) highlighted the emergence of new forms of decentred subjects emerging from the schizoid institutions of cap-italism. The development of a 'dynamic unconscious' was determined by a process of 'becoming' based on the decentred subjects of the 'schizoid' and the 'nomad' that were free from fixed identities, modern subjectivities and organized bodies.

According to Bauman (1996), the problem of identity in the modern world was fixed on the maintenance of existential and ontological security. The creation and maintenance of a fixed and stable identity was a necessary pilgrimage or 'life project' undertaken by the modern individual. The fluid and fragmenting melting pot constituted by the modern metropolis demanded that individuals constructed a fixed identity in order to avoid becoming lost in the urban desert of 'noth-ingness'. In contrast, the problem of identity in the postmodern world is fixed on avoiding a fixed identity. In a world of 'timeless time' and the 'ever-present', identity as a fixed and stable life project has become increasingly problematic and has been replaced by a series of lifestyle projects or life strategies. The modern 'pilgrim' who spent a lifetime building a single, coherent and 'centred' *life project* has been replaced by a fragmented being constituted by a series of alternative postmod-ern life strategies that are based on short-term mini-projects and fluid, decentred identities. These identities were assumed to be marginal in modern societies but have become the dominant life strategies in postmodern society. The *Stroller* or *Flâneur* is an itinerant who searches fo meaning in the urban environment where all meaning is found in appearance. The *Vagabond* is the constantly moving stranger unable to settle down because of the scarcity of settled places. The *Tourist* is an individual who moves constantly from home in search of new experiences and to escape the boredom of home. The *Player* is an individual who treats life as a game and treats nothing as serious, controllable or predictable. For such an individual, the only point to life is to stay ahead and embrace the rules of the game. In the context of these post-modern life strategies, life has become shallow, fragmented and discontinuous. The fragmentation of modern culture has resulted in a proliferation of cultural artefacts, orientations and practices through which it is possible to construct self-identity. Individuals have become 'entrepreneurs of the self' and utilize the resulting autonomy to change fundamental aspects of their identity including physical appearance, gender alignment and political orientation (Wagner, 1994). Living becomes an increasingly skilled activity as individuals consciously direct a route through the fragments that constitute human existence. These processes and dynamics underpin the development of postmodern politics.

The development of postmodern politics has involved the decreasing importance of social class as the basis for social identity and the declining importance of metanarratives as a basis for understanding the world. The postmodern condition involves a rejection of what Jean-François Lyotard has termed *metanarratives* – the myths and stories or ideologies that legitimate political institutions and activities (Lyotard, 1984). These metanarratives included socialism, communism and feminism and provided universal models of how to think and how to act politically to supporters of these projects. These metanarratives defined a community in relation to itself and its environment and told people what to think and how to think it – assumed truths that needed no proof or justification, with dissent being defined as a form of *political incorrectness*. Modern metanarratives are dissolved and deconstructed by the postmodern condition. Postmodernity involves the deconstruction of modernity or modernity coming to terms with its own impossibility (Bauman, 1991: 272), and the essential characteristics of postmodernity and postmodern politics are institutionalized pluralism, contingency and ambivalence (Bauman, 1992: 187). Bauman (1997: 22) has described postmodern politics as a form of neo-medievalism that has involved a reversal or deconstruction of political modernity and a return to a 'medieval world of beggars, plagues, conflagrations and superstitions'. This includes the decline of the centralized state; the decline of participatory democracy;

importance of political violence; the emergence of
tities; and the development of politics without rules.
(1994b), the recycling of medieval values recreates old
lighlights the extent to which history is now in reverse.
ing reached its speculative limits and extrapolated its virtual developments is disintegrating into its simple, constituent elements
in a catastrophic process of recurrence and turbulence that Baudrillard
defines as 'rehabilitation by bricolage' and 'eclectic sentimentality' (Baudrillard, 1994b: 10–11, 35). Postmodern politics involves a rejection of
'totality', 'unity' and 'universalism', and individual freedom has become
the yardstick by which beliefs, ideas and practices should be measured.
Postmodern politics is the politics of single-issue movements and the
replacement of party politics by the politics of 'imagined communities'
or groups of people who *feel* that they have something in common.
In a social and political system in which everything is open to negotiation and subject to change, there is a tendency towards irrationality
and instability. The ambivalence at the heart of the postmodern condition results in an identity politics in which politics is created by
individuals rather than being imposed on them.

Bauman (1997) has argued that the following forms of politics mark
the postmodern condition. First, there is a 'tribal politics', where tribes
are imagined communities formed by individuals with shared values,
attitudes and beliefs. This often involves a return to fundamentalism as
communities draw on shared symbols to construct a common self-
identity. Second, there is a 'politics of desire', which involves the need
to acquire tribal tokens by the members of imagined communities.
This results in the merging of citizen and consumer as articles such as
food, clothes and music become highly politicized and the political
becomes personal. Third, there is a 'politics of fear', which involves the
avoidance of potentially harmful effects. In this case, uncertainty
results in an increasing dependence on experts and an increasing ques-
tioning of the advice of experts. Fourth, there is a 'politics of certainty',
which is concerned with trust and the way experts attempt to produce
and distribute certainty. Individuals are mostly unable to challenge or
endorse the arguments of experts, but exercise choices on the basis of
trust, and the manipulation of trust becomes the basis for the politics
of certainty. In the postmodern world, a loss of trust can be seen as
a major threat to identity. Postmodern politics is thus premised on
liberty, diversity and tolerance: although this may become manifest as
a liberty reduced to consumer choice, a diversity reducible to lifestyle
choice and a tolerance based on spectator curiosity in front of a TV

screen. This is what Bauman (1991) refers to as the 'dark side' of post-modernity. Imagined communities develop tribal conceptions of right, truth and beauty, and without the constraints of reason it is possible that barbarism and brutality will be applied to those outside the community. In this context, privatization and selfishness are intrinsic parts of the postmodern condition.

Postmodern political culture: degraded democracy or do-it-yourself culture?

The tendency towards privatization and selfishness associated with the 'dark side' of postmodernity has been highlighted by a number of commentators concerned with the degradation of democracy in contemporary politics. Skocpol (1993) charts a decline in the democratic vibrancy of civic organizations in the USA. Increasingly, membership organizations in the community have become memberless organizations that are dependent on professional managers and large-scale funding bodies. Previously, these groups 'taught democracy' through their imitative federal structures and provided members with important organizational and communication skills. Membership mattered and the leaders of organizations were forced to mobilize members and interact with a diversity of people from divergent occupational, social and ethnic backgrounds. The main beneficiaries of the shift from membership to memberless organizations have been the upper tiers of US society who have gained both leverage and voice as membership organizations have been professionalized. Putnam (2001) has also highlighted a trend towards the declining vibrancy of American civil society in recent years. The decline in civic engagement can be traced along a variety of indices: voting in local and national elections, attendance at public meetings or political rallies, or serving on the committee of a local organization such as a parent–teacher association (PTA) or church group, membership of labour unions, involvement in voluntary organizations such as Boy Scouts or Red Cross, fraternal organizations such as Lions or Elks and significantly for Putnam bowling in organized leagues. The tendency for Americans to be 'bowling alone' has not been mitigated by the emergence of new mass membership organizations such as The Sierra Club or the National Organization for Women, which tend to foster dues-paying passivity, or self-help groups such as Alcoholics Anonymous (AA) which tend to foster individual self-reflection. The decline in civic engagement has resulted in a declining level of social trust and 'social capital'. Putnam suggests a number of possible explanations for these developments: including the movement of women into the labour force; an increase in geographical mobility; demographic changes that have weakened the middle-class nuclear family; and the technological transformation of leisure in the form of the home entertainment provided by TV, DVD and PCs (Putnam, 2001: 277–84).

The crisis of modern political culture is linked to a wider crisis of modernity and the way in which this has generated a dynamic process of individualization. Individualization is a product of the structural hyper-differentiation that marks late modernity and the increasing impossibility of integrating fragmented individuals within functional systems with competing logics of action. Formerly, the nation state played a central role in this process owing to the ways in which the regulation of welfare encouraged self-reliance and self-organization. The intensification of modernity has involved the transformation of modern biographies into 'elective' or 'risk' biographies and, in the context of increasing uncertainty, the constant threat of biographical slippage (Beck & Beck-Gernsheim, 2002: 24). In this context, failure becomes personal failure, and social crises, such as structural unemployment, poverty and the increasing precariousness of middle-class living, are 'collectively individualized' and transformed into the risk burdens of individuals (Sennett, 1998). This is particularly evident in the discourse of the 'underclass' that has developed in the context of deindustrialization and the crisis of the social democratic state (Lash & Urry, 1994: 165–70). Within this discourse, the underclass has come to represent a dangerous internalized 'other' (Bauman, 1998: 67). The political project of neo-liberalism is of course committed deeply to a process of 'atomization' in which risk is intensified by the dismantling of those institutional resources such as welfare systems, education and human rights that are vital to the maintenance of risk biographies. This is resulting in the sub-politicization of society and the depoliticization of national politics (Beck & Beck-Gernsheim, 2002: 27–8). Hence, there is an increasing crisis of representative democracy owing to a lack of trust in collective actors and the hollowing out and reconstitution of collective actors as a result of the processes of globalization and individualization. The consequences of radicalized or 'second' modernity are characterized by two contradictory phenomena. On the one hand, the (re)emergence of new forms of nationalism, fundamentalism and terrorism based on ethnic and religious tribalism. On the other hand, demands for radicalized democracy premised on a reflexive recognition of the ways in which political parties, trade unions and the institutions of the welfare state negate freedom and self-realization and the way in which 'altruistic individualism' is made possible by the defence of the 'lifeworld' from the market and communal regulation.

In contrast to the 'dark' side of postmodern politics outlined by Bauman, it is possible to outline a possible 'light' or 'progressive' side based on demands for radical democracy by new social movements motivated by emergent forms of altruistic individualism. As I will argue in Chapter 6, the emergence of NSMs highlights the ways in which values are replacing class as the principal determinant of political identity and alignment (Inglehart, 1990). NSM politics poses a cultural challenge to the dominant language of an increasingly complex civil society. The actors within NSMs are presented as the transformative and prefigurative agents of post-industrial society or 'prophets of the present' that articulate alternative futures in the form of new values, identities and lifestyles (Melucci, 1989). Maffesoli (1996) has highlighted the tribal nature of new social movement politics, where 'the tribe' is not so much a fixed group as a certain ambiance or state of mind expressed through lifestyles, appearance and form. To what extent, therefore, are NSM politics simply a reflex of the tribal politics of desire, fear and certainty? There are many signs that the implosion of 'consumer' and 'citizen' associated with the process of hyper-differentiation has resulted in the politicization of articles such as food, music and clothing. The 'politics of desire' is manifested in a range of 'new age' quasi-religions or the aestheticization of politics around post-material issues such as gender, sexuality, human rights and the environment (Bagguley, 1995). NSMs attract participants through 'emotional recruitment' or through the way in which NSMs 'frame' personal experiences into individual meanings and organizational perspectives (McAllister-Groves, 1995). An examination of the phenomenon of 'DIY' culture that emerged during the 1990s highlights the ambiguous nature of contemporary political cultures and identities.

During the 1990s, radical forms of environmentalism emerged as part of a broader phenomenon of DIY culture: a youth-centred and youth-directed counter-culture premised on direct action politics and new musical sounds and experiences. The counter-culture included radical environmental groups such as Earth First! and Reclaim the Streets that were linked to alternative media such as Indymedia and Squall and new spaces of protest, pleasure and living such as rave music and free parties (McKay, 1998). In many ways, this was a paradigm case of postmodern politics with a number of distinctive features in comparison with earlier examples of counter-cultural politics (McKay, 1996). DIY culture resulted in forms of sub-national and localized tribal politics focused on the politics of desire, fear and certainty. This included the use of music and dress to subvert mainstream consumer culture and the refocusing of politics around 'fun', 'self-development' and affective micro-communities (Jowers *et al.*, 1999). DIY culture tended to be vicarious and anti-intellectual and to articulate a culture of immediacy that tended towards forms of narcissistic hedonism and lifestyle anarchism associated with single-issue campaigns and 'new age' spirituality. However, DIY culture also provided a reflexive challenge to 'expert systems' with regard to the environmental implications of global warming or road building and the reconstitution of trust through the development of direct and unmediated forms of media. Furthermore, DIY culture emerged as an important example of 'solidary individualism' (Berking, 1996) formed through a practical critique of the spectacular forms of mainstream politics and culture (Plant, 1992) and the demand for unmediated forms of radicalized cultural politics. DIY culture was essentially ambiguous and its form can be located somewhere between a reflexive 'risk community' that has emerged through a critique of scientific rationality and an articulation of counterfactual reason (Beck, 1992; Giddens, 1990) and the intersubjective identity politics suggested by Bauman (1992). DIY culture can be understood as a form of postmodern politics within modern society (Heller & Fehér, 1988): a form of politics premised on a rejection of grand narratives, the privileging of function over structure and a weakening of class politics. The development of postmodern politics has also been highlighted by commentators working within the 'global turn' who highlight the ways in which the dynamic flows of the global cultural economy have resulted in the de-territorialization of modern political cultures and identities.

Globalization and the de-territorialization of culture and identity

As I mentioned earlier, the precise relationship between globalization and the transformation of self-identity is highly contested and rests on divergent understandings of the relationship between globalization and modernity. In contrast to the position of Giddens, the process of globalization can be equated with a radical rupture from modernity and the emergence of a postmodern global society. In this context, the transformation of modern socio-political culture and identity has been focused on the emergence of a global cultural economy that has emerged through the complex and contradictory tension between cultural homogenization and cultural heterogenization. Appadurai (1990) presents the new global cultural economy as a complex, overlapping order determined by the disjunctures between the economy, culture and politics. These disjunctures are explored as the relationship between five dimensions of

global cultural flow which Appadurai terms 'scapes': ethnoscapes, technoscapes, financescapes, mediascapes and ideoscapes. These scapes are
deeply perspectival and form the building blocks of the 'imagined
worlds' that produce fluid and irregular landscapes of meaning and
have the potential to subvert the 'official' imagined worlds of fixed and
stable nation states. Ethnoscapes are constituted by landscapes of shifting people such as tourists, immigrants, refugees and guestworkers.
While stable communities still exist, ethnoscapes highlight the greater
number of people who are either forced to move or have the desire
or fantasy of wanting to move. Technoscapes are constituted by fluid
configurations of technology that cross national boundaries and take
the form of a technological infrastructure of transnational satellite and
cable networks. Financescapes are fluid movements of currency, stocks
and shares that cross national boundaries. The relationship between
ethnoscapes, technoscapes and financescapes is deeply disjunctive such
that each acts as both a constraint and a parameter for the others
and each has its own set of constraints and incentives. The resulting
disjunctive order is built on a series of mediascapes and ideoscapes
that result in a further series of disjunctures. A mediascape is constituted by the distribution of electronic capabilities to produce and dis-
seminate information and images of the world created by the media.
Mediascapes help to constitute narratives of the 'other' and the proto-
narratives of possible lives based on the fantasies or desires for acquisition or movement. Ideoscapes are also constituted by a distribution
of images that are often directly political and relate to the ideologies of
states or the counter-ideologies of movements oriented to capturing
states. Ideoscapes are composed of elements of Enlightenment thought
such as welfare, rights and sovereignty organized by the master term
of democracy. The global diffusion of these concepts and images has
undermined their internal coherence, and communication between elites
and followers on the basis of these concepts and images is increasingly
semantic and pragmatic in nature.

Appadurai (1990: 301–2) has argued that global flows occur in and
through the growing disjunctures between ethnoscapes, technoscapes,
financescapes, mediascapes and ideoscapes. These flows increasingly
follow non-isomorphic paths owing to the speed, scale and volume of
flows, and the resulting disjunctures contribute to the constitution of
global culture. The central problematic of global culture has become the
process of cultural reproduction in a context of de-territorialization.
The process of de-territorialization tends to bring labouring populations
into the spaces of relatively wealthy societies and tends to promote an

exaggerated sense of criticism or attachment to the politics of the home state. De-territorialization is, therefore, both a seedbed for the emergence of global fundamentalism and the basis of new markets through which media companies and travel agencies are able to exploit the need for de-territorialized communities to have contact with their homelands. The process of de-territorialization is the basis for the fractured and fragmented nature of mediascapes and ideoscapes. The disjunctive nature of the global cultural economy and the dynamic of de-territorialization have resulted in the increasing disarticulation between 'state' and 'nation'. In many places, nations or groups with ideas about nationhood seek to capture or co-opt state power, while existing states seek to capture and monopolize ideas about nationhood (Baruah, 1986). Imagined communities such as Sikhs, Tamils, Basques and Québécois constitute nations in search of a state. Existing states seek to monopolize the moral resources of community either by maintaining the alignment of 'state' and 'nation' or through forms of 'heritage politics' that serve to 'museumize' the origins of nationhood. Appadurai (1990: 304) argues that the disjunctive relationship between state and nation exists on two levels. First, it exists as a battle of imaginations based on the mutual cannibalization of state and nation. Second, it exists as a disjunctive relationship that is deeply entangled with global disjunctions. This is illustrated by the case of the Kurds whose claim for nationhood overstretches existing nation state boundaries. The increasingly 'disorganized' nature of capitalism also impacts on the disarticulation of state and nation. The state is forced to remain 'open' through the dynamics of media, technology and travel which can fuel consumerism and result in cravings for new commodities and spectacles. However, these cravings can become caught up in new ethnoscapes, mediascapes and ideoscapes in ways that threaten the integrity of the nation state. States are thus under siege where contests over ideoscapes of democracy are fierce or where there are disjunctures between ideoscapes and technoscapes or ideoscapes and financescapes.

The paradox of contemporary ethnic politics is the way in which the primordial categories of language, skin colour, neighbourhood and kinship have become globalized. These categories generate sentiments which have the ability to ignite intimacy into political sentiments and turn loyalty into a staging ground for patterns of identity that have become spread over vast and irregular global spaces. In this context, ethnic groups move but remain linked through sophisticated media capabilities. Globalization is not the same as homogenization but does involve instruments of homogenization. These instruments include clothing styles, advertising, language hegemonies and armaments which are absorbed into local political and cultural economies only to be repatriated into heterogeneous dialogues of national sovereignty, free enterprise and fundamentalism in which the state plays an increasingly delicate role (Appadurai, 1990: 305). In cases where there is too much openness, the state is threatened by internal revolt. Where there is too little openness the state may exit the international state system. Examples of the latter include North Korea and Burma. Global culture is thus a process through which sameness and difference attempt to cannibalize one another. This involves the hijacking of the twin Enlightenment ideas of the triumph-antly universal and the resiliently particular. The ugly side of this process can be witnessed in refugee flows, riots, state torture and terrorism. The light side is manifested in the form of fantasies generated by the hope for alternative imagined worlds. The relationship between culture, identity and irregular and disjunctive global flows has been developed further within the 'complexity turn'.

Complex cultures and identities: glocalization as a 'strange attractor'

The development of the 'complexity turn' has resulted in the analysis of global culture and global identities as part of a process of global emergence connected to the phenomena of 'strange attractors'. Strange attractors are defined as 'systems where spaces are unstable and to which the trajectory of dynamical systems is attracted over time through bil-lions of iterations and processes of positive feedback' (Urry, 2003: 83). The 'complexity turn' has built upon earlier work which highlighted the ways in which social systems were attracted to the 'centriphery' attractor: a dynamic and irreversible relationship between centre and periphery that simultaneously centres and peripheralizes and creates new patterns of order and disorder (Baker, 1993; Stewart, 2001). Urry (2003: 84) has reformulated this to suggest that the specific form taken by the centriphery attractor is 'glocalization'. This highlights the ways in which the global and the local are bound together in a dynamic relationship with massive flows of resources moving between the two and where the global and the local exist in a symbiotic, unstable and irreversible set of relationships where each is transformed through billions of iterations over time. These attractor effects are presumed to have led to a massive increase in the scale, intensity and range of information flows over the past two decades and have resulted in the increasing dematerialization of information flows. The process of dig-itization allows information to travel instantaneously within a fluid network of global communications. In this context, social relations across the world are transformed as diverse social practices are irreversibly 'drawn into' or 'sucked into' the glocalizing attractor (Urry, 2003: 85). The 'glocalization attractor' developed as information flows were intensified by the collapse of the former USSR, the increasingly global reach of international news agencies such as CNN, the deregulation of financial markets and most notably the development of the World Wide Web. These developments have enabled social relationships to be drawn into the attractor and in the process be irreversibly remade. The attractor does not presuppose a single coordinating centre but constitutes 'complexity without telos' as local changes induce wider populations to 'cooperate' in the emergence of new forms of behaviour (Kwa, 2002: 42).

The operation of the glocalization attractor has fundamentally changed the nature of nationality. As frontiers have become more permeable and cultural life interchangeable across national borders, territory has become a less important determinant of national self-definition (Maier, 1994: 149). Nationality is increasingly constituted through local places, symbols and landscapes which become icons of national culture within the context of global travel, business and branding. The nation has become a free-floating signifier that is detached from the state and which is central to the process of 'branding' within the swirling contours of the global order (Harvey, 1996; Delanty, 2000). The glocalization attractor is also important with regard to the more general development of and opposition to global brands (Klein, 2002). Brands flow in and out of cultures: downwards from the centre and outwards from local street life and cultures; a process through which local resistance is turned into new opportunities for global rebranding. Globalization generates its own opposition through networks and flows that resist global ordering through the organization of 'resistance identities' (Castells, 1997: 356). Resistance identities exist only as virtual communities linked by identifications constituted in the non-geographic spaces of activist discourses, cultural products and media images (Rose, 1996: 333) and partly through their resistance to flows which they seek to de-totalize and localize (Urry, 2003: 89). These developments have resulted in the disarticulation of civil societies. Important discontinuities have emerged between the logic of power-making in the global network and the logic of association and representation in specific societies and cultures (Castells, 1997: 11). De-territorialized global entitities are vulnerable to democratic mobilization by mobile, de-territorialized social movements. This was demonstrated in the effective resistance of 'anti-globalization' campaigners to the global liberalization agenda of the WTO. The anti-globalization movements are globally mediated and are both 'imagined communities' maintained by tribal symbols of consumption and internet communication and, through the 'compulsion to proximity', come together in contexts of intense fellow-feeling at events such as demonstrations, social forums and festivals.

The strange attractor of glocalization is held to be responsible for the disruptive and conflictual social and political relations that characterize the new global (dis)order. This is often presented in the apocalyptic terms of an emergent global disorder locked in conflict between a consumerist 'McWorld' and the identity politics of jihad (Barber, 1996). Barber has demonstrated the spiralling social disequilibrium that threatens existing forms of democratic public spheres and civil societies and contributes to new forms of inadvertent tyranny that range from the invisible constraints of global consumerism to increasingly palpable forms of barbarism (Barber, 1996: 220). This is presented as part of a more general process whereby established forms of citizenship are eroded and bifurcated into global consumerism and local identity politics. National forms of citizenship are drawn into the strange attractor of glocalization alongside Islam, Hinduism, evangelical Christianity and other local religions; thoroughly transforming the former and imbuing the latter with global characteristics. In the era of global complexity, according to Urry (2003: 107–8), the 'banal nationalism' of the modern era is increasingly played out on the global stage or global screen and it becomes a form of 'branded nationalism' that circulates amongst global information and communications systems. The resulting complexity is compounded by the fact that most 'societies' are not separate nation states, particularly in the case of 'nation peoples' affected by various forms of displacement and migration. The most notable of these non-nation state societies is constituted by the Chinese Diaspora. These groups are drawn into the glocalization attractor and rebranded within global complexity. This results in the emergence of multiple identities owing to the decline of the 'true national self'. Similarly, the Latino community not only forms the largest ethnic grouping in Los Angeles, but Latinos in the USA form the fifth largest 'nation' in Latin America. This has developed through the movement of transnationalized communities between Mexico and the USA: communities that exist like quantum particles in two places at once (Davis, 2000: 77). Hence, global complexity comprises multiple 'islands of order' made up of nation states, complex diasporas and other networked, fluid polities such as supranational states, global religions, NGOs and cross-border regions (Urry, 2003: 108; Habermas, 2001). Contemporary cultures and identities are seen as emerging from the 'strange attractor' of glocalization that is determined by these complex and contradictory networks and flows.

The postmodern political condition: the liminality of political-cultural identity

The 'cultural', 'global' and 'complexity' turns have highlighted important changes in the socio-political cultures and identities that dominate the contemporary world. The 'cultural turn' has highlighted how the rejection of 'grand narratives', the decentring of the self and the marginalization of the nation state have resulted in a political culture marked by ambivalence and the emergence of a 'pluriverse' of fragmented and fluid political identities. These developments are associated with the degrading of democratic political culture and the emergence of a 'neomedieval' political culture dominated by 'neo-tribal' political identities. The 'global turn' has highlighted the ways in which political culture and identities have become 'de-territorialized' as a result of the dynamics of globalization and the resulting disarticulation of 'nation' and 'state'. In the global cultural economy, political cultures and identities have become increasingly fluid and unstable owing to the disjunctures between flows of people, money, ideologies, technology and media images. The 'complexity turn' has explored the disruptive and conflictual global cultures and identities that have developed as a result of the 'strange attractor' of 'glocalization'. The strange attractor of glocalization determines an increasingly complex array of cultural identities through the emergent and non-linear flows between the local and the global. The focus has thus been on the decentring, de-territorialization and complexification of culture and identity rather than on the ways in which culture and identities are 'lived' and experienced. Consequently, the essentially ambiguous nature of contemporary political cultures and identities has been overlooked.

The origins of this ambiguity can be found in the fact that we live in a modern society dominated by constantly evolving forms of postmodern politics. As Heller and Fehér (1988: 1–13) have argued, postmodernity is neither a historical period nor a cultural or political trend with well-defined characteristics, but a 'private-collective time and space within the wider time and space of modernity'. Postmodern politics is a form of politics within modernity constituted by those who have problems with modernity and wish to take modernity to task and those who wish to make an inventory of the achievements and dilemmas of modernity. Postmodernism is a way of thinking about the world premised on the notion of 'being after' the 'event' of the modern: beyond the grand narrative, beyond class, beyond the revolution but not beyond history (Heller & Fehér, 1988: 3). In the postmodern imagination, there is nothing outside of the 'historical' because there is nothing beyond the contingency of human action that impels or creates 'necessity' (Tormey, 2001: 168). The modern is not less complex than the pre-modern nor is it less difficult to understand or submit to the human will. Indeed, modernity is 'decentred' and constitutes an unstable equilibrium and is becoming increasingly 'opaque', 'pluralistic' and 'heterogeneous'. Heller and Fehér (1988: 35) have argued that this 'opacity' is no barrier to emancipatory political action as long as action is not devised as totalizing. Postmodern politics involves a rejection of a revolutionary politics with the potential to 'revise' modernity as a totality in favour of a politics in which individuals acting singularly or together through political parties and movements act for themselves and others in order to transform the here and now (Tormey, 2001: 170). The postmodern political condition is marked by a Janus-faced relationship between politics and morality. Postmodern politics is underpinned by an irrationalism and an unpredictability which, in the context of total moral relativism, can lead inexorably towards the emergence of the negative identities of racial and ethnic hatred. Hence, there is an intense ambiguity underpinning postmodern culture and political identities.

The 'cultural', 'global' and 'complexity' turns in political sociology have charted the evolution and development of postmodern political culture and identities but have failed to grasp adequately that these new forms of culture and identity have developed *within* modernity. Postmodern political-cultural identities are, therefore, premised internally on communicative identity formation and premised externally on the instrumental pursuit of interests (Cohen, 1985). The 'decentring' and globalization of modernity have resulted in the decentring and marginalization of the nation state and problematized the instrumental pursuit of interests through political parties and movements. As I demonstrated in Chapter 4, this has resulted in an increasing tendency towards the politics of refusal and autonomy: the politics of anti-power rather than forms of politics that confront and attempt to challenge and transform the institutional power of capital and the state. These forms of institutional power have, however, been intensified by the processes of neo-liberal restructuring and through the dynamics of hypermodernity which, through the commercialization of lifestyles and the emergence of a rampant individualism, have had a corrosive effect on social identities and political cultures (Lipovetsky, 2005). Political cultures and indentities are thus between the modern and the postmodern, between the global and the local, and as a consequence highly ambiguous and complex. This complexity is not determined by a systemic 'attractor' but through the ways in which these ambiguities or liminal cultures are 'lived' and used to construct equally ambiguous and liminal forms of identity. In Chapter 6, I explore the ways in which these ambiguous forms of culture and identity are manifested in the politics of new social movements.

Summary and conclusion

In this chapter, I have explored how modern forms of political-cultural identity have been challenged and transformed by the 'cultural', 'global' and 'complexity' turns in political sociology. The chapter began by stressing the extent to which modern political culture and identity were always contingent and prone to disintegration but various forms of community stretching from the locale to the nation state provided a degree of institutional solidity and fixity. The 'cultural turn' in political sociology has explored the ways in which the postmodern condition and the 'decentring' of the modern nation state have shattered the solidity of modern culture and generated increasingly fragmented and individualized forms of political-cultural identity. The impact of globalization on modern political culture and identity remains contentious and there is an ongoing debate between sociological accounts that conceptualize globalization in terms of the expansion and intensification of modernity and approaches which present globalization as a dynamic leading to a global society that is beyond modernity. The former approach highlights the ways in which identity formation is an increasingly individualized process owing to the reflexive nature of globalized late modernity. The latter approach highlights the fluid and non-linear processes of identity formation that result from the disjunctions that underpin the global cultural economy. The chapter then explored the ways in which the 'complexity turn' has employed the metaphor of the 'strange attractor' of glocalization to highlight how identities emerge from the complex and non-linear relationship between the global and the local. In the final section, I established the case for analysing contemporary political-cultural identity as the ambiguous and liminal product determined by the way in which postmodern forms of politics are lived and experienced within modern society.

6
Networks of Resistance: Global Complexity and the Politics of New Social Movements

The labour movement was *the* social movement of modern society. The labour movement emerged during the nineteenth century as the principal oppositional movement in civil society that articulated a collective resistance to the individualizing dynamics of the capitalist market. The principal objective of the labour movement was to politicize the employment relation and social welfare. The successful expression of this was the KWS and nationally specific forms of institutional corporatism which resulted in the labour movement becoming integrated or incorporated into the institutions of the state. The resulting contradictions were responsible for both the long-term crisis of state welfare (Offe, 1984) and the erosion of the legitimacy and mobilizing capacity of the labour movement (Offe & Wiesenthal, 1985). This crisis of 'institutional politics' was the context for the emergence of the 'new right' and the 'disorganized capitalism' (Offe, 1985a) associated with globalization. The social democratic and socialist left decomposed into a series of radical new social movements concerned with rolling back the state, not in favour of the market, but in favour of advanced welfare ideals based on self-management in civil society (Offe, 1985b). The 'new social movement paradigm' is premised on the proposition that the labour movement belongs to a past era of industrial capitalism. The shift from old social movements has been presented in terms of both important changes in the nature of society and economy and changes in the values and orientations of individuals in contemporary society. Important structural changes include the process of deindustrialization in advanced Western societies and the shift towards a post-industrial or informational economy. This has coincided with an important shift in the dominant values in these societies away from class-based material and instrumentalist orientations towards the post-material values of autonomy, personal self-esteem and intellectual and aesthetic satisfaction (Inglehart, 1990). This shift has been the principal focus of the 'cultural turn' which has focused on the emergence of a range of new social movements based on issues such as sexual orientation, gender, race and ethnicity and the environment. These movements form the basis of a new form of identity politics based on claims for cultural autonomy and the recognition of difference. The 'global turn' has developed these themes further by highlighting the ways in which transnational dynamics and forces increasingly bypass the nation state and established forms of nationally organized interest-group politics. The 'complexity turn' has focused on the way in which new social movements constitute emergent 'fluids' in a system of global complexity. The 'cultural', 'global' and 'complexity' turns thus highlight a tendency for social movements to become increasingly fragmented, de-territorialized and fluid in organizational form.

In this chapter, I develop a detailed analysis of the ways in which the 'cultural', 'global' and 'complexity' turns have impacted on the sociological study of social movements. The following section, 'Social movements and modern sociology', explores the paradigms and perspectives of modern political sociology that were applied to the analysis of social movements. I focus in particular on resource mobilization theory (RMT) and a range of alternative approaches inspired by Marxism and critical theory. The next section, 'Social movements and the cultural turn', explores the 'cultural turn' in social movement theory and contains a critical evaluation of the work of Alberto Melucci and his argument that new social movements constitute a symbolic challenge to the cultural logic of post-industrial society. The section 'Social movements and the global turn' explores the 'global turn' in the analysis of new social movements. A distinction is made between analyses which explore NSMs within the analytical framework of globalized modernity and those approaches which analyse NSMs as important components of a globalized or postmodern social order. These approaches are illustrated through a discussion of Ulrich Beck's analysis of the 'sub-politics' evoked by globalized ecological risks and Manuel Castell's analysis of NSMs as a form of networked resistance to informationalized global capitalism. The section 'Social movements and complexity' explores the 'complexity' turn in social movement theory. A number of recent commentaries are explored which focus on NSMs' emergent fluids that swarm across the increasingly borderless world of global complexity. In the final section, 'The ambiguities of social movement politics', I use the example of the labour movement, as the most extreme example of a modern social movement, to highlight the all-pervasive nature of the postmodernization of social protest, and the ambiguous and liminal forms and spaces that result from the development of these new forms within the decomposing institutions of political modernity.

Social movements and modern sociology

Within the paradigm of modern 'mainstream' political sociology, social movement mobilization was presented as psychologically motivated and irrational. In the work of functionalists such as Neil Smelser, for example, the mobilization of social movements was a sign of social strain and dysfunction (Smelser, 1959, 1962). More psychologically focused accounts presented social movement mobilization in terms of an aggregated psychological response to the relative deprivation of ongoing social conditions (Davies, 1971; Gurr, 1971). The main departure from these types of approach took the form of RMT which developed a rational-choice approach to the analysis of social movements focused on individual decisions to participate in social movement activity. This approach took the existence of social grievances for granted and, therefore, rejected the existence of social problems as the principal dynamic explaining participation in collective action. The focus of RMT was on why individuals become involved in collective action on the basis of a rational calculation of their own interests. The initial focus of RMT was on the question of why individuals fail to get involved in collective action based on the rational propensity for individuals to maximize benefits and minimize costs. Olson (1965) argued that there was no necessary relationship between collective interests and collective action in an attempt to address the rational preferences underpinning the so-called 'free-rider' problem. This developed into an explicit focus on how resources are mobilized in order to make participation rational for self-interested individuals. The development of RMT marked a shift away from the narrow application of a marginal utility approach to an explicit focus on the social context in which social movements mobilize. There was an interest in the social and community pressure on individuals to become involved in social movement activism and the high rewards in terms of social prestige and power accruing to social movement leaders (Oberschall, 1973). There was also a focus on how a generalized increase in societal affluence had encouraged the development of a professionalized social movement sector providing both a career structure for social movement activists and an increase in the resources available to social movements (Zald & McCarthy, 1987).

According to Zald and McCarthy, the free-rider problem ceases to exist where the costs of participation are virtually zero and where considerable potential benefits exist for those individuals that take an active role.

The tendency for resources to accrue to members of elite networks made it difficult to explain why social movements should mobilize on a programme advocating radical social change. This problem was addressed by Tilly (1978) who highlighted the important role of the state in accommodating or repressing social movements on the basis of the perceived interests of state elites. In the US context, Tilly argued that this process determined three main destinations for social movements: the dissolution or repression of a movement; the absorption of a movement into the polity; or the constitution of a movement as an enduring pressure group. The growth of electoral politics had shifted social movement activity away from the 'national movements' that marked the nineteenth century towards a focus on learning 'repertoires of collective action' in order to engage with 'political opportunity structures'. There is a sense in which the approach of Tilly is incompatible with that of Zald and McCarthy, particularly with regard to the focus on grassroots activists rather than formal political settings and his rejection of the notion that 'interests' are reducible to individual preferences (Nash, 2000: 121). However, it is also possible to present these approaches as being relevant to different periods of social movement mobilization (McAdam *et al.*, 1996) and different stages of what Tarrow (1998) terms 'cycles of contention'. This cycle is marked by existing social movement networks undergoing a process of diffusion leading to a rapid period of social movement building marked by direct forms of action and heightened demands on time and resources followed by a period of consolidation and institutionalization. The genesis of the upturn is related to heightened social grievances or the emergence of new political opportunity structures. This however presumes that individuals are motivated by factors other than self-interest and takes the analysis beyond the concerns of rational-choice theory (Nash, 2000: 123).

During the 1960s, the focus of social movement studies started to change owing to both the novel and distinctive features displayed by a range of 'new' social movements and the changing social context in which social movements mobilized (Nash, 2000: 102–12). The emergence of libertarian politics around issues such as civil rights, gender, sexuality, the environment and US involvement in the Vietnam War seemed to herald a new age of social movement politics. In contrast to the 'old' social movement politics associated with the labour movement, the 'new' social movement politics was non-instrumental, oriented towards civil society rather than the state and involved a focus on the symbolic politics of culture, lifestyle and participation rather than the centralized and bureaucratic politics of the nation state. There were several attempts to highlight the changing social context in which the 'new' social movement politics was developing. Post-Marxist comment- ators highlighted the changing social composition and crisis tendencies of post-industrial capitalism. For Offe (1987), new social movement pol- itics had developed in a context of social democratic prosperity, the growth of the service sector and an expansion of the education system. In this context, 'decommodified' groups rejected the materialistic parti- cularism of the labour movement and embraced the universalism of new social movements. New social movements mobilization constituted a politics of class but not politics on behalf of a class (Offe, 1987: 77). Similarly, Habermas (1976) presented new social movement politics in terms of a defence of the 'lifeworld' of family and community values from the dynamics of commodification and bureaucratization. Habermas focused initially on new social movements in terms of a demand for rational accountability in order to realign individual motivations and social reproduction. This functionalist approach was later modified in order to present the 'lifeworld' as a sphere with its own rationalizing dynamic of de-traditionalization that facilitated rational criticism and democratic deliberation in the public sphere (Habermas, 1983, 1987).

There were also a number of accounts that presaged the emergence of the 'cultural' and 'global' turns in social movement analysis. There were attempts to trace the emergence of new social movements in terms of the relative affluence of the post-war period. This period, it was suggested, had shaped the experiences and values of a generation in the direction of a new form of post-material politics based on per- sonal self-esteem and intellectual and aesthetic satisfaction (Inglehart, 1990). Hence, the new social movements were a generational phenom- enon, and a series of studies focused on the age profile of new social movement activists (Pakulski, 1995). The shift towards the cultural turn was completed by a series of accounts which focused on new social movements as products of post-industrial or postmodern society. Hence, Touraine (1971, 1981) focused on new social movements as products of the shift from industrial to 'programmed' or 'informational' society; an approach which was developed further by Melucci (1989, 1996) to take account of the dynamics of globalization and individualization. The shift towards the cultural turn was completed by analyses focused on new social movements as products of postmodernity. Hence, new social movements emerged from the fragmentation of politics and reflected a deep disillusionment with institutional politics, the weakening of the social milieu of communities and occupations as sites for political mobilization, and the increasing importance of culture as the sphere through which identities and communities are formed and stabilized (Crook *et al.*, 1992). The focus on new social movements was also partially determined by important changes within the discipline of sociology itself. Modern sociology was seen as having ignored social movements other than the labour movement owing to the rationalist and instrumental bias of the modern discipline (Calhoon, 1995). However, this should not obscure the extent to which the labour movement did indeed marginalize other social movements for much of the late nineteenth and twentieth centuries through the symbiotic developmental logics of labour movement mobilization and nation state building (Tilly, 1984). In this context, the emergence of a new form of social movement politics centred on civil society rather than the state required a fundamental revision of the key concepts and methodologies of political sociology.

Social movements and the cultural turn

The cultural turn in social movement analysis involved an increasing interest in the role of new social movements in processes of cultural contestation. The most important departure can be found in the work of Alain Touraine, who applied the cultural turn to an essentially Marxist analysis of social movements. For Touraine, social movements are and should be the central focus of sociology as social relations emerge from social action and social movements are collective agents of social action. Touraine takes from Marxism the notions that every type of society is marked by conflict between dominating and dominated classes and that social movement activity is premised on systemic change, but rejects the functionalism of Marxism in favour of a social action approach. Touraine argues that the struggle between opposing classes is over control of what he terms 'historicity': the reflexive processes through which society is produced and reproduced through conscious reflection and action on social action and its conditions. The shift from industrial to 'programmed society' had shifted the focus of class struggle away from issues of political citizenship and workers' rights towards a struggle over the control of knowledge and information, and issues of autonomy and self-control. It is, however, the focus of Touraine on culture that has contributed most to the postmodern turn in social movement theory. Control over historicity involves control of the cultural orientations through which social relationships are normatively organized. The model of power utilized by Touraine is similar to the early position of Foucault which involved the denunciation of the power inherent in all social relations. Social relations are relations of power because they remain fixed in patterns of class domination. Engaging with the political system at the level of the state amounts to the co-option of social movements and a diversion from the key struggle over norms and values within civil society. The main problems with Touraine's analysis are an overemphasis on ideology in the framing of identity and a determinism that creates a tension between structure and action and downplays the important diversity of social movements that mobilize on issues less than systemic transformation (Nash, 2000: 135–7).

These weaknesses were addressed by Alberto Melucci who attempted to synthesize Touraine's analysis with important aspects of RMT. Melucci rejected the notion that there is a single progressive movement for each type of society as an unwarranted reification of social movements as 'personages'. Rather, collective action was presented as an ongoing process through which social actors negotiated and constructed meanings from a diversity of ends, means and forms of solidarity and organization. Melucci is also critical of RMT and the notion that social movements exist in relation to an external field of opportunities. Rather, goals and opportunities are defined by collective actors in an ongoing process through which the social movement is constructed. The motivation to participate emerges through the process of social interaction including the calculation of costs and benefits. Melucci downplays the importance of social movement leaders in favour of a focus on social movements as invisible and latent submerged networks. These networks take the form of experiments in alternative ways of living and lifestyle that challenge the dominant cultural codes of society. New social movements thus constitute a cultural challenge to the logic of post-industrial society. The control of information is the key to this challenge owing to the ways it which it mediates the individual awareness of global processes. The symbolic mediation of 'signs' is central to post-industrial society, and new social movements are primarily concerned with access to information and the contestation of symbolic resources in the cultural sphere. Struggle takes the form of innovative forms of organization and lifestyle that are viewed as important ends in themselves in a merging of private lives and public commitment. New social movements are thus struggles over identity which has become increasingly important owing to the increasing reflexivity of complex societies. While control has increased over intimate aspects of everyday life, the organizations that regulate such behaviour also provide resources in the form of knowledge and communication skills that facilitate increased autonomy and self-regulation. Hence, in post-industrial society, there is a greater emphasis to act on action itself in order to intervene in the biological and motivational structure of human beings in order to change oneself as an individual. Melucci is thus critical of the one-dimensionality of Foucault's model of power: power involves the administration of subjectivity, but networks of individuals are able to utilize the power resources of powerful organizations in ways unintended by bureaucrats and managers (Melucci, 1989: 208–9).

The work of Melucci involves an attempt to establish the connection between individual identity and collective action. Individuals participate in social movements only to the extent that it makes sense for them to do so. Collective action is constructed in interaction through individuals working on themselves in conflict or cooperation with others. Social movement identity cannot be constructed outside the relationships that give it meaning. New social movements have a tangential relationship with institutional politics: publicizing meta-political dilemmas and defining new public spaces between the state and civil society. Melucci's approach is postmodern to the extent that it involves a rejection of the dualism between the way in which social life is defined and the way in which it is lived. Collective identity is forged through the manipulation of signs and symbols to provide common meanings, and the question for social movements is 'how and for what purpose we should use the power of naming in order to fabricate the world and to subsume it to the signs with which we express (or do not express) it' (Melucci, 1996: 131). The main problem with Melucci's analysis is his dogmatic refusal to take seriously politics at the level of the state. This tends to downplay both the substantive struggle of social movements for citizenship rights and the internal plurality of social movements (Nash, 2000: 145). As Nash argues, it should be possible to conceive social movements mobilizing between the state and civil society and working towards both the democratization of everyday life and the extension of citizenship rights.

There has also been something of a cultural turn within the RMT perspective based on the recognition that the focus on rational self-interest ignored the feelings, emotions and values of social movement actors and which resulted in a tendency to focus on the 'ends' rather than the 'means' of collective action. An attempt to overcome these problems has been to utilize Goffman's concept of 'framing' in order to synthesize social constructionism and methodological individualism. A 'frame' simplifies the world through the selective punctuation and encoding of objects, situations and experiences. This is applied to the study of social movements through the concept of 'collective action frame' which emphasizes or punctuates the intolerability of a group's social condition (Snow *et al.*, 1986). This involves 'diagnostic attributions' which attribute blame for the situation and 'prognostic attributions' which provide solutions to overcome the condition and 'encode' observations and experiences into meaningful packages which can be translated into targets for mobilization (Snow & Benford, 1992: 137–8). The focus is thus on micro-mobilization based on face-to-face interaction (Snow *et al.*, 1980). Through a process of 'frame alignment', individual interpretations of the situation are linked with those of the movement as a whole as part of an ongoing process that involves 'frame bridging', 'frame amplification', 'frame extension' and 'frame transformation' (Snow *et al.*, 1986). This is combined with the notion of 'master frames' which are more universal and less context specific and which provide the mechanism through which movements are formed and constrained and provide an explanation for the cyclical nature of social movement mobilization (Snow & Benford, 1988, 1992). There have been attempts to integrate the framing approach with the analysis of 'political opportunity' and 'mobilizing' structures (McAdam *et al.*, 1996). Hence, a dynamic relationship exists between the form and timing of mobilization and perceptions of political opportunities. Indeed, the perception of opportunities can result in further opportunities in a dynamic tension in which social movements are increasingly authors of their own fate. As Nash (2000: 126) argues, this tends to overemphasize the control social movements have over their own definitions and opportunities and tends to present culture as an external resource that can be manipulated by social movements. This leaves unanswered the question as to why social actors become involved in social movements in the first place: the framing of cultural understandings is posited as prior to individual decisions on costs and benefits (McAdam *et al.*, 1996). Ultimately, it remains questionable as to whether the focus on framing is consistent with rational-choice theory and the realist epistemology that underpins RMT. If individuals are motivated by the internal validity of frames then the link between collective action and political opportunities is broken. Further, the notion that cultural framing takes place prior to collective behaviour and action fails to take seriously the notion that cultural contestation and transformation emerge from the meaning and interpretations that social actors attribute to collective action and events.

Social movements and the global turn

The analysis of the relationship between globalization and changes in the nature of new social movement politics can be divided between approaches which remain within the modernist framework and approaches which reject the modernist framework in favour of a global society or postmodern perspective. An important example of the former can be found in the work of Ulrich Beck on the politics of risk in 'second modernity' (Beck, 1992, 1995, 1997). Beck argues that globalization, driven primarily by the globalization of capital, results in nothing less than the death and rebirth of politics. The emergence of 'sub-politics' is linked to the decentring of the nation state and the emergence of new forms of public engagement in response to the human-generated risks of 'second modernity'. These risks are generated by the unexpected 'boomerang effects' of modern development, including the unwanted ecological side effects of industrial development and the unwanted social and economic effects of global capitalism. The development of sub-politics is linked to the migration of political decisions away from established modes of national governance in the economic, technological and scientific domains. In these domains, unaccountable elites fix the boundaries of acceptable scientific development, and public involvement is limited to a superficial choice of political representatives and hierarchically organized 'consultation'. In the context of rapid technological change, governments have become reactive on the issue of social risks and are increasingly forced into a position of defending and legitimating decisions that were not made by them in the first place. Risks are produced by industry, externalized by economics, individualized by legal systems, legitimated by science and made to appear harmless by politics. The resulting 'glocal issues' cannot be adequately resolved by the nation state and consequently politics has divided into globalization from above in the form of transnational forms of governance and international treaties and globalization from below in the form of collective action by groups outside the formal democratic arena (Beck, 2000: 37). The development of sub-politics marks the emergence of a generalized and centreless form of politics (Beck, 1992: 227) marked by the possibility of more deliberative and inclusive forms of democracy. The resulting forms of 'direct politics' are *ad hoc* forms of participation that bypass institutional forms of opinion formation and decision-making and are constituted as *ad hoc* coalitions of oppositions that are open and susceptible to the forging of new links (Beck, 1999: 40). The traditional political affiliations of class, gender and ethnicity have become increasingly outmoded alongside the meta-narratives of liberalism, socialism and conservatism. Sub-politics is classless and inclusive and reflects the universality of social 'bads'. Hence, social actors from a diversity of backgrounds meet in sub-political space in an attempt to coordinate the system and reset and realign the switches (Beck, 1998a: 104). Beck's notion of sub-politics is thus congruous with the notion of 'life politics' developed by Anthony Giddens or the notion of the 'public sphere' developed by Habermas (Giddens, 1994; Habermas, 1983). The diffusion of risk undermines traditional power bases rendering society susceptible to political restructuring and the emergence of new forms of cosmopolitan democracy.

There are a number of commentators writing from a Foucauldian perspective who are critical of Beck's model of risk politics and who question the progressive potential of 'discourses' of risk (Castel, 1991; Culpitt, 1999; Dean, 1999). The focus of these commentators is on the privatization of politics through the deployment of risk as a discourse and hence on the disciplinary and restrictive functions of risk. A discourse is a set of ideas, beliefs and practices that provide representations of knowledge. As a discourse, therefore, risk becomes a tool of regulation and surveillance (Caplan, 2000: 3) and shapes the way reality is experienced through the generation of 'truths' that are internalized by individuals and which provide parameters of appropriate action. It is argued that Beck underestimates the role of risk in the regulation of everyday behaviour and, consequently, the importance of risk as a discourse in the stifling of oppositional movements and the closing down rather than opening up of political possibilities (Allen, 2000: 39). The institutional attribution of responsibility for risk indicates that a distrust of 'otherness' can be conveniently forged in the direction of blame (Lash, 2000: 51). The two accounts are ultimately premised on two opposing conceptualizations of power. Beck presents power as top-down or 'laddered' with institutions losing credence to sub-political movements, while commentators inspired by Foucault focus on risk as a form of power that is circular and networked (Mythen, 2004: 170).

As Mythen (2004: 171) notes, risk is ultimately polythemic and capable of producing diverse effects from opposition to social control. Undoubtedly, the language of risk has been used to intensify social control and reinforce unequal social relations and has, therefore, generated conservative responses that restrain autonomy and creativity (Caplan, 2000;

Furedi, 1997), and there are, therefore, limits to the emancipatory possibilities of the politics of risk (Abbinnett, 2000; Nugent, 2000; Rustin,
1994). Direct politics may also be a product of disenchantment with
liberal democracy and cannot therefore be detached from formal political
processes. The ability of the state to repress sub-politics is also downplayed by Beck. For Beck, the practice of sub-politics takes place in
abstract global space as constituted by the 'upper house of technology' at
the macro level and within deliberative democratic frameworks at the
micro level. Case studies suggest that enhanced forms of democracy do
not necessarily result in the elimination or reduction of environmental
risk (Hajer & Kesselring, 1999) and the numerous examples of 'green-
wash' highlight the ways in which deliberative processes can be hijacked
by corporate capital. Beck accepts that sub-politics is not a panacea in
isolation, but fails to take seriously alternative political routes to political
mobilization in the form of nationalism, violence and scapegoating
(Mythen, 2004: 176). Political perceptions of risk are mediated by existing
opinions and cultures and, therefore, are likely to be ambiguous and
fluid. In this context, political reflexivity is one response amongst many.
Ultimately, both Beck and his Foucauldian critics have led the politics
of risk into the impasse of opposing positions based on realism and
relativism and have increasingly talked past each other: Beck has over-
emphasized agency and underemphasized the coercive capacity of social
structures, while the Foucauldian approach treats the risk subject as an
empty vessel activated by risk (Lupton, 1999: 6).

Anti-globalism: networks of resistance and the globalization of politics

The most ambitious attempt to explore the changing form of social
movements in a networked global society can be found in the work of
Castells (1997). The restructuring of the global economy has combined
with the informational mode of development to transform all areas of
social and personal life according to the social logic of the network.
While these developments have the positive effects of enhancing the
productive capacity, cultural creativity and communications potential of human society, they also result in the disenfranchisement of
societies. The mechanisms of social control and political representation
are disintegrating in the face of the abstract power of a global web of
computers. The 'place-bound' institutions of state and civil society
based on 'flows of power' are superseded by the 'power of flows' between
nodes in the network and the elites that control the network. In this
context, individuals have lost control of their jobs, their environment,

their lives and even their governments. In the face of this domination, new forms of 'resistance identities' have emerged to challenge the logic of the network and take revenge on their domination by global flows (Castells, 1997: 71–2). Social actors attempt to resist the ahistorical domination of timeless time and overcome the particularities of place (Castells, 2000a). The success of a social movement can be gauged by its ability to assume the reflexive form of the network in order to make demands communicable in the space of flows. I will explore the work of Castells on the Zapatista rebels in Mexico and the subsequent debate on the World Social Forum (WSF) in order to demonstrate the contribution and limitations of the 'global turn' to the understanding of contemporary social movements.

Castells has argued that the success of the Zapatistas was largely down to their communication strategy in which they emerged as the first 'informational guerrilla movement'. The Zapatistas were part of a broader network of struggle that can be defined as a movement against globalism. In the global South, these struggles originated in response to the negative impact of global institutions such as the 'IMF Riots' that have developed in response to 'structural adjustment' programmes of the IMF (Walton & Seddon, 1994). In the global North, the initial resistance took the form of defensive struggles around welfare and employment rights by organized labour. More recently, however, these national forms of resistance have developed into new forms of international resistance that not only link national struggles, but also create new terrains of struggle at the transnational level. This movement achieved global visibility with the insurrection of the Zapatistas in Chiapas, Mexico (Cunninghame & Ballesteros Corona, 1998; Esteva, 1999). The Zapatistas emerged on 1 January 1994 as the Zapatistas National Liberation Army (EZLN) on the day the North American Free Trade Agreement (NAFTA) came into effect. The aim of the EZLN was to make visible the forgotten victims of neo-liberal globalism to the world through the publication of a series of communiqués on the internet. The demands of the Zapatistas are foundational and premised on the demand for autonomy. These demands include work, land, shelter, food, health, education, independence, freedom, democracy, justice and peace in the context of municipal self-government. The distinctiveness of this guerrilla movement is that it eschews Marxism and 'vanguardism' and, in contrast to other Latin American guerrilla movements such as Shining Path in Peru, does not resort to random violence, fear and intimidation. The Zapatistas are anti-patriarchal, and stand for the rights of self-determination and local democracy, ecology and preservation of the environment.

The Zapatistas created a media event in order to diffuse their message, while trying to avoid a violent and bloody confrontation. While they had arms, they did not pursue a military strategy. The use of arms was used to make a statement and force negotiations with the Mexican Government around a set of demands that found widespread support throughout Mexican society. Leading figures in the movement such as sub-commander Marcos provided an image, based on the wearing of a ski mask and the smoking of the pipe in the jungle location, which acted as a communications bridge with the media. This involved drawing on indigenous culture to provide a spectacle or display of theatrics that linked past, present and future. These images were displayed through video, telecommunications and internet media to generate a worldwide network of solidarity that was then deployed to control and limit the repression of the Zapatistas by the Mexican state. The Zapatistas thus highlighted the way in which 'weak ties' between activists can build effective 'social bridges' between diverse movements through the deliberate construction of new political spaces (Granovetter, 1973). The Zapatistas provided the first example of a 'netwar' – the worst nightmare of the architects of the new global order – a multi-organizational network arising from civil society to contest neo-liberal globalism.

The Zapatistas defined a new form of internationalism that blurred the line between global and local issues and involved the construction of alliances amongst a plurality of movements (De Angelis, 2000). In contrast to 'socialist internationalism' of the modern era, the goals of political action were not framed outside the unification process, but emerged from the unification process and generated new radical claims and social subjects. This form of internationalism grasps the multi-dimensionality of human needs and articulates a new emancipatory philosophy rooted in the universality of the human condition. The contradictions between the demands of different movements are the object of political practice and are transcended through communications and alliances in civil society (Esteva, 1999: 158–9). The Zapatistas inspired solidarity from activists around the world and unleashed an international insurrection of hope against the forces of global capitalism. The Zapatistas cry of *Ya Basta!* (enough) announced 'the end of the end of history' and their communiqués posted on the internet began to unite a diverse band of marginal people: vagabonds, sweatshop workers, sex workers, indigenous peoples, intellectuals, factory workers, illegal immigrants and squatters (Notes from Nowhere, 2003: 24–5). The Zapatistas inspired the growth of electronic NGO networks: the so-called 'Zapatista effect' that has posed an increasing symbolic threat to global neo-liberalism within a media-generated public sphere (Cleaver, 1998). However, this success story highlights clearly the ambiguity between cultural innovation and symbolic contestation on the one hand, and political and economic contestation on the other. The mere existence of the Zapatistas as a potential alternative had a huge impact on the generation of a counter-power within global civil society. Yet this rhetoric of global resistance has had minimal impact on the lived poverty of the indigenous peoples of Chiapas (Chandler, 2004: 327). Ten years after the start of the Zapatistas' rebellion, the Mexican Government continues to ignore their demands. This is not, however, to deny the symbolic significance of the Zapatistas' uprising and the motivation the rebellion provided to protestors around the globe.

The form of politics initiated by the Zapatistas provided a language and a form of action that informed and inspired a new wave of protests towards the end of the 1990s. During this period, coordinated action spread throughout the developing world culminating in days of action against the WTO in 1998 and the G8 in 1999 with a global *Carnival against Capital*. The anti-capitalist movement only became visible to the media in the global North when protestors began to mobilize at the global summits in the developed world. The global justice movement (GJM) burst onto the scene during the protest at the 1999 WTO summit in Seattle, when 40,000 demonstrators drawn from a wide spectrum of movements interrupted a meeting of the WTO that had been convened to discuss the liberalization of trade in services. The protestors ranged from core sections of the American labour movement, such as the Teamsters and the Longshoremen, to a range of NGO and activist coalitions campaigning around environmental issues, fair trade and third world debt. In the wake of Seattle, a plethora of protests targeted the global summits of institutions such as the WTO, IMF, EU, APEC, G8 and FTAA, including mobilizations in Washington (2000), Millau (2000), Melbourne (2000), Seoul (2000), Nice (2000), Prague (2000), Washington (2001), Gothenburg (2001) and Genoa (2001). The emergence of the Zapatistas and the GJM is part of a process through which a new transnational political space has been forged in which alternatives to neo-liberalism can be discussed by globalized political actors.

The World Social Forum (WSF) emerged from the GJM and originated from an initiative by a group of Belgian activists to develop a forum that could bring together groups and movements from around the world that shared an opposition to neo-liberalism. The first forum was held in Porto Alegre, Brazil during 2001 in opposition to the World Economic Forum that was being held in Davos, Switzerland. The WSF is a 'worldwide, movement-based, multi-scale and multi-sited cultural process' (Conway, 2004) or a space that is open, diverse and pluralistic and oriented to the generation and communication of movement-based ideas and practices. However, a key source of contention within the WSF remains whether it represents merely an 'open space' to encourage discourse and dialogue or a 'movement of movements' premised on the translation of diversity and plurality of opinion into common political will and action (Patomäki and Teivainen, 2004; Marcuse, 2005; Conway, 2005). The values of diversity, pluralism and participation are foundational and definitive and the WSFs have comprised forms of coordinated self-organization that include meetings, parades, protests, music, dance and exhibitions. In 2001, 2002 and 2003 the WSF was held in Porto Alegre, Brazil and was dominated by Latin American groups concerned with issues such as the FTAA and landlessness. In 2004, the WSF was held in Mumbai, India where there was a greater focus on the historically marginal such as indigenous peoples, AIDS sufferers and sex-trade workers. At this forum, there were discussions around the issues that linked social and biological diversity such as access to water, environmental destruction and the control of nature.

The WSF is producing new forms of political participation, deliberation and popular power and a new geography of social movement organizing. The development of the WSF highlights the extent to which the contemporary world order is increasingly comprised of multiple and overlapping sovereignties, and the lack of a recognizable or unified global sovereign constitutes the fundamental challenge to the global movement. Hence:

> global-citizens-in-the-making might also be creating a global sovereignty ... over an increasingly privatized sphere that is monopolistic in tendency, individualizing, intrusive and destructive of human sociality and creativity. (Waterman, 2000: 145)

Citizenship thus remains 'a conflictive practice related to power' (Jelin, 2000: 53). The objects of contention are the World Bank, IMF, WTO, G8, FTAA, EU and MNCs that are challenged in the name of popular sovereignty at the local, national and global levels. The new citizenship is premised on the 'right to have rights': an idea that has developed through the anti-hegemonic struggles of the excluded by social movements claiming political subjectivity. These movements demand the right to participate in order to create new forms of egalitarian sociability and reciprocal recognition in civil society (Dagnino, 1998: 50–2). The WSF embodies an emergent 'alternative, post bourgeois conception of the public sphere' (Fraser, 1997: 72): the space is thus 'placed but transnational, localized but characterized by expanding globality' (Conway, 2004: 376). This space is not constituted by a public sphere of rational democratic deliberation (cf. Habermas, 1983, 1987), but a plurality of subaltern counterpublics (Fraser, 1997: 81) which express their exclusion from the formal universality of the liberal public sphere. The WSF is thus part of the consolidation of an emergent 'transnational civil society' (Keck & Sikkink, 1998). The new anti-globalization movements go beyond the politics of identity and difference to issues of democracy and a search for collective solutions to common problems (Gill, 2000). The WSF highlights the possibility of inclusive, egalitarian, multicultural and anti-oppressive political spaces. However, there remain significant obstacles to this process including the huge chasms across civilizational divides, regional outlooks, religions, gendered orders and world-views.

Despite these limitations, the WSF has played a central role in the convergence of the anti-globalization and anti-war movements worldwide through the promotion of pluralism. The demands for democracy, rights and participation are not being marginalized but transformed from legal and institutional claims to claims based on cultural practices (Isin & Turner, 2002; Gilbert & Philips, 2003). Citizenship is increasingly about 'being political': entering conflicts over power and recognizing the agnostic nature of citizenship (Isin, 2002). This, however, is contested terrain focused on a set of uneven, crisis-ridden processes that are established by transnational practices. The liberal paradigm is in decline while the new paradigm is still under construction. The anti-globalization movement represents a form of postmodern politics within modern society (Heller & Fehér, 1988): a form of politics premised on a rejection of grand narratives, the privileging of function over structure and a weakening of class politics. The content of the struggle, however, remains foundational and we see the liminality inherent in contemporary global politics. Hence, the WSF could be best described as a form of participatory communication and engagement 'that is *in movement*, even if it is not *a movement* of a traditional kind' (Patomäki & Teivainen, 2004: 152). However, the WSF will eventually have to face up to the insight that global democratic change will not be achievable without concrete strategies of political change and engagement with state actors and the need to engage with more traditional forms of politics (Patomäki & Teivainen, 2004: 151).

Social movements and complexity

The complexity turn in social movement analysis has taken the form of an increasing tendency to apply metaphors from complexity theory to the development and form of social movements. In the process, the social actor tends to disappear to become part of a complex structure of liquefied and irregular movement. There has thus been an increasing tendency to portray social movements as fluid-like and marked by irregular and unexpected upsurges in activity and protest (Urry, 2003: 71–4). Rapid mobilization is presented as the result of endogenous, self-reinforcing processes where small events and changes are amplified by positive feedback loops towards a 'contagion effect' and protest spreads like a forest fire. Social movements are thus portrayed as global fluids that flow in webs and networks (Jasper, 1997; Jordan, 1998) and take the form of amorphous nebula with indistinct shapes and variable density (Melucci, 1996: 113–14). These fluids, it is suggested, can only be explored effectively through the prism of non-Euclidean sticky spaces and bending time (Sheller, 2001). Social movements are portrayed as having no beginning or end, with multiple temporalities that flow through multiple channels and may 'overflow' or 'ebb away'. The existence of free space allows movement through borders and boundaries such that social movements are able to transmute in unexpected locations. This has been presented as an example of 'network switching' (White, 1995) that involves the movement of people, objects and images that coalesce, disperse, concentrate and dissolve and thereby switch the point of attack through the flooding of spaces. Complex social movements are conceptualized as leaderless, non-organization. The 'fuel protests' that emerged in the UK during 2000 in opposition to perceived high excise duty on vehicle fuels illustrated how the fluidity of petrol supplies was susceptible to blockage by protestors and how a small movement of 2000 protestors could cause chaos and almost bring the British economy to its knees (Urry, 2003: 71–2). The reasons for this were localized refining of petrol with just-in-time delivery to petrol-station forecourts, the possibilities for instantaneous real-time communication via mobile phones and the internet, and the wider context of a globalized media system, the universalization of motorized mobility and the 'demonstration effect' of simultaneous protests across Europe. Hence, the complexity of 'netwars' in an age of complexity whereby threats in the information age are more diffuse, dispersed, multidimensional, non-linear and ambiguous (Arquilla & Ronfeldt, 2001: 2).

The complexity approach has also been applied to the analysis of the global justice movement by Chesters and Welsh (2005, 2006) in an analysis of the 'alternative globalization movement' (AGM). Following Deleuze and Guattari (2002), life is presented as a process of 'becoming' rather than 'being' and this allows social movements to be conceptualized as the connection of heterogeneous elements forged into new assemblages with emergent properties. Similar to Deleuze and Guattari's 'war machine', the AGM constitutes an antagonistic potential of forces that resist or escape processes of stratification, over-coding and control by global capitalism. The AGM is thus an anti-capitalist agitator in global civil society (Chesters, 2004) that creates de-territorializing 'lines of flight' (Deleuze & Guattari, 2002: 55) through practices of discovery and artistic invention in order to synthesize forces immanent to the subversive practices of resistance, refusal and escape. This process occurs in 'fractal movement space' where modes of symbolic contestation, discursive democracy and antagonistic conflict overflow borders and are iterated at various scales from the local to the global. The antagonism that inheres in the AGM derives from its capacity for cultural intervention and experimentation. Hence, the importance of a 'hacker class' (Walk, 2004) subverting and reappropriating the virtual singularities of global capital combined with an affective desire for co-presence and collaboration contributes to the emergence of new modes of cultural intervention and production. The AGM works on and through the raw material of subjectivity and the symbolic in the form of a 'carnival of collectivism' (Protevi, 2001: 3) that cannot be grasped within either nation state or 'frame' analysis which tend to focus on collective identity as a mechanism for expressing political claims or grievances. Rather, a model is developed which links subjectivity and social action to the planetary action system through non-linear dynamics of space, meaning and time.

The complexity turn problematizes the key propositions of social movement theory including the use of collective identity to explain social movement cohesion (McDonald, 2002); the use of national political opportunity structures to explore the orientations of social movement actors (McAdam *et al.*, 2001); the use of a left–right binary divide to explore dynamics of contention; and the exploration of social movement activity in cyclical terms. These approaches have problems in dealing with the latency period in social movement activity (Melucci, 1989, 1996) marked by 'identity work' in submerged networks. Complexity theory facilitates the exploration of internal complexity derived from multilinear social evolution or social movements as 'becoming minorities' (Deleuze & Guattari, 2002: 471). The stage for the emergence of the AGM is a 'planetary action system' (Melucci, 1989) marked by increasing complexity owing to the systemic feedback facilitated by the application of ICT to all aspects of life and unprecedented levels of social and spatial mobility. In this context, the struggle against capitalism is an iterative rather than a cyclical process. Iteration is congruent with the Deleuzian notion of becoming and the notion that something that is truly new can emerge only through repetition (Žižek, 2004). The emergence of the anti-globalization movement highlights the emergence of new democratic spaces and the 'reflexive framing' of issues in ways that contribute to 'ontological security' through the linking of personal and planetary milieux. The framing repertoires within the anti-globalization movement have been radically extended by the extensive use of ICT and the occurrence of 'events' or 'encounters' that involve processes of intense networking around nodal points of contestation such as protest events or social forums (Chesters & Welsh, 2005: 192). The Deleuzian perspective, however, eschews the restructuration of protest and contestation, and there is a tendency to focus on the anti-globalization movement as a form of 'disorganization' that articulates an aesthetic form of reflexivity.

The ambiguities of social movement politics: liminal spaces of struggle

Modern political sociology focused on social movements as collective agents that pursued instrumental goals in nationally determined political opportunity structures. The 'cultural', 'global' and 'complexity' turns in political sociology have highlighted the shift from instrumentalism towards complex forms of de-territorialized identity politics. The 'cultural turn' highlighted the ways in which the shift towards the postmodern condition had resulted in social movement politics taking the form of struggles over the autonomy of identities and lifestyles. Hence, 'new' social movements were defined in opposition to the 'old' social movement *qua* the labour movement which remained locked into the universal and instrumentalist paradigm of political modernity and was, therefore, destined to decline and decompose. The 'global turn' has focused on the de-territorialization of social movement mobilization as a result of the decentring of the nation state and the ways in which the demands of social movements can be articulated through the global networks of the 'space of flows'. The global justice movement provides an example of how new political spaces have emerged between the local and the global based on foundational struggles for social rights. The 'complexity turn' has presented new social movements as important 'global fluids' which have emergent and non-linear properties and which swarm in the webs and networks of the global planetary system. The global justice movement has been presented as being constituted by forms of disorganization that frame an opposition to neo-liberal globalism through aesthetic forms of reflexivity. These 'turns' have highlighted the postmodern nature of social movement organization and protest without a consideration of the extent to which these developments have occurred within the decomposing framework of political modernity. As result, the essential ambiguities of contemporary social movement politics as a 'lived' or 'existential' category are either downplayed or ignored. These ambiguities can be highlighted through an exploration of recent trends and developments in respect of the labour movement: the most modern of social movements which has developed an increasingly postmodern orientation in response to the intensification and globalization of modernity and the development of postmodern political forms.

During the past decade, the labour movement has emerged as an active agent rather than a passive victim in the process of neo-liberal globalization (Munck, 2004). There have been examples of new interventions by organized labour at the global, regional, national and local levels in which organized labour has both emerged as a key moment of resistance against neo-liberalism and as part of a progressive alliance of actors in global civil society. The ambiguity and complexity of labour movement politics is a result of the ambiguous conflation of an instrumentalist modern agenda to engage with capital and the state in an attempt to bend the future trajectory of capitalist modernity and an altruistic postmodern agenda of 'identity work' that has involved building progressive alliances with diverse campaigns and movements in civil society. The instrumental elements of reorientation have been largely defensive and tend to confirm the rather pessimistic prognosis of Castells that the interests of labour are place-bound and incommunicable in the 'space of flows' (Castells, 1997). This has involved an attempt to re-embed political relations along the glocalized configurations of capital and the state. The most interesting developments are in Europe where globalization, in the form of European integration, has produced transnational labour movement actors in the form of the European Trade Union Confederation (ETUC) and a range of European industry federations (EIFs) at the sectoral level. The ETUC is a social partner within the institutions of the EU and in that role has consultation rights with the European Commission and the European Central Bank and limited negotiating rights with UNICE – the European employers' confederation. These developments are part of a top-down social democratic strategy to resolve the contradictions between globalization and social democracy through international cooperation and coordination and the construction of a Social Europe (Clift, 2002: 495). These developments highlight the construction of a 'public sphere' by the EU and thus the undeveloped nature of European civil society and the enduring 'democratic deficit within the institutions of the EU' (Rumford, 2003).

There is, however, a contrary tendency to the above instrumental defensiveness in the form of 'social movement unionism'. The development of 'second' or 'reflexive' modernity has resulted in the 'opening up' of civil society as the increasing importance of 'risk biographies' has generated new forms of 'altruistic individualism' (Beck & Beck-Gernsheim, 2002: 24). We can see this dynamic operating within the European labour movement where opposition to European integration has resulted in both instrumental actions at the national level and new forms of transnational solidarity. The latter link the global and local struggles of activists and build bridges between the labour movement and other movements and actors in the global public sphere. The process of European integration provoked militant forms of industrial action in the form of strikes, particularly amongst public-sector workers, in France, Germany, Italy and Spain, and the emergence of new unions or union factions opposed to neo-liberal restructuring such as SUD in France or Sin Cobas in Italy (Taylor & Mathers, 2002a, 2002b). The latter development formed the basis for the development of a transnational network of resistance between oppositional trade unions and a range of campaigns involving movements representing women, black people, environmentalists, pensioners, migrants and the homeless. These became manifested in phenomena such as Euromarches, a network of movements that organized marches and demonstrations at key European summits to highlight the plight of the marginal and excluded in Europe (Mathers, 1999), ATTAC that campaigns for a tax on movements of capital (Patomäki, 2000) and the involvement of trade unions in the WSF and European social forums (Lee, 2004). Neo-liberal globalism has encouraged a 'logic of participation' between trade unions and social actors beyond the workplace (Robinson, 2000) and the emergence of 'social movement unionism' as a global phenomenon (Munck & Waterman, 1998; Robinson, 2002). Manifestations of altruistic individualism in the form of 'community unionism' have developed in the USA (Ness & Eimer, 2001; Fantasia & Voss, 2004), Canada (Cranford, 2003), Australia (Ellem, 2003; Tattershall, 2005) and the UK (Wills, 2001; Wills & Simms, 2004). In the USA, trade unions organizing through local 'central labor councils' have made alliances with faith groups and groups representing the low paid and the marginalized to make citizenship claims on a range of issues from minimum wages to public transport (Johnston, 2000, 2002). These developments highlight the dominant tendency towards the development of postmodern politics in modern society (Heller & Fehér,

1988) and the ways in which contemporary social movements increasingly mobilize in the liminal social spaces between the modern and the postmodern and between the local and the global.

Summary and conclusion

In this chapter, I have explored how the rapid social changes of recent decades have impacted on the organization and mobilization of social movements. The instrumentalist, materialist and bureaucratic orientation of modern social movements, represented by the paradigmatic case of the labour or workers' movement, has been increasingly marginalized and decentred by a range of 'new' social movements which articulate non-instrumentalist values and are organized in non-hierarchical and informal ways. Modern political sociology tended to stress either the class-based nature of social movement activity or the extent to which collective action was the product of the individual 'rational' decisions of social movement actors. The 'cultural turn' in political sociology shifted the focus of social movement studies towards a consideration of the relationship between social action and social meaning and the ways in which social movements were constitutive of social identity. The 'global turn' has involved both attempts to highlight the potentially progressive role of new social movements in a globalized 'reflexive' modernity and their potential to generate new forms of postmodern identity politics in the transnational spaces opened up within a networked global society. The 'complexity turn' has suggested that new social movements can be understood through the metaphor of 'global fluid' in an attempt to highlight the non-linear and unpredictable affects of social movement mobilization in contemporary society. The chapter concluded with an illustration of the ambiguous or liminal spaces occupied by social movement organizations in the contemporary era and the analytical promise associated with an 'existential turn' in social movement studies.

7
Networks of Terror: Globalization, Fundamentalism and Political Violence

A defining feature of political modernity was the centralization of legitimate violence within the unitary and sovereign form of the modern nation state. The sociological analysis of violence and terror was conducted in terms of an 'episodic' conceptualization of power and tended to focus on how violence underpinned the structural capacities of economic and political elites. In an era marked by warfare, revolution and violent social upheaval the 'objective' characteristics of military and physical violence were accentuated and the important role of violence in the constitution of social meaning and identity tended to be marginalized or ignored. The events of 9/11 2001 in New York highlighted the extent to which violence always has a context that shapes both the protagonists and victims of violence and those that represent them (Lawrence & Karim, 2007). The political memory is never simply a neutral lens of human history and experience: the context of violence determines and defines the range of public memory and the political uses of the past. Hence, the contrast between the moral and media panic generated by the attack on the World Trade Center, New York and that generated by the political violence and genocide committed in the African nations of Rwanda and the Sudan. In the contemporary age, the media does not simply report violence but both creates and responds to public expectations and concerns about violence and terror. The events in both New York and Africa highlight the extent to which violence remains a daily reflex of twenty-first-century life: the end of the Cold War has not resulted in a new world order of peace and harmony. The focus of this chapter is the question as to why violence and terror prevail in the new millennium.

In this chapter, I explore the above problem through an analysis of the conceptualizations of violence and terror developed by modern political sociology and an exploration of the ways in which this paradigm has been challenged and transformed by the 'cultural', 'global' and 'complexity' turns. In the next section, 'Political violence and modern sociology', there is an exploration of political violence and terror within the modern paradigm of political sociology, focusing in particular on Marxist and Weberian approaches and the relationship between war, violence and the development of the modern state and economy. In the following section, 'Violence and the cultural turn', I explore the ways in which the 'cultural turn' has resulted in a shifting focus away from violence and the nation state towards the ways in which forms of symbolic and metaphorical violence underpin the discourses and practices of everyday life. This is approached through a discussion of the work of Michel Foucault on violence and terror. The 'cultural turn' has also involved an increasing focus on the ways in which the shift to an increasingly informationalized economy and society has resulted in the tendency towards the mediatization of violence and the increasing importance of simulated violence and violent simulations. This will be approached through a consideration of the work of Jean Baudrillard on war and simulation. In the section 'The global matrix' I explore the impact of the 'global turn' on the sociological analysis of violence and terror. The main focus is on the way in which the dynamics of globalization have resulted in the de-territorialization of violence and terror and the subsequent intensification of violence and terror as a global threat or 'risk'. This is illustrated through the work of Ulrich Beck on terrorism in the 'world risk society'. This is followed by a discussion of the relationship between globalization and the emergence of new forms of identity politics which have fuelled the intensification of religious fundamentalism, virulent and extreme forms of nationalism and violent terrorism. In the section 'Complex terror' I explore how the 'complexity turn' has resulted in the reconceptualization of violence and terror as emergent and unpredictable 'fluids' in a system of global complexity and the ways in which the application of a post-panoptical model of power transforms the arena in which violent terrorism develops into a 'planetary frontierland' marked by the symbolic end to the era of space. In the final section, 'The ambiguities of complex violence and terror', the limits of the 'cultural', 'global' and 'complexity' turns are explored and the ambiguous and liminal characteristics of contemporary political violence and terrorism investigated.

Political violence and modern sociology

The treatment of violence in modern political sociology reflected the broader debates and disagreements that emerged from the conceptual antinomies of state–society and conflict–consensus debates. In general terms, the Marxist approach has tended to analyse violence as under-pinning the historical origins and structural form of the capitalist economy, while Weberian approaches highlighted the ways in which violence and warfare underpinned the development of the modern nation state. The Marxist approach focused on social structure and conflict and portrayed violence as a structure and a fundamental and inevitable force in the process of historical change. In *Capital*, Marx (1976: 873–940) explored the process of primitive accumulation and the ways in which violence underpinned the historical evolution of capital. The prehistory of capital was written in the annals of mankind in 'blood and fire', and capital came into the world 'dripping from head to toe, from every pore, with blood and dirt' (Marx, 1976: 875, 926). The external violence and force of primitive accumulation became internalized through the process of capital accumulation in the form of the internalized discipline of wage labour. The violence inflicted by the colonizer on the colonized was an important ante-cedent of the capitalist mode of production and instrumental to its success. For Engels, violence and warfare played a pivotal role in the dialectic of history. In *Anti-Dühring*, Engels highlighted the importance of the economic as a force for subjugation and the ways in which the violence of bourgeois revolutions was historically necessary in order to create the context for the new capitalist economy to develop. Engels also argued that military innovations were always instrumental to eco-nomic gains, although making the use of arms familiar to the masses could be risky as the armies of warlords could be transformed into an army of the people in the struggle for socialism (Engels, 1987).

The development of the modern state involved the centralization of violence in a unitary, sovereign and legitimate social institution. The focus on violence and the state can be traced to Thomas Hobbes and the argument that a generalized fear of death in the state of nature pro-vided the context for the emergence of a powerful state or *Leviathan* to prevent the violence of all against all. For Hobbes, the state contains within itself that state of violence which it suppressed by means of a concomitant violence. Amongst sociologists influenced by the Weberian tradition there has been a concern to explore the relationship between violence and warfare and the origins and development of the nation state. Anthony Giddens, for example, has argued that the main dynamic underpinning the development of the modern system of nation states were important changes in the organization of warfare. The need to fund modern warfare was, according to Giddens (1985: 115–16), responsible for the development of the modern monetary and credit systems. Michael Mann has also illustrated the way in which the development of the British state was closely related to increases in military capacity at times of war: between 70 per cent and 90 per cent of state expenditure was devoted to warfare between the twelfth and the nineteenth centuries (Mann, 1993). Robert Dahl (1989) has argued that warfare and nation-hood are intimately related: mass wars required active and supportive citizens which strengthened the legitimacy of the state and contributed to the integration of political communities. Notwithstanding these historical developments and dynamics, the relationship between the contemporary modern democratic state and political violence is less clear. Hannah Arendt, for example, suggested that in the modern era state violence has been associated only with a particular manifestation of the state in the form of totalitarianism (Arendt, 1973). The totalitarian state did not replace older forms of violent law with its own sense of legality. Rather, it constituted a 'movement' rather than a government and was marked by a duplication of authority between party and state. Arendt argued that totalitarianism constituted a form of 'radical evil' based on an 'all or nothing' programme of subjugation or self-annihilation. Totalitarianism worked through violence and the generation of lawlessness rather than through state violence. The central institutions of totalitarianism were the concentration and extermination camps which emerged in a context in which all men had become superfluous or lacked the fear of death. Totalitarianism thus marked the end of Hobbes's Leviathan as a protector against violent death, a change in the material conditions of humanity and the emergence of a new form of humanity based on alternative ways of organizing power.

In contrast to legitimate state violence, and lacking the intensity and universality of revolution, is the phenomenon of terrorism. Terrorism can be defined as the premeditated use of violence to achieve political ends. Terrorism is a pejorative term and is used by both democracies and autocracies to delegitimize political enemies. In contrast, terrorist groups often describe themselves with such positively laden labels as revolutionary cell, urban guerrillas and freedom fighters (Lia, 2005: 9). The perpetrators of terrorism tend to legitimate their actions on the basis of the violent or aggressive behaviour of their opponents. Terrorism has been divided into 'domestic' and 'international' or 'transnational' according to its reach beyond particular national boundaries and sub-divided into four main types corresponding to the ideological motivation of the perpetrators: socio-revolutionary terrorism (left-wing and right-wing), separatist terrorism (usually ethnic minority groups seeking autonomy or independence), single-issue terrorism (anti-abortion, animal rights and environmental activists) and religious terrorism (Lia, 2005: 11). In modern political sociology, acts of terrorism tended not to be treated separately from acts of collective political violence and, as a consequence, modern political sociology had little to tell the world about the nature or causes of terrorism (Lia, 2005: 10–11). However, since the 1990s, and particularly after the events of 9/11, the study of terrorism has thrived. The most important contributions to the sociological study of terror have been conducted within the 'cultural', global' and 'complexity' turns of the discipline.

Violence and the cultural turn: symbolic and simulated violence

The 'cultural turn' has provoked a shift in focus away from the central-ization of violence within the institutional form of the nation state towards a focus on the ways in which symbolic or metaphorical viol-ence is inscribed within everyday discourses and practices. The work of Foucault, in particular, has highlighted the origins of violence in the practices of human consciousness or in the context of the inter-subjective network of texts, institutions and discursive practices. Foucault developed an archaeology and a genealogy of violence in order to provide a historical context for the reading of text and an understanding of the networks of power that produce text. This amounted to an inversion of the liberal project as it enabled the hidden assumptions underlying human identity and the masking of hierarchy to be uncovered:

> It is because subjectivity is marked and masked that violence seems to escape its own analysis: it lives in the shapes it appears to sub-vert. Violence is not opposed to structure as something that exists external to structure; it is another form of structure, of processes, of practices. It is shadow to light, but without shadow how can one see light. (Lawrence & Karim, 2007: 7)

There is no general theory of violence, and theories of violence can be as varied as the practices within which they occur. Violence exists through social and scientific practices such as the family, law, religion and the state. Foucault (1977b) presented the panopticon as a form of metaphorical totalitarianism constituted as an all-embracing, all-pervasive state. In tracing the genealogy of the prison, Foucault described how the medieval punishments which involved the graphic tearing of a criminal's body in order to inscribe the wrath of the sovereign developed into the 'gentle way' of punishment that involved the transformation and reintegration of the individual. The *epistemes* for reading this shift can be found in the 'leper colony' and the 'plague'. While the leper colony involved the fantasy of exclusion and invisibility, the plague articulated the 'will to order': the fantasy of a society based on disciplinary mechanisms of total arrest and total surveillance. The society of spectacular violence thus became the panoptical state which sublimated violence onto the non-corporal or symbolic plane and in the process cut up the body politic into segmented individuals. The panopticon is thus the defining feature of a society where the principal organizing logic has shifted from public life and the community towards private individuals and the state. In the work of Deleuze and Guattari (1983), spectacle and the panopticon are arranged as a continuity rather than as an opposition. In primitive society, cruelty was the foundation of culture. Through rites of initiation, the individual body was marked as being of a certain tribe and the body lost its apartness from culture and became a 'body without organs'. This 'terrible alphabet' constituted a collective memory of word/ language that pulled the individual to the collective. The initiation into the cultural/linguistic body without organs was based on a creditor/ debtor relationship, where the debtor owed a debt of initiation to the *socius*. In the context of the modern state, however, the debt has become internalized and infinite. This is based on an inward spiritualization which has entailed a repressed cruelty of the animal-man made inward and scared back into himself in order to tame the creature imprisoned in the state. The state became internalized in a field of increasingly decoded social forces. Hence, a physical system became spiritualized into a super-terrestrial field that became increasingly over-coded and formed a meta-physical system. The relationship between despot and people became a relationship between classes based on decoded rather than over-coded flows. The state machine determined by the social system rather than the state machine determining the social system. In the modern world, individual consciousness is thus the product of the sublimated symbolic violence of capital and the state.

The 'cultural turn' has resulted in an increasing concern to explore the representation of violence. The representation of violence raises important questions concerning the relationship between violence and identity and in particular the question as to whether we find the subject of violence so alluring that we become embraced by its magic even when we attempt to disavow it (Lawrence & Karim, 2007: 492). In the colonial context, for example, Taussig (1996) highlighted the role of violence as a phantasmic social force. Stories of native violence were used in order to foster a culture of terror which in turn became an integral component in the maintenance of order. More recently, Osama bin Laden, leader of the al-Qaida terror network, has utilized the media in order to wage jihad and emblematize collective bodies of evil for destruction in the name of moral purity. The entire infidel world has been subjected to religious sanction and bin Laden has become the primary icon of terror for the entire Western world as well as a primary icon of hope for entire swaths of the developing world. The most important attempt to capture the relationship between war, terror and the media in the postmodern world can be found in the work of Jean Baudrillard. In his analysis of the first Gulf War, Baudrillard argued that a war in the conventional sense did not take place. The Gulf War was a media event in the form of simulated hyperreality (Baudrillard, 1983b). The hyperreal is constituted by what Baudrillard presents as a third level of simulation. The first level of simulation is an artificial representation of the real. The second level of simulation involves a blurring of the boundaries between representation and reality. The third level of simulation is hyperreality, which is generated by models that have no origins in reality or is constituted as the real fake: the model precedes the real and is generated algorithmically via mathematic models or computer codes.

The hyperreal is beyond good and evil and is measured in terms of performivity: what works or appears good is good. According to Baudrillard (1995), the 'gulf war did not take place' but was detached from the real and constituted a third-order simulation. There was an important illustration of this during the conflict when a CNN television report switched to a group of reporters 'live' in the Gulf, who were revealed to be watching CNN in order to discover recent developments. This highlighted the ways in which news was being generated by the news. The media were producing the 'reality' of the war for both the viewers and those involved. This development has taken propaganda to a new level: the media were not involved in misrepresenting what *is* happening but actively constructing what *will* happen. The Gulf War did not take place primarily in the form of physical combat between comparative powers, but was fought through projections and simulations. For Baudrillard, therefore, the Gulf War was hyperreal and a war in the conventional sense of the word never occurred. The war was *programmed* by the USA and generated by computer systems. The second-order simulation did not precede a real war, but involved the deterrence of the real by the virtual. The war was ultimately about itself: a self-reflexive act to discover whether war is possible in the post-modern era.

The Gulf War and, one may project, all war and acts of terror including 9/11, are for Baudrillard a media spectacle. Unlike earlier commentators on the 'society of the spectacle' such as Guy Debord (see Debord, 1995), Baudrillard does not maintain the division between the empowered and the disempowered in the spectacular society and does not develop a moral critique of the spectacle. The distance between spectacle and spectator has collapsed or *imploded* to the extent that the viewer is also part of the scene. There is no normative or realistic 'third position' from which to evaluate the spectacle. The hyperreal involves simultaneously both total involvement and submersion and total alienation and detachment. In contrast to Foucault's panopticon, which involves perspectival space, in hyperreality the active seeing and the passive being seen are an identical position. There is therefore a transformation of traditional modes of power and subjugation into a circulation of interchangeable positions. The focus on the symbolic and simulated nature of violence has been further complexified by the 'global turn' which has focused on the de-territorialization and relativization of violence and terror.

The global matrix: transnational terror and violence

The 'global turn' has resulted in a concern to explore the ways in which the dynamics of globalization have led to the increasing de-territorialization of violence and the ways in which the risks associated with violence and terror have become increasingly de-bound and global in their reach. The relationship between globalization, violence and terror has economic, geopolitical, socio-spatial and cultural determinants. The economic and geopolitical determinants of this relationship have been explored by Mann (2001), who highlights the patterns of integration and disintegration that result from the complex interplay of globalization processes. Globalization defuses onto a world scale the uneven development and contradictions of the West and North and then combines them with those emanating from South and North–South relations. Globalization is essentially Janus-faced and has provided both order and disorder. Global development has involved the expansion of economic, military, political and ideological networks along different boundaries and according to different rhythms, and this has resulted in the emergence of distinctive forms of integration and disintegration. This is evident with regard to the global economy where a system that is formally capitalist is cut across by regional, national, religious and other boundaries. Mann (2001: 53–7) has suggested that global economic power is marked by the contradictions of 'ostracizing imperialism' through which one part of the world both avoids and dominates the economy of the other. International trade and investment have become increasingly concentrated within the North and hence in economic terms globalization is mostly Northernization. The ostracism is only partial as the North continues to trade with and invest in the South which it continues to dominate. This domination is based on two mechanisms of unequal exchange: a secular downward trend in the price of raw materials and fluctuating exchange rates. The latter have generated large levels of debt in the South and encouraged neo-liberal intervention by the North through the 'structural adjustment programmes' of the IMF and the World Bank. In the South, however, the dominance of political realists and Chicago School economists has had the effect of deflecting North–South tensions and divisions onto the internal politics of each Southern nation state. There are, therefore, powerful tendencies towards disintegration and instability in the global South as a result of the uneven development of the global capitalist economy.

These instabilities are compounded by geopolitical developments generated by the impact of globalization on the world distribution of military power (Mann, 2001: 57–61). In general, the North is becoming integrated as a single military system as states increasingly take cover beneath the US umbrella. The USA does not, however, have the capacity or inclination to dominate militarily China or Russia, and has limited influence over India and Pakistan, which are both nuclear powers. Russia, India and Pakistan all have a common interest in redefining some of their own enemies as 'Islamic fundamentalists' in order to legitimate their oppression. The military dominance of the USA has, however, been in decline in recent years owing to the internal pacification of the North and a subversive revolution in the 'weapons of the weak', of which 9/11 provided a spectacular example. In essence, a dual military world has emerged comprising 'zones of peace' in a largely pacified North alongside 'zones of turmoil' elsewhere. Thus, while there are indeed signs of the development of a single political culture across the North premised on liberal democracy, development and democracy are spread unevenly across the global South. The history of the twentieth century demonstrated the problems of establishing democracy in multiethnic or multi-religious environments. The dominant pattern was the political domination by one religious or ethnic group over others followed by resistance, civil war and ethnic cleansing. These factors have combined with economic failure to ignite the flames within zones of turmoil. In the context of global consumerism, developmental failure weakens regime legitimacy and intensifies political conflict. This has been exacerbated by three forms of Northern interventionism: declining terms of trade and debt crises; the propping up of unpopular or corrupt regimes; and intervention in local ethnic/religious conflicts. The US policy in the Middle East demonstrates the exacerbation of conflict along all three dimensions – although this is unusual and exceptional. Sub-Saharan Africa suffers mainly from ostracism rather than imperialism which has resulted in the emergence of a number of political 'black holes' such as Somalia and Southern Sudan marked by fragmented political relations, civil wars and ethnic conflict.

Ethno-nationalist and religious resistance movements are emerging across the global South. There is a religious faultline emerging between Islam and other religions across great swaths of Asia and Africa. According to Mann (2001: 66), the two main reasons for the pre-eminence of Islam amongst these conflicts are not doctrinal but social and historical: namely, the historical importance of Muslim movements in the resistance to Western imperialism, and the historical legacy provided by Muslim 'warrior sects' who conquered Muslim cities and states in order to reassert the fundamentals of the Koran. In places, fundamentalists are reviving this tradition and adding the emphasis on *qital* (combat) against the enemies of Islam as part of a broader injunction of jihad (struggle) in the name of Allah where violence is not necessarily implied. These 'combat fundamentalists' (Mann, 2001: 67) offer an explanation of real social conditions and a plausible, albeit high-risk, strategy for remedying them. Fundamentalism resonates most strongly where Southern poverty meets Northern imperialism – in places such as Palestine or Chechnya. While fundamentalist regimes tend to be authoritarian and based on harsh religious dictatorships, fundamentalist movements tend to be highly populist as opposition movements. These movements advocate 'theo-democracy' based on the self-rule of the *umma* or religious community. The pressure of these movements has persuaded increasing numbers of Muslims to define their enemies in religious terms giving the global struggle a more global cosmology. The struggle ranges Muslim against infidel, good against evil, God against the Great Satan (Barber, 1996). Military power will not successfully defeat fundamentalism as it merely fans the flames of the fundamentalist resentment. The status of the USA as the principal enemy of combat fundamentalism was not inevitable but is a product of the unforeseen consequences of US policy on communism, Israel and oil (Mann, 2001: 70).

The socio-spatial determinants of the relationship between globalization, violence and terror can be explored through a focus on the intense risks unleashed by the territorial de-bounding of violence and terror in an increasingly globalized world. For Beck (2002b), global terror networks are one of the three principal axes of conflict in world risk society alongside ecological conflicts and global financial crises. In 'second modernity', uncontrollable, human-made and manufactured uncertainties and risks have become 'de-bound'. This de-bounding takes a spatial, temporal and social form. Risks are no longer bounded by the nation state, have long latency periods and it is increasingly difficult to establish liability for their genesis. Global risks are unequally distributed and in the periphery appear as an exogenous process. Individuals feel like hostages to processes that are beyond local correction. In this context, ecological and terrorist threats flourish with a particular virulence owing to the weak states that define the periphery. In important ways, however, terrorist-network threats are distinct from ecological and financial risks. Ecological and financial conflicts result from the accumulation and distribution of 'bads' associated with the production of goods. In contrast, terrorist activity is an intentional 'bad' and aims intentionally to produce the effects that the others produce only unintentionally: the 'principle of intention' has replaced the 'principle of accident'. The perception of the terrorist threat has undermined further the 'active trust' that underpins the economy, everyday life and democracy and replaced it with 'active mistrust'. The dissolution of trust multiplies risks and thus the terrorist threat triggers a self-multiplication of risks by the de-bounding of risk perceptions and fantasies (Beck, 2002b: 44).

This process has important implications for the form and scale of state intervention in the management of risk, as the principle of private insurance has been replaced by the principle of state insurance. The world of individual risk is challenged by a world of systemic risks and this has opened up a range of new conflicts concerning the distribution of costs from terrorist activity. The terrorist threat has a transnational and hybrid character that has reinforced the hegemony of existing powerful states: states have empowered themselves through the definition of *their* terrorist enemy. In this context, the traditional distinctions between war and peace and attack and self-defence start to dissolve. The images of the terrorist threat have become de-territorialized and denationalized and flexible nation state constructions of the threat have emerged which legitimate the global intervention of military powers in the name of self-defence

(Beck, 2002b: 44). The rhetoric around the war on terror and the threat of al-Qaida practised by Western leaders such as George W. Bush or Tony Blair has provided the Islamic terrorist with what they crave the most: recognition of their power. A relationship of mutual enforcement between Western powers and Islamic terrorists has thus developed. In contrast to the pluralization of experts and expert rationalities that are associated with financial and ecological risks, the response to the risk of terrorist attack has involved the gross simplification of enemy images by government and intelligence agencies. The scale and intensity of terrorist risks are instantly established and reproduced through the global media. The dangers associated with terrorism have expanded exponentially with advances in communications and financial technology. The same technology that has served to individualize financial risks has also individualized war (Beck, 2002b: 45). Most horrifying is the potential for terrorism to unleash all the risk conflicts that are currently stored up from the rapid processes of technological and scientific advance. Every advance in gene and nanotechnology provides a further addition to the terrorist toolkit.

Globalization, political violence and 'identity thirst'

The cultural determinants of the relationship between globalization, violence and terror can be explored through a focus on the ways in which the dynamics of globalization have intensified the already complex relationship between violence and identity. The modern matrix of nationalism and globalism was dealt a deathblow by the global events following 9/11, and a new global matrix has emerged which overlays the old matrix in complex and contradictory ways (Nairn & James, 2005). The source of this dynamic is the aggressive assertion of neo-liberal globalism since 1989 that has simultaneously dissolved national boundaries and reduced the power and status of nation states. The result has been elite and mass resentment and the mobilization of often-aggressive forms of non-economic power. This reflects the human cost of destroying national boundaries. The process of neo-liberal restructuring and the attempt to undermine these borders have magnified the importance of 'identity politics'. Within the resulting national–global matrix, culture, language, feeling and religion have assumed equal importance to economics and the internationalization of *homo economicus* as desired by the Washington Consensus. Hence, the relationship between ICT-led globalization, political violence and terrorism:

> Technology has fused with lowered borders, increased migratory movements, rising expectations and correspondingly inflamed resentments,

to create a militant *identity-thirst*. People that despair of neo-liberal lackeys and Third Way hypocrites do not lose their wish for meaningful lives and transcendent purpose. They go elsewhere: in the West, religion, reheated xenophobia and reality TV are evident candidates ... The meaning-nexus undermined by boundary loss is reclaimed by strident affirmation of identity, or even more splendid martyrdom. (Nairn, 2005: 45–6; *my emphasis*)

The Islamic suicide bombers who hit the World Trade Center, New York with passenger aircraft on 9/11 2001 and its aftermath are an unintended side effect of neo-liberal globalism. The post-2001 'war on terror' or 'meta-war' unleashed by the Bush regime in the USA marked an attempt to reimpose US leadership on a globalization process that has become increasingly divergent from and dysfunctional for a US-led neo-imperialist foreign policy premised on 'one market under God' (Nairn, 2005: 31). Neo-liberal globalism creates new inequalities and novel ways of both connecting places and bypassing and ignoring them (Ferguson, 2002). Hence, an engine of conflagration has developed which transforms liberal democratic capitalism into ethnic hatred (Chua, 2002). In a fluid and fragmented world, individuals fasten onto material interests and prejudice in order to satisfy their 'identity thirst'.

The events of 9/11 are the most spectacular manifestation of a form of fundamentalist politics associated with Islam that has spread throughout the developing world. This form of politics has become a state ideology in Iran and is posing a serious challenge to secular regimes in Indonesia, Egypt and Pakistan (Bruce, 2000: 40–65). In the context of weakening civil and national bonds, there has been the development of aggressive forms of ethnic sub-nationalism that exploit the particularities of place, religion or ethnicity (Alter, 1994: 91–119). This resurgence of nationalism has involved either the implosion of nation states or sub-national challenges to the legitimacy and integrity of nation states. These new forms of nationalism are often based on 'cultural' or even mystical forms of identity based on romanticism, ritual, tradition and legend. In the global South, an important legacy of colonialism was the drawing of national boundaries in ways that ignored ethnic, cultural and tribal divisions. These divisions have re-emerged in the form of serious sub-national conflicts in Burundi, Nigeria, Rwanda, Eritrea, Iran, Iraq, India, Pakistan and Indonesia (Forrest, 2003; Pfaff-Czainecka, 2005). The collapse of the Soviet bloc and the Soviet Union has revitalized ancient nationalities and ethnicities and resulted in serious ethnic conflict in Moldova, Chechnya, Georgia and Azerbaijan and civil war in the former Yugoslavia (Zisserman-Brodsky, 2003; Fowkes, 1996). These intense ethnic conflicts have often been the scene of violent and bloody episodes of ethnic cleansing and genocide. There has also been the emergence of important separatist movements in North America in the form of Quebec nationalism in Canada, and in Europe in the form of Basques (Spain), Breton (France), Welsh and Scottish (UK) nationalisms (Keating, 1988; Reinharz & Mosse, 1992). The re-emergence of nationalism has coincided with the resurgence in far-right politics and the increasing popularity of a range of neo-fascist parties and movements. In Europe, for example, far-right movements have developed a fervent nationalism in order to oppose immigration, 'big government' and European integration. Important examples include the Austrian Freedom Party, the British National Party, the Front National in France, the German People's Union and the National Alliance in Italy (Eatwell, 2000; Payne, 1999; Veugelers, 1999). In the USA, a range of white supremacist, neo-Nazi and anti-Semitic groups, including the Ku-Klux-Klan (Castells, 1997: 84–97), constitutes the 'Patriot' movement.

The cultural dynamics linking globalization to the growth of ethnic hatred and violence and the decade of political super-violence which culminated in the events of 9/11 in New York and the subsequent US-led war on terror have been explored by Appadurai (2006). First, Appadurai notes the fundamental and dangerous idea behind the very notion of the modern nation state: the idea of the 'national ethnos'. There is, he suggests, a direct route from notions of a 'national genius' to a totalized cosmology of the sacred nation and further to ethnic purity and cleansing. Second, Appadurai (2006: 15; 1998b) notes the intense social uncertainty generated by globalization. This uncertainty is generated by the migratory movements of ethnic groups and the resulting mixture of cultural styles and media representations which generate profound doubts with regard to the differentiation between 'we' and 'they'. This uncertainty creates high levels of anxiety with regard to the relationship between individuals and state-provided goods such as health, housing and safety. In this context, violence can create a macabre form of certainty and brutal techniques to establish and maintain the distinction between 'them' and 'us'. In a context where globalization has unglued fixed and stable categories of modernity, violence has thus become one of the ways in which the illusion of fixed and charged identities can be (re)produced (Appadurai, 1996). Hence, fundamentalism and violence can be seen as an emerging cultural repertoire of 'full attachment' (Appadurai, 1998a) which produces previously unrequired levels of certainty with regard to questions of identity, values and dignity. Third, the roots of new ideological forms of majoritarian and racialized nationalism in democratic societies can be located in the inner-reciprocity between the categories of 'majority' and 'minority' in liberal thought. The result of this inner-reciprocity is the generation of an 'anxiety of incompleteness' through which numerical majorities can become predatory and ethnocidal. This is particularly the case in relation to 'small numbers' as small minorities remind them of the gap between their condition as a majority and the possible horizon of an unsullied national whole based on a pure and untainted national ethnos. The resulting incompleteness can result in the exercise of violence against minorities. Fourth, the large-scale violence of the 1990s was underpinned by a 'surplus of rage' produced by the 'narcism of minor difference'. The lines between major and minor difference became increasingly uncertain in a context where the elimination of difference was rendered increasingly problematic by the dynamics of globalization and this often resulted in intense levels of frustration. The development of terrorist organizations such as al-Qaida, the growth of asymmetric violence against civilian populations and the phenomena of suicide bombings and hostage taking and execution can thus be seen through the lens of a global rage against neo-liberal marketization, the specificities of anti-Americanism on a global scale and the unexpected return of the patriot, martyr and sacrificial victim into the spaces of mass political violence. The analysis of the ambiguous, unexpected and asymmetrical threat posed by contemporary manifestations of violence and terror has been developed further using the vocabulary of 'complexity', and this is discussed further in the following section.

Complex terror: the asymmetric threat of unequal powers

The 'complexity turn' has explored the extent to which violent terror constitutes an emergent and unpredictable 'global fluid' that evades control by the institutions and agencies of the nation state system. Urry (2002) has argued that the events of 9/11 highlighted the complex ambiguities of the contemporary world. We live in a fluctuating, noisy, chaotic world marked by varied possibilities and a world where systems are characterized by an irreversible arrow of time producing complex structures within which small events can produce large outcomes (Prigogine, 1997: 26–7, 127). The events of 9/11 demonstrated the importance of 'asymmetric threats' and the ways in which contemporary 'wars' are fought between highly unequal powers. Terrorism is political communications by other means, and the message being communicated was an intense hatred of the USA. In the context of global complexity, the powerless are able to inflict intense violence on institutions of power and the bodies and buildings in which that power is condensed. The origins of this asymmetric warfare can be found in the 'wild zones' or 'zones of turmoil' (Mann, 2001: 61) that are generated by neo-liberal globalism and which are marked by 'absence', 'gap' and 'lack' (Urry, 2002: 62). Here charismatic leaders are able to mobilize alternative armies on the basis of plausible solutions to the problems of inequality associated with the domination of Islamic societies.

The threat of asymmetric threats is exacerbated by contemporary urban forms marked by 'splintering urbanism' and the resulting chaotic juxta-position of 'wild zones' and 'tame zones' which have become highly proximate through curvatures of time-space (Urry, 2002: 62–4). The power of the 9/11 event resulted from the linking together of people, objects and technologies in a deadly, non-failing network which was able to unleash a new and unique form of warfare against the USA focused on the killing of innocent civilians. The war involved the 'attractor' of mediated power and the sense that everything is visible within the global panopticon. The world watched as planes flew into the World Trade Center and the buildings instantaneously collapsed. There has been spec-ulation that the 20-minute gap between the planes crashing into the World Trade Center was designed to maximize the media impact of the event. Hence, the wild and safe zones collided in the sky above New York on 11 September 2001 in a way no one in the safe zone had predicted (Urry, 2002: 64). These events occurred because of the actions of a terror-ist network, al-Qaida. In contrast to global networks such as McDonald's or Disney which are complex but stable and enduring connections between people, objects and technologies across multiple times and spaces, terrorist networks take the form of 'global fluids'. These fluids, it is suggested, move according to novel shapes and temporalities in ways that break free from linear or clock time. These fluids act on local information but their local actions are, through numerous iterations, captured, moved, represented, marketed and generalized and are able to impact chaotically on distant people and places. These fluids demonstrate no clear point of departure but rather de-territorialized movement at different levels of speed and viscosity with no necessary end-state or purpose.

Hence, global fluids create their own context for action rather than being 'caused' by context. Al-Qaida can be seen as a self-organizing system at the edge of chaos. The network is hard to defeat owing to its ability to mutate in shape, form and activities. This self-mutating capacity renders the network invisible and, on occasions, awesomely present

(Urry, 2002: 66). In this context, the state and transnational state agencies have become more rather than less important. Intensified regulatory capacities are required to deal with multiple and overlapping fluids that move across borders and through time-space in 'dizzying, discrepant and transmuting form'. States are forced to act as regulators or gamekeepers of networks and fluids generated by the unpredictable consequences of other economic, social and political entities including global terrorist networks. The new 'other' has resulted in the emergence of new forms of warfare described as 'swarming' (Dillon, 2000) or 'networked military mobility' (Castells, 2001: 161–2): a form of non-linear warfare that eliminates the notion of a 'front line' in favour of high-tech guerrilla struggles dependent on secure communication. The new global disorder is premised upon the mutually reinforcing relationship between what Barber (1996) describes as a consumerist 'McWorld' and the identity politics of patriarchal jihad. These two worlds constitute a 'strange attractor' which draws a huge array of other relations into its orbit (Urry, 2002: 67). Thus, existing notions of democracy and citizenship are drawn into and transformed through this strange attractor, and the attractor polarizes the global system between McWorld and jihad.

The ability of the nation state to contain the de-territorialized fluid of global terror has, however, been questioned by Bauman (2002), who has argued that the events of 9/11 marked the symbolic end to the era of space in an era of post-panoptical power. In the era of space, territory was the most coveted of resources as it was the prime guarantee of security. Power was territorial and so were privacy and freedom from the interference of power. The events of 9/11 highlighted that this era had drawn to a close. In the era of post-panoptical power, the protective capacity of space had been annihilated and, in this context, no one can cut themselves off from the rest of the world. This annihilation of space is a double-edged sword as no one can hide from blows, and blows can be plotted from an enormous distance. In this context, strength and weakness, threat and security have become extraterritorial issues that evade territorial solutions. The origins of 9/11 lie in the massive insecurities generated within the uncolonized, politically uncontrolled and thoroughly deregulated 'space of flows'. The event translated a threat from the difficult-to-master language of global insecurity into the familiar and easy-to-understand language of personal safety. The degree of vulnerability can no longer be measured on the basis of the defence provided by arsenals of high-tech weaponry. The world can no longer be divided between a part secure behind modern anti-missile systems and a part abandoned to war and anarchism. Global space has taken the form of a frontierland in which agility and cunning count for more than sophisticated weapons systems. In the frontierlands, war is not fought in trenches, but on the move, and the might and nuisance capacity of adversaries is marked by speed, inconspicuousness and randomness. Adversaries are extraterritorial. Frontierlands are simultaneously factories of displacement and recycling plants for the displaced.

In the frontierland, the adversaries and the battle lines that separate them are in constant flux. In a context marked by a generalized lack of trust and loyalties there are only 'confluent alliances' and 'confluent enmities'. In this context, while the war against some terrorists can be won given an adequate supply of money and weapons to bribe 'flexible allies', the war on terrorism remains unwinnable as long as global space retains its frontierland characteristics. This is unlikely in the present context of an avoidance of institutionalized structures empowered to elicit obedience to universal rules and deliver a politically controlled global order. It is unlikely as both sides in the conflict have a vested interest in the perpetuation of frontierland conditions. There is no new Westphalian settlement designed to overcome the neo-medieval chaos of the current situation. In contrast to Clausewitz's famous axiom that war is but a continuation of politics by other means, the war on terror amounts to the ongoing absence of politics by any other means (Baudrillard, 2001). The nature of war in the frontierlands is reflexive and experimental: the random search for a lucky move (Bauman, 2002: 87–8). In these reconnaissance battles, units are not sent out to capture enemy territory but to explore the endurance, determination and resources of the enemy. Reconnaissance battles are the principal form of battle in an unregulated environment. The principal causes of under-regulation are the collapse of established authority structures and the emergence of new sites where the question of legitimate authority has never been raised (Bauman, 2002: 88–9). The collapse of established authority structures has particular importance at the global and life-political levels as both lack traditions that can be evoked and relied on in new conditions. At the planetary level, the resulting political void is a constant invitation to bargain by force as neither the outcomes of the global game nor its rules are predetermined and no global authority exists in order to determine or enforce such rules. In this context, lawlessness is self-perpetuating whenever a successful attempt to use it for partisan advantage takes place and is undertaken with increasing zeal by those attempting to maintain their privileges and those intent on usurping them.

The ambiguities of complex violence and terror

In modern political sociology, political violence was analysed as a structural property of capital or the state that played a key role in the institutional development of modernity. The 'cultural', 'global' and 'complexity' turns have shifted the focus to the increasing importance of symbolic and simulated violence, the de-territorialized nature of global terror networks and the asymmetric threat posed by extraterritorial terroristic 'fluids'. The 'cultural turn' highlighted the decentring of state violence and the tendency for violence to be sublimated onto the symbolic plane. In this context, the representation and 'performivity' of warfare and terrorism have become the most important manifestations of these phenomena. The 'global turn' has focused on the de-territorialization of political violence and terrorism and the ways in which the inequalities emanating from the uneven development of the global system are creating tensions and conflicts that are being translated into an array of violent 'combat fundamentalisms'. In this context, terrorism has become a de-bounded global risk that has expanded exponentially with the development and growth of the global media industry. The ideological projection of neoliberal globalism through global networks has created new levels of resentment, uncertainty, anxiety and rage and a militant 'identity thirst' that has been satiated by the growth of ethnic hatred, religious fundamentalism and global terror. The 'complexity turn' has highlighted how emergent terror networks constitute an asymmetric and unpredictable threat in the context of global complexity. Global terror networks have been presented as unstable global fluids which swarm around an increasingly borderless world and constantly mutate into new forms in ways that avoid their control and elimination by regulatory agencies. The 'cultural', 'global' and 'complexity' turns have provided a range of illuminating insights into the changing form of political violence and terrorism in the contemporary world. The work of Appadurai (2006) explored earlier highlighted how globalization had created a new 'geography of anger' based on increasingly complex and ambiguous forms of identity. In order to understand the ways in which violence and terror are 'lived' as existential categories we need to delve more deeply into an analysis of the liminal forms in which this ambiguous complexity is manifested in contemporary society. This liminality is not located between the modern and the pre-modern but as a result of the ways in which traditional world-views and beliefs are articulated in postmodern forms within globalized hypermodernity: the resulting repertoires of violence and terror are neither pre-modern, modern nor postmodern and are lived between the local and the global.

The US 'war on terror' which followed 9/11 has been legitimated by a discourse which presents the perpetrators and supporters of Islamic terror as evil individuals motivated by a hatred of freedom and the American way of life. As Mazarr (2007) has noted, however, al-Qaida and similar terror groups and networks have emerged from the same orientation towards modernity that fuelled the emergence of virulent forms of fascism, nationalism and religious fundamentalism throughout the twentieth century. In the mid-nineteenth century, Hoffer (1951) noted that both radical and reactionary movements appealed to a particular mindset: one besieged, thwarted, filled with real and invented grievances, overwhelmed with the existential demands of modernity and thrilled with the prospect of revalidating a humiliated nation or ethnic group by recapturing age-old values and glories (Mazarr, 2007: 9). In this context, Islamic terror networks have emerged from the reaction of people to the Western-shaped world and the anger and confusion of individuals to that reaction, together with a fury at the inability of their governments to secure the welfare and interests of their people in a globalized world. These psychological factors are nestled in a larger context of geopolitical, socio-economic, cultural, demographic and other realities to produce forms of frustration, rage and ultimately terrorism which spring forth as the modern collides with the traditional (Mazarr, 2007: 10–11). Into the resulting mêlée step charismatic 'identity entrepreneurs' offering a cure for popular alienation and anxiety in the form of narratives or stories populated by the heroes and villains of local and global conspiracies that link a glorified past to a feculent present and then to a reglorified future. The identity entrepreneurs accumulate an ideology through the writing of books and manifestoes in an attempt to rally support for their cause, conspire through the formation of secret cabals and eventually act, forcing either large-scale social change and the formation of state terrorist regimes, as occurred in Iran following the 1979 Islamic Revolution, or engage in small-scale terrorist acts in order to bring attention to their cause. The content of these ideologies are a reverence for past glories, moral absolutism and the scapegoating of outside forces which, in the case of Radical Islam, is directed at the West or the Great Satan.

Barber (1996) has conceptualized this civilizational schism in terms of the conflict between 'jihad' and 'McWorld': the latter a product of developments in technology and communication that have facilitated the global diffusion of Westernized consumer capitalism. However, as Barber (1996: 156) has noted, jihad is not only the adversary of the McWorld but its progeny: the two being locked together in an ongoing Freudian struggle, with neither willing to coexist with the other, but neither being complete without the other. Jihad represents a permanent war of reaction against the present in the name of the past: a fight for religious conceptions of the world against secularism and relativism; a fight using weapons of every kind including those borrowed from the enemy, carefully chosen to secure their identity; and a fight under God for a cause that, because it is holy, cannot be lost even when it is not yet won (Barber, 1996: 206). As Castells (1997: 16–19) has noted, Islamic fundamentalism is not a traditionalist movement but a contemporary form of identity politics that has developed in reaction against unreachable modernization, the evils of globalization and the collapse of postcolonial nationalism. Religious fundamentalism is thus a culturally constituted defensive reaction against the individualizing dynamics of the 'network society' and a form of identity politics based on specific codes of self-identification, a community of believers and an external truth that cannot be virtualized because it is embodied in its believers (Castells, 1997: 64–6). The complexity of contemporary manifestations of violence and terror is, therefore, a product of the ways in which the existential uncertainty associated with rapid social and political change are 'lived' by individuals in an increasingly unequal and bifurcated world. The desperate search for meaning and identity generates forms of postmodern identity politics in the context of a hypermodern global system whose institutional architecture continues to be dominated by neo-liberal capitalism and the international state system. In the liminal and ambiguous spaces that have resulted from this disjuncture, violence and terrorism are real and vital responses to the lack of identity and meaning that have been generated by the abstract processes of globalization.

Summary and conclusion

In this chapter, I have explored the development of violence and terrorism in modern society and the ways in which the 'cultural', 'global' and 'complexity' turns in political sociology have attempted to understand the changing forms and manifestations of violence and terror in contemporary society. In modern society, political violence and terror were objective manifestations of power exercised through and/or against the modern nation state. The crisis and decomposition of political modernity has resulted in violence and terror becoming increasingly virtualized, symbolic and de-territorialized. The 'cultural turn' has served to highlight the extent to which the exercise of violence and terror can no longer be effectively separated from its symbolic representation and mediation, and this has enabled insights into the ways in which the threat and risks of violence and terror have become increasingly internalized as important components of postmodern identity. The 'global turn' has demonstrated how the uneven and contradictory impact of globalization has simultaneously intensified and de-territorialized violence and terror as a result of the uneven development of neo-liberal capitalism, the spatially unbound nature of risks and threats in 'second' or 'reflexive' modernity and the ways in which violence and terror have become important mechanisms through which the anxieties of identity-loss can be expressed in a context of neo-liberal globalism. The 'complexity turn' has usefully employed the metaphors of complexity and chaos theory to characterize violence and terror as unpredictable 'global fluids' that pose an asymmetric threat to global order. The chapter concluded with the argument that violence and terror can only be adequately understood as existential categories through an understanding of the ways in which they constitute liminal forms of culture and identity between the modern and the postmodern and between the global and the local.

8
Complex Citizenships: Between Universalism and Particularism?

The concept of citizenship is intrinsically complex and ambiguous as a result of the different and historically specific ways in which the concept has been used. The concept developed originally in the city states of ancient Greece and Rome. The etymology of the word from the Latin *civitas* or 'body of citizens' highlights the extent to which the original conception of citizenship was connected to *membership* of a city and this was reflected in the modern meaning of citizenship which was constituted by 'membership' of a *nation* with settled and stable boundaries. The social membership associated with modern citizenship implied a set of *rights* and *obligations* between individual citizens and the state. Throughout the modern period, however, the scope of membership and the composition of the political community were highly contested, and a central objective of social and political mobilization by subaltern social movements was to widen the definition of citizenship to include hitherto excluded groups and individuals. In the Western world, the apogee of modern citizenship occurred in the immediate postwar period with the development of the Keynesian Welfare State (KWS) and the development of universal systems of social rights and social protection. The universalism of the Enlightenment ideologies that underpinned the KWS were never realized in practice, and during the past three decades the model of universal modern citizenship has been challenged and marginalized by alternative conceptions of citizenship. During the 1960s, the emergence of 'new' social movements led sociologists to question the centrality of the relationship between class and citizenship and there was an increasing focus on the relationship between citizenship and inequalities based on gender, sexuality and race and ethnicity. The 'cultural turn' in sociology thus shifted the focus of the debate on citizenship from *universalism* to *difference* or *otherness*. The 'global turn' in political sociology has focused on the extent to which the processes associated with globalization have disarticulated social and political rights and the nation state, and resulted in the development of a range of post-national forms of citizenship beyond the nation state. In the context of global complexity there have also been challenges to the anthropo-centric bias of modern citizenship and the notion that social and polit-ical rights can be attributed to natural and hybrid phenomena such as animals or the environment.

The purpose of this chapter is thus to explore the ways in which the analysis and representation of citizenship have been transformed by the 'cultural', 'global' and 'complexity' turns in political sociology. In the next section, 'Modern citizenship', I explore the key contributions to the debate on modern citizenship with a particular focus on the model of universal citizenship established in the work of T.H. Marshall. The key arguments of Marshall are outlined, followed by a discussion of the weaknesses and limitations of the model and the ways in which this conceptualization of citizenship has been further undermined by the crisis and globalization of modernity. The section 'Cultural citizen-ships' explores how the 'cultural turn' has shifted the debate on cit-izenship away from the universal nature of rights and obligations towards a focus on diversity, particularism and support for 'different-iated' or 'multicultural' citizenship based on 'group' rights and oblig-ations. The work of the key contributors to this debate such as Iris Young and Will Kymlicka is explored followed by a critical appraisal of the strengths and weaknesses of this approach. In the section 'Global citizenships' I explore how the 'global turn' has resulted in an increas-ing focus on the de-territorialization of citizenship rights and oblig-ations and the emergence of new forms of citizenship beyond the territorial confines of the nation state. There is an exploration of the work of Yasemin Soysal on post-national citizenship and human rights, followed by a critical discussion on the limits and possibilities of transnational citizenship. This is illustrated through an exploration of environmental and European citizenship. The section 'Complex cit-izenships' explores how the 'complexity turn' has shifted the focus towards the rights and obligations of global flows and hybrids. In the final section, 'Liminal citizenships', I employ the example of the struggle for rights by the global justice movement against transnational insti-tutions such as the WTO and EU to highlight the ambiguous and liminal forms of citizenship which result from the increasing dom-inance of postmodern political forms within a hypermodern global system.

Modern citizenship: the foundations and limits of universalism

Throughout the modern era, citizenship was a key constituting feature of the modern state. There were four key elements to modern citizenship: a system of membership; a type of status; a set of rights; and a set of duties (Pierson, 1996: 128–42). During the modern period, citizenship implied membership of a political community defined by the nation state, and hence citizenship was intertwined with nationhood. In this context, citizenship developed as both a status that implied a series of rights and responsibilities and as an important source of personal identity. Citizenship was also a system of social closure defining 'insider' and 'outsider' groups. The nation state discriminated between different groups with regard to the granting of full citizenship status within their territories, and the 'inclusion' of outsider groups was regulated by complex procedures and rituals. Citizenship constituted a somewhat paradoxical form of status in modern society owing to the fact that it was *ascribed* rather than *achieved* by existing members of the political community. Citizenship was ascribed either on the basis of the citizenship of one's parents (*jus sanguinis*) or on the basis of being born within the territory of a particular state (*jus soli*). Citizenship was thus an achieved status only for outsiders and incomers. The practice of modern citizenship highlighted the limits of contractarian thought as developed within modern political philosophy. Modern citizenship was essentially an involuntary status and the state had the capacity to withdraw citizenship in a unilateral way as a sanction against law breaking. In essence, modern citizenship was a form of identity that was either ascribed or achieved but in both cases was compulsory.

Universal citizenship and the welfare state: the critique of T.H. Marshall

The most important element of citizenship is with regard to its juridical status as a set of rights and obligations. The most important attempt to chart citizenship as an expanding and increasingly universal system of rights can be found in the work of T.H. Marshall. Marshall (1981, 1992) was concerned with the failure of classical liberal theorists such as J.S. Mill to explore adequately the contradiction between *formal* political equality and citizenship rights expressed through the franchise and the persistence of *substantive* social inequalities as expressed through the capitalist market and capitalist private property. Marshall argued that these contradictions had been resolved through the historical development and extension of citizenship which had culminated in the development of the KWS in the post-war period. In what amounted to an ideological apologia for the post-war mixed economy, Marshall argued that capitalism provided the best 'economic' guarantor for citizenship, as capitalist growth provided the resources to fund welfare benefits which could be provided by the state thus alleviating the inequalities of market provision. The model of citizenship developed by Marshall was premised on the assumption that the modern nation state was underpinned by territorial integrity and cultural homogeneity. Marshall outlined a theory of citizenship which explored the social-welfare history of Britain in the eighteenth, nineteenth and twentieth centuries. The growth of citizenship rights in each of these centuries corresponded to a particular dimension of citizenship: *civil*, *political* and *social*. The eighteenth century witnessed the development of civil rights defended and upheld by a system of law courts. These rights included freedom of speech, the right to a fair trial, and equal and fair access to the legal system. During the nineteenth century, there was a marked development of political and electoral rights upheld and enshrined within the institutions of parliamentary democracy. These rights emerged from the struggles of the emergent working class for political equality in terms of the extension of the electoral franchise and greater access to the parliamentary process. During the twentieth century, there was an expansion of social rights which were premised on claims to welfare and were upheld and enshrined within the institutions of the welfare state. Social rights were constituted by rights such as the entitlement to social security in periods of unemployment and sickness, and access to universal health and education systems. According to Marshall, the development of social citizenship rights to welfare resulted in a movement towards a greater 'equality of status' between individuals.

The model of citizenship developed by T.H. Marshall was subjected to a range of criticisms which highlighted the evolutionary nature of his analysis and his failure to pay sufficient attention to social struggle and agency in the construction of citizenship rights. The account of citizenship developed by Marshall was accused of being evolutionary and historicist in a way that ignored politics and the way in which each of the rights he identified was the product of a protracted phase of struggle and conflict (Giddens, 1982; Bottomore, 1992). The evolutionary nature of Marshall's argument is particularly problematic given the way in which social rights have been reversed and destroyed by neo-liberal restructuring since the 1980s (Delanty, 2000: 20–1). Critics also argued that modern citizenship developed in a circuitous rather than a linear fashion (Birnbaum, 1997). Marshall's account was accused of being Anglocentric and based on the assumption that the development of citizenship in the UK provided a universal model for the development of citizenship in other countries. Michael Mann has highlighted how the early acquisition of political rights by individuals in the USA prevented the wide-scale demand for social rights and the way this contributed to the relatively undeveloped nature of universal social welfare in the USA (Mann, 1996). Marshall's account was also accused of being universalist and premised on the assumption that modern citizenship rights developed in opposition to class inequality. This ignored the significance of gender, race and ethnic inequalities as forms of inequality that undermined the universalism of modern citizenship (Turner, 1986). The duties associated with citizenship were a key element of both classical and modern conceptualizations of citizenship, but were not taken seriously in the work of Marshall (Hay, 1996: 77). In recent years, there has been an increasing focus on the responsibilities of citizenship owing to the way in which the obligations associated with citizenship are prominent within both New Right and communitarian political discourse. In modern societies, the obligations associated with citizenship were deeply gendered and this undermined further the universal model of citizenship developed by Marshall. For men, the focus was often on the duty to perform military service and this was often a key dynamic in the extension of the franchise (Therborn, 1978). For women, responsibilities were focused on the rearing of children and these were articulated within pro-natalist state policies. These differential responsibilities were reflected in differential rights as women were either excluded from full citizenship rights or granted only partial citizenship rights. The right to full citizenship has also been associated with the duty to perform paid employment and, in the post-war period, this was reflected in the commitment of national governments to a policy of full employment. In the context of neo-liberal globalization, however, this has become increasingly problematic, leading to New Right policies that negate social citizenship rights and claims by radical social movements for a minimum income for citizens guaranteed by the state.

Feminist critics of Marshall argued that he took the male citizen as the 'norm' and ignored the ways in which the development of the rights of women took a trajectory different from the development of the rights of men. The feminist critique was premised on the ways in which the liberal state and the rule of law institutionalized the power of men over women and thereby institutionalized power in a male form. The critique has highlighted the ways in which modern citizenship privileged the public

sphere populated by men at the expense of the private sphere populated by women and as a result excluded or marginalized women from
full citizenship rights (Pateman, 1988). This is related to the institution
of marriage and the ways in which traditional forms of the family constrained the citizenship rights of women (Vogel, 1991). Pateman (1989)
has highlighted the patriarchal nature of the welfare state and the ways
in which the post-war settlement associated with the KWS was underpinned by the unpaid domestic labour of women. Women had a disproportionate importance within the welfare state and the welfare state
had a disproportionate importance for women as the everyday practices of the welfare state served to establish a relationship of structural
dependency between women and welfare agencies (Fraser, 1989b; Gordon,
1990; Hernes, 1987). In the case of racial and ethnic minorities, the
possession of formal citizenship did nothing to prevent exclusion from
full participation in society (Brubaker, 1989, 1990). Marshall wrote his
account of citizenship at the height of post-war prosperity, which was
a time when the welfare state was still being developed and expanded.
Since the 1970s, the economic assumptions of Marshall concerning the
compatibility between capitalism and citizenship have been increasingly questioned by the New Right. These critics have highlighted how
high taxation and welfare spending undermined the market economy
and corporate profits. These arguments have been emphasized with the
intensification of globalization and the increasing mobility of TNCs and
MNCs. The critique of Marshall and the demonstration that enduring
patterns of inequality and marginalization were reproduced by 'universal'
models of citizenship were an important dynamic in the development of
the 'cultural turn' in citizenship studies.

Cultural citizenships: towards particularism, diversity and difference?

The 'cultural turn' in citizenship studies followed the challenge to
universalist models of citizenship by the liberation movements which
developed in the 1960s and 1970s. The universalist claims of modern citizenship have been deconstructed in order to highlight the ways in which
the 'universalist' discourse articulated a powerful exclusionary dynamic.
The 'cultural turn' has focused on the increasing importance of a postmodern politics of difference premised on a responsibility towards 'otherness' (Nash, 2000: 157). The politics of the feminist movement, the gay
and lesbian liberation movement and the civil rights and anti-racist movement involved not only a challenge to the exclusion of certain groups

from the citizenship rights enjoyed by 'normal' citizens, but a challenge to notions of normalcy and the development of a pluralist politics that pursued different forms of citizenship for different social groups. Feminist writers have argued that liberal models of citizenship played an important role in legitimating the inequalities associated with patriarchal capitalism. Chantal Mouffe has argued that the notion of citizenship has been constructed in the male image and that, while women are theoretically equal to men as citizens, the continuing sexual division of labour, the feminization of poverty and the enduring domestic duties of women contradict this formal parity (Mouffe, 1993). The welfare state reflected the patriarchal division of labour in which full citizenship was based on full-time employment and the benefit system was premised on the proposed superiority of this model. Caring and domestic work were seen as 'private' and not contributing to the 'public good'. Hence, women were caught in the so-called 'Wollstonecraft dilemma' or same-difference dilemma: should the women's movement struggle to be treated equally with rights defined according to male norms, or struggle for gender-specific rights enabling women's differences to be valued and recognized? The 'cultural turn' has involved the attempt to resolve this problem through the notion of 'group-differentiated' citizenship rights that recognize social difference and diversity. Examples of group-differentiated citizenship rights include 'affirmative action' programmes designed to overcome the unequal rights of minorities in the workplace, the 're-districting' of electoral constituencies in the USA in an attempt to generate areas with African-American or Hispanic majorities and the electoral procedures designed to ensure the parliamentary representation of aboriginal peoples in New Zealand (Isin & Wood, 1999: 45, *passim*).

The case for group-differentiated citizenship rights has been developed through a critique of the universalism underpinning the liberal conception of citizenship. Iris Young (1989: 274) has argued that liberalism articulated a model of citizenship which denied the existence of social difference and articulated a universalism both in terms of equality of participation and in the abstract sense of individuals adopting a 'universal point of view'. The adoption of this universal viewpoint compelled individual citizens to deny their particular identity when exercising the rights and responsibilities of citizenship. The 'democratic' institutions of liberal democracy denied an effective voice to social identities that deviated from the 'norm' of white, heterosexual male, and the laws generated by the liberal democratic polity applied to everyone regardless of the diversity of their needs or the enduring nature of social inequalities. Liberalism affirmed the domination of the ideal of equality over the ideal of difference. This domination reflected a series of deep-rooted power relationships that have their historical origins in the dynamics of imperialism and patriarchy. The historical development of liberal citizenship was bound up with the celebration of objective reason and in opposition to emotion and the body. Hence, the 'uncivilized', 'irrational' or 'emotional' were deemed incapable of assuming the full responsibilities of citizenship. These inequalities were often reproduced at an unconscious level through a structure of power that produced and reproduced 'five faces of oppression': 'exploitation, marginalization, powerlessness, cultural imperialism and violence' (Young, 1990: 39–65). In order to overcome these forms of oppression, Young has advocated a 'politics of difference' based on the incorporation of group identities into the decision-making institutions of the community and the development of institutional mechanisms and public resources to ensure the recognition and representation of distant voices (Young, 1990: 184). The importance of group identity and group-differentiated rights resulted from the ways in which groups 'constitute individuals' and the difficulty for non-group members to understand the oppression that a particular group faces. The concept of 'differentiated citizenship' is thus based on group rights rather than individual rights and the notion that citizenship should celebrate and protect difference rather than seeking to transcend difference through universal equality.

The politics of multiculturalism rests upon the notion that the maintenance of individual freedom is dependent on the maintenance of cultural differences and alternative lifestyles (Kymlicka, 1995). In this context, Will Kymlicka has also advocated a 'differentiated' or 'multicultural' citizenship which recognizes the importance of culture to an individual's sense of place or identity. The work of Kymlicka is more narrowly focused on 'ethnic identity', which is important because it provides the cultural context within which individuals develop and which, therefore, set the parameters for individual choice. The problem with liberal conceptualizations of citizenship, he argued, was the tendency to treat the relationship between ethnicity and the state in the same manner as the relationship between religion and the state. This resulted in the notion that particularistic identities should be confined to the private sphere while citizenship inhabited the universal and culture-blind public sphere. This rendered minorities susceptible to the injustices perpetrated by the majority and resulted in the exacerbation of ethno-cultural conflict (Kymlicka, 1995: 5). In order to overcome these injustices, Kymlicka advocated a theory of justice for the multicultural state that involved both universal rights for all individuals and certain group-differentiated rights or 'special status' for minority cultures. These included three forms of group rights (Faulks, 2000: 89). First, there is the right to self-government including the devolution of powers to minorities within the state. Second, there are polyethnic rights which protect group identity through the legal protection and public financing of minority cultures. Third, there is the provision of special representational rights which ensure the inclusion of minorities in political institutions. This position is based on the notion that liberal citizenship has been traditionally defined 'by and for white, able-bodied, Christian men' and thus that citizenship is a 'group differentiated notion' (Kymlicka, 1995: 124).

The work of both Young and Kymlicka represents an attempt to develop a theory of differentiated-group citizenship by building on the strengths of liberalism in order to identify and overcome the limits of liberal citizenship. There are, however, a number of weaknesses with the group-citizenship approach that undermine its theoretical coherence and potential to enhance citizenship (Faulks, 2000: 91–8). First, the approach replaces the essentialist individualism of liberal citizenship with an equally essentialist definition of the social group. The problem with this essentialism is the way in which it denies the internal differences within groups and the complexity of individual identity. Hence, a theory of citizenship based on group rights risks freezing social differences and creating a fragmented and highly static model of politics that is unlikely to overcome the oppression of minority groups. A further problem relates to the question of which groups are to be awarded special or differentiated status. The criteria cited are ultimately quite arbitrary and this has the potential to exacerbate the tensions between social groups. Furthermore, the argument that only members of a particular group can understand the oppression faced by that group undermines the prospects for deliberative democracy and the reconciliation of disputes between different groups (Miller, 1995: 446). There is also the danger that social groups can violate the individual freedom of their members or behave in illiberal or oppressive ways towards individuals on the basis of their group membership. The ultimate problem with differentiated citizenship is that it assumes that equality and difference are irreconcilable. This is a result of the way in which advocates of this position accept the abstract individualism of a liberal citizenship built on the defence of a market-dominated private sphere (Faulks, 2000: 99). The assertion of difference over equality denies the possibility of a project of citizenship premised on the pursuit of equality through the peaceful accommodation of difference. The philosophy of difference is ultimately a politics of defeat: a politics which is disillusioned with the possibilities and prospects for radical social change and which celebrates marginality, parochialism and oppression (Malik, 1996: 265). In contrast, the 'global turn' has demonstrated the possibility for marginalized groups to attain new forms of transnational citizenship based on universal human rights.

Global citizenships: towards a post-national citizenship?

The processes associated with globalization have blurred the material and psychological boundaries that defined citizenship in the modern era. The boundaries of fixed and stable political communities based on the nation state have become increasingly porous. The stable political communities of the modern era have been undermined by the development of ICT, the emergence of a global consumer culture and the increasing power of MNCs in the international economy. The increasing dominance of MNCs is not linked in a straightforward way with the marginalization of the nation state. The increasing power of MNCs is linked to the development of neo-liberal globalism which has privileged the interests of Western states over developing nations and intensified social and economic inequalities on a global scale. In this context, neo-liberal globalism can be seen as a particular state strategy that aims to secure and protect the interests of elites in Western liberal states (Faulks, 2000: 135). The processes associated with globalization heighten the existing contradictions between capitalism and citizenship in two main ways (Faulks, 2000: 136–9). First, neo-liberal globalism involves weak or minimal regulation of key actors such as MNCs, and in the competition for global trade nation states curtail democratic scrutiny over MNC activity and rein back social and civil rights such as welfare entitlement and trade union membership. Second, the dominance of the market over citizenship has important implications for both the generation of global risks and the ability of the nation state to guarantee citizenship rights in the face of global risks. In the face of risks generated by migration, infectious disease, international crime, nuclear power and environmental degradation, the Hobbesian logic of the state as a guarantor of security to its citizens is increasingly undermined. The 'global turn' in citizenship studies has focused on how neo-liberal restructuring and the crisis of the KWS have decomposed nationally determined forms of citizenship and resulted in increasingly de-territorialized claims for citizenship rights at both sub-national and transnational levels. The forms of citizenship associated with the KWS are undermined by three processes associated with globalization (Conway, 2004). First, intensifying transnational economic and cultural flows have expanded the reach of human rights norms and thereby eroded the administrative capacity and legitimacy of national political institutions. Second, in the context of the global institutionalization of the human rights discourse, individuals and groups are able to raise claims against states regardless of their citizenship status. Third, processes of immigration have created multiple allegiances amongst diasporic communities and instantiations of dual and multiple citizenships.

The past decades have seen a massive increase in various forms of spontaneous migration. The main trends have been a growth in the level of migration from Mexico and the Caribbean basin into the USA and migration of individuals from regions such as North Africa into Southern Europe. There has also been an increase in refugees and asylum-seekers who are currently estimated to number 23 million worldwide. These developments have produced something of a political and moral panic in Europe and North America and a concerted effort to police national borders more rigorously and increase the sanctions on people traffickers and employers who employ illegal and undocumented workers. These developments are often referred to as the development of 'Fortress Europe' or 'Fortress America'. However, these developments have occurred in the context of the ratification by national governments of a series of international conventions and protocols that seriously restrict the ability of nation states to discriminate against non-nationals, guest workers, illegal migrants and asylum-seekers. The *Universal Declaration of Human Rights*, for example, prevents nation states from distinguishing between persons on the grounds of nationality in respect of civil, social and political rights. The *Covenant on Economic, Social and Cultural Rights* imposes an obligation on nation states to provide a range of rights to such things as health, housing and welfare to all people within their territorial jurisdiction. The *International Covenant on Civil and Political Rights* imposes an obligation on nation states to protect the rights of minorities. This includes illegal migrants who have the right to appeal against deportation and to be treated humanely. These developments highlight how the processes and dynamics associated with globalization are resulting in the development of post-national citizenship rights.

Post-national citizenship: towards a system of universal human rights?

Yasemin Soysal has argued that international treaties and conventions are important examples of post-national citizenship rights that are increasingly based on notions of *universal personhood* rather than on membership of a particular nation state (Soysal, 1994). The language of human rights has become increasingly central to the governance of world affairs. Respect for the person has challenged the idea that the nation state has sovereign jurisdiction over its citizens and bolstered the notion that international or transnational bodies can legitimately interfere in this relationship when the human rights of individuals are threatened. Soysal has used the example of so-called 'guest workers' in Europe to develop the argument that the successful mobilization of these workers for social and civil rights has reduced the importance of citizenship to the point where the rights of 'non-citizens' do not differ significantly from those of citizens and thus that social membership is increasingly 'post-national' (Soysal, 1994: 119, 44). There has been an increasing disarticulation of nationality and rights, and national states are increasingly caught between competing claims for legitimacy. The legitimacy of the nation state with regard to its indigenous population requires it to regulate immigration in a way that preserves national sovereignty, while its legitimacy amongst the international community of nation states requires nation states to respect human rights conventions that grant rights to non-nationals. Hence, the inconsistency of nation states in the regulation of immigration and human rights and the resulting tensions produce an arena in which groups and individuals are able to compete for post-national citizenship rights. These struggles are not beyond nationalism as the globalization process also implies the disarticulation of nationhood and national identity. Hence, the struggle for post-national citizenship rights may involve intense ethnic struggles and assertive claims to national identity.

The extent to which human rights have the capacity to replace citizenship rights is questioned by critics of Soysal. Faulks (2000: 142–5) outlines three limitations to Soysal's thesis. First, while guest workers may possess social and civil rights they do not possess political rights, which are necessary to develop and sustain the participatory networks underpinning common institutions of governance. These networks are crucial with regard to the integration of immigrant groups into the dominant culture. Furthermore, in contrast to citizenship rights, human rights do not imply a reciprocal set of obligations and, for migrant groups, the receipt of rights without reciprocal obligations could be a recipe for social unrest and the hostility of indigenous populations. Second, Soysal tends to overstate the extent to which immigrants do indeed enjoy the same level of social and civil rights as 'native' populations. In Europe, racial harassment and violence continue to result in discriminatory behaviour in the fields of employment and public-service provision (Bhabha, 1998: 602–3). Beyond Europe, the notion of post-national citizenship is even more difficult to sustain. In the USA, the millions of illegal immigrants employed in low-wage sectors have limited access to welfare benefits following 1996 welfare legislation (Schuck, 1998). Third, the question of human rights cannot be separated from wider political questions relating to governance and the structures that sustain social, political and economic rights. Soysal has developed and defended a highly abstract model of citizenship rights in order to demonstrate the 'limits of citizenship'. According to Faulks (2000: 145–6), citizenship remains an important component of global governance for two main reasons. First, while globalization has altered the context in which states govern, the state is nevertheless *the* institution which can concentrate most effectively economic, military and communicative power. Transnational actors such as MNCs, the World Bank and the IMF are not rootless actors, but are ultimately dependent on frameworks of rules established and maintained by nation states. Hence, the pressure to enhance citizenship will continue to be located principally in the further democratization of nation states and the further embedding of the principles of citizenship at the national level. Second, citizenship expresses a relationship between rights, responsibilities and participation that is central to any system of governance. Human rights that are divorced from any notion of political community provide a flimsy basis for social and political order.

There is, therefore, no generally accepted notion that universal human rights are either possible or desirable. Advocates of the notion such as Soysol, or Turner who advocates human rights on the basis of the universal frailty of human existence in the face of global risks (Turner, 1993), are accused of advocating a highly abstract and passive model of social rights. Indeed, Huntington (1998) has argued that the pursuit of universal standards of justice in the form of human rights is counter-productive as the world is divided into distinct civilizations that are mutually suspicious of one another. Through the development and diffusion of ICT associated with globalization, the differences between these civilizations have been accentuated. The chief protectors of these civilizations are nation states and thus any attempt to undermine these alternative civilizations through universal standards of justice is likely to result in conflict and violence. Huntington has argued that global security requires the development of 'global multiculturality' rather than universal human rights. This is necessary to prevent the growth of aggressive forms of fundamentalism – particularly Islamic fundamentalism. The alternative, according to Huntington, is a rejection of multiculturalism by nation states at the domestic level and an assertion of national identity at the international level. However, as Faulks (2000: 147) has noted, Huntington overlooks the fact that the majority of conflicts since 1945 have been between states that share ostensibly the same culture and that conflict is built into the nation state system. The position of Huntington tends to suffer from cultural determinism and ignores the ways in which the interaction between states is responsible for conflict and the growth of both fundamentalism in the developing world and the growth of neo-liberal fundamentalism in Western societies. The West is responsible for the hypocritical advocacy of universal human rights, while at the same time championing the deregulation of the global economy in ways that have resulted in the undermining of basic citizenship rights. Furthermore, liberal states have hypocritically supported corrupt and authoritarian regimes in the developing world for geopolitical or economic reasons. During the 1980s, the West supported the regime of Saddam Hussein in Iraq during the time of the Iran–Iraq War and the USA supported the Afghan warlords in their struggle against the USSR. However, both the Iraqi regime and the Taliban in Afghanistan were subsequently redefined as part of an 'axis of evil' in the US-led war against global terror. This hypocrisy and the resulting inequalities and violence have obviously played a key role in the radicalization of alienated minorities in the developing world and the widespread rejection of Western 'liberal' values.

There have been attempts to rescue the concept of citizenship for the global age in ways that avoid both the neo-conservatism of Huntington and the recourse to abstract and universal human rights by theorists such as Soysal and Turner. This has involved the advocacy of a form of citizenship that not only remains rooted in a local context but which reaches outwards to encompass obligations to other communities and to establish rights across a range of contexts. Hence, Lister (1997) has argued for a form of citizenship that is both internationalist and multi-layered and which stretches from the local to the global. This formula suggests that the egalitarian potential of liberal forms of citizenship can only be achieved if citizenship is detached from limiting cultural identities such as nationality or ethnicity. The argument is for a complex and multi-textured citizenship based on multiple civic identities and multiple loyalties (Heater, 1990: 320). The development of citizenship beyond the nation state has also been a focus of advocates of 'cosmopolitan democracy'. Held (1995) has attempted to theorize a form of citizenship that has a global orientation, but which also advocates the establishment of participatory forms of governance beyond the nation state. The challenge for advocates of cosmopolitan democracy is to find ways of translating the rights, responsibilities and participation associated with national citizenship beyond the nation. In the liberal tradition, rights have often

been formulated in a highly abstract and disembodied way that failed
to recognize the gap between *de jure* and *de facto* rights and hence the
relational and reciprocal nature of social and political rights. However,
according to Faulks (2000: 150–2) the processes associated with globalization are changing our perception of the character of citizenship
rights. First, the risks and threats associated with nuclear warfare or
ecological destruction are making states more sensitive to the rights of
others. This is reflected in the increasingly proactive humanitarian role
of the UN, which increasingly involves intervention in the internal
affairs of individual nation states. In Europe, the Maastricht Treaty of
1992 formally established citizenship at the European level in order
to balance economic integration with the maintenance of social and
political rights within the EU. While there is undoubtedly an ongoing
'democratic deficit' in relation to the institutions of the EU, European
directives and legislation now supersede the law of member states and
have delivered material rights to European citizens across a range of
employment and social protection issues. Second, globalization has
resulted in a heightened awareness of the environmental threats to the
ecosystem and the frailty of humanity in the context of environmental
damage. In this context, it has become increasingly apparent that
rights are only sustainable when based on a sense of responsibility to
other communities and towards the natural environment. In the following sections the examples of environmental citizenship and European
citizenship are considered in more detail.

Environmental citizenship

Environmental problems do not respect the artificial boundaries of nation
states as is demonstrated by contemporary phenomena such as global
warming and climate change. The emergence of the Green or ecology
movement has, therefore, resulted in attempts to refine or reformulate
citizenship in ways that could contribute to sustainable development.
Traditional conceptions of citizenship are anthropocentric or human-
centred even when stretched to the global level in the form of 'human
rights' that compensate for human frailty (Turner, 1993: 178). As Beck
(1992) has argued, citizenship is not always protected by societal institutions as these institutions often reinforce the conditions of human
frailty. This has resulted in an increasing focus on the rights of inanimate
nature. An ecological dimension to citizenship involves extending the
'ethic of care' to the environment in order to facilitate the conservation
of natural resources and the conditions for sustainable development.
There are three main dimensions of ecological citizenship (Faulks, 2000:

152–3). First, the ecological citizen recognizes his or her organic process of birth and growth out of the earth as a living organism (van Steenbergen, 1994: 150). Second, a link is developed between intimate citizenship and global problems in ways that facilitate a shift from quantitative measures of success based on economic prosperity and welfare towards qualitative measures of success based on the food we eat, the air we breathe and the beauty of our natural surroundings (Steward, 1991). Hence, there is a recognition that economic wellbeing does not necessarily promote civility, social cohesion or even a sense of enlightened self-interest (Newby, 1996: 210). Third, ecological citizenship requires a rebalancing of 'conservation' and 'progress' and the expansion of citizenship rights to future generations, other species of animals and inanimate objects. Ecological citizenship is underpinned by eco-centric rather than anthropocentric values. Even if the doctrine of speciesism, which suggests that animals have equal moral worth and therefore equal rights with humans, is rejected, it involves a recognition that humans have responsibilities towards other species (Smith, 1998). The development of ecological citizenship highlights the ways in which citizenship is becoming uncoupled from the nation state and the ways in which the boundaries between the public and private domains are breaking down. The concerned ecological citizen has responsibilities in the formally private spheres of the family, consumption and the workplace: the responsibility to recycle bottles, cans and newspapers, to purchase commodities produced in sustainable and non-harmful ways, and to prevent and reduce wastage in the workplace. In a world in which nation states remain the dominant actors, states too have responsibilities in the global order, particularly in relation to the ways in which environmental degradation is linked to issues of structured debt and dependence between the developed and developing world.

As a form of 'global citizenship', environmental citizenship is more of a process than a set of institutionalized practices. It is based on challenging dominant cultures and identities in a form of politics that is pluralist, egalitarian and globally oriented. Hence, while national politics was *spatially bound*, post-national citizenship operates *temporally* in ways that open up the possibility of an alternative future based on ecological sustainability and fairness. The development of ecological citizenship involves an implosion of the 'social', 'political' and 'civil' rights outlined by Marshall (Urry, 2000: 170). While there may be a duty to protect the environment, there is no corresponding right to an adequate environment (Batty & Gray, 1996) and, as a consequence, global citizenship can only be developed on the basis of trust between diverse communities and the democratization of the bodies which govern world affairs. The development of global citizenship does not, however, imply the development of a world state. Multiple citizenships do not imply the end of independent and autonomous political communities, but a transformation in the nature of the relationship between these communities in the form of overlapping networks of power (Held, 1995: 267–86). There is, however, an inconsistency in Held's position. As Hoffmann (1998: 62) has argued, while Held's theory has an underlying post-statist logic, Held is ultimately unwilling to detach sovereignty from the state. The ambiguities that develop when the 'idea' of the modern state is applied at the transnational level can be exemplified with regard to the political dimension of European integration associated with the development of European citizenship (see Faulks, 2000: 150–60).

European citizenship

Since the 1980s, the principal objective of European integration has shifted from economic and political cooperation between sovereign nation states to the social and political integration of European nation states. The Maastricht Treaty of 1992 stated that 'every citizen holding the nationality of a member state shall be a citizen of the Union'. The act thus conferred a new level of citizenship to the people of Europe. The act conferred rights relating to the free movement of people, goods, services and capital and the right for EU citizens to vote and stand for election in local and European elections. Soysal (1994: 148) has argued that EU citizenship is post-national membership in its most elaborate legal form. The existence of a growing political space at the European level has become evident alongside an emergent European civil society. There has been a marked increase in the volume of European legislation resulting in rights associated with employment and social protection, including right to workplace consultation, and health and safety, and rights to holiday, sickness, maternity and paternity pay (Taylor, 2008). However, the forms and consequences of European citizenship are complex. The processes through which European citizenship have been created are essentially an elite project and are distinctly statist and exclusive in nature. While every citizen of an EU member state is a citizen of the EU, the determination and delivery of European citizenship remains at the national level owing to the principle of subsidiarity and, therefore, European citizenship does not really exist outside the traditional context of nation and state (O'Leary, 1998: 91). The main dynamic operating within the EU is *intergovernmental* rather than *federal*. The way in which the EU works is through the European Commission recommending EU 'directives' that have to be approved by the Council of Ministers before they can be transposed into nation state law. O'Leary (1998: 100) also highlights the ways in which European integration involves the construction of an exclusive and mystical European identity that sets legal and cultural limits to the expansion of European citizenship.

The institutional development of the project of European integration has resulted in the emergence of post-national citizenship in at least two important respects. First, the *European Convention on Human Rights* established by the Council of Europe has been incorporated into the legal systems of member states, and member states are bound by the decision of the European Court of Justice (ECJ). Second, the transposition of an EU directive into domestic law results in EU law overriding nation state law. In this context, many commentators have highlighted the emergence of a 'democratic deficit' in Europe. Democratically elected governments at the national level are increasingly constrained by the decisions of unelected officials at the European level. The powers of the European Parliament are limited with regard to holding the Commission and Council to account. Membership of the EU has, therefore, eroded many substantive citizenship rights at the national level and national forms of regulation have been replaced by 'soft' forms of 'framework' governance that lack democratic accountability. An example of this can be found in the way in which the so-called 'open method of coordination' has been used to coordinate the reform social policy in EU member states according to the neo-liberal logic of 'employability' (Taylor, 2006). Delanty (2000: 110–11) has argued that four main objections can be raised against the notion that the EU constitutes an important locus of post-national citizenship rights and obligations. The 'liberal critique' has developed the argument that the development of the EU involves a loss of political sovereignty and legitimation amongst European nation states. The 'civil society' critique is based on the civic republican position that the EU is devoid of a politics of participation owing to the non-existence of 'civil society' at the European level. The 'communitarian critique' is based on the argument that the European level is devoid of political identity and culture and that the development of a European political culture is impossible in the absence of a substantive political identity at the European level. The 'radical critique' is based on the argument that the EU is generating new forms of exclusion based on 'Fortress Europe' and a subsequent decline in social solidarity as the neo-liberal policies of the EU have eroded established forms of social welfare at the national level. However, Delanty (2000: 112) has argued that the problems highlighted by these critiques can be compensated for if European integration is conceptualized as a form of governance that can no longer be realized at the national level and thus the extent to which it can be seen as an important stepping stone towards the establishment of a system of global governance based on post-national or cosmopolitan citizenship. Hence, the loss of democratic legitimacy can be compensated for by the development of an institutionalized discourse on sustainability at the European level; the loss of active participation can be compensated for by the creation of a transnational civil society based on flows of communication and 'voice'; the loss of cultural identity can be compensated for by the creation of a legal identity based on a citizenship of residence; and the loss of social solidarity can be compensated for by a commitment to human rights. However, the lack of progress along these dimensions highlights the essentially normative nature of Delanty's position, which neatly sidesteps the contradictions underlying the already existing EU. Clearly, the 'cultural' and 'global' turns have highlighted the complexity of citizenship in an increasingly fragmented and mobile world. This theme has been developed further through the application of the 'complexity' turn to the study of citizenship.

Complex citizenships: towards a citizenship of 'flow'?

According to Urry (2000), the form of citizenship conceptualized by Marshall was a 'citizenship of stasis' and this can be contrasted with the 'citizenship of flow' concerned with mobilities across borders, of risks, travellers, consumer goods and services, cultures, migrants and visitors. Urry (2000: 167) has outlined six forms of the 'citizenship of flow'. First, there is *cultural citizenship* which involves the right of all social groups to full cultural participation in their society. Second, there is *minority citizenship* that involves the right to enter another society and remain there with appropriate rights and duties. Third, there is *ecological citizenship* concerned with the rights and duties of the citizen to the earth. Fourth, there is *cosmopolitan citizenship* concerned with how people develop an orientation to other citizens, societies and cultures. Fifth, there is *consumer citizenship* concerned with rights to goods and services provided by both the public and private sectors. Finally, there is *mobility citizenship* concerned with the rights and responsibility of visitors to other places and cultures. While this is not articulated explicitly as an example of complex citizenship, the approach assumes that citizenship is non-linear and emergent and divorced from spatial and temporal determinations and constraints. Urry (2000: 172–3) suggests that it is possible to outline seven types of global citizen (cf. Falk, 1994; van Steenbergen,

1994). First, there are *global capitalists* who attempt to unify the world on the basis of global corporate interests and who are implicated in the use of science and technology in ways that generate unpredictable hazards. Second, there are *global reformers* implicated in large international organizations who are concerned to regulate and moderate global capitalism through a discourse of both science and rights. Third, there are *global managers* who are involved in managerial, scientific and technical solutions to ameliorate hazards. Fourth, there are *global networkers* who establish and sustain work, professional and leisure networks across national boundaries through imagined or virtual travel. Fifth, there are earth *citizens* concerned to take responsibility for the global through an ethics of localized care. Sixth, there are *global cosmopolitans* who exhibit an ideology of openness towards other cultures and environments often through extensive travel. Seventh, there are organizations and individuals that constitute a *global green environmental backlash* which use environmentalists and 'political correctness' as the new global scapegoats and which mobilize through anti-environmentalist demonstrations and media events.

In this complex model of citizenship, the securing of rights by world populations depends upon the balance of forces between these global hybrids and the extent to which any is able to achieve global hegemony (Urry, 2000: 173). Each articulates a different notion of citizenship with a different configuration of hazards, rights and duties within a citizenship of flow defined by the movement of people and images in new cultural contexts through time and space (Stevenson, 1997: 51). Hazards include environmental bads, cultural homogenization, disease pandemics and the instability of the global economy. Rights include migration, cultural autonomy and participation, access to goods and services across the globe, the right to form social movements, the right to travel and migrate for leisure purposes and the right to inhabit environments that are relatively free of risks. Obligations include awareness of global hazards and the state of the globe, to display a cosmopolitan attitude towards other cultures, peoples and environments, to live in a social and environmentally sustainable way and to act in the global public interest. Globality thus involves the development of a new kind of 'performance citizenship' that is constructed from below and involves duties that are based on conscience rather than imposed by national statutory bodies (Albrow, 1996: 178).

Citizenship has always involved the communication and distribution of symbolic resources. The shift from the local and the national to the global requires the creation, circulation and consumption of cultural resources and a 'glacial' sense of time which resists instant-aneous time and seeks to slow time down to nature's speed in order to create an imagined community at the global level (Urry, 2000: 178). At the national level, citizenship requires the 'depiction' of the nation and institutions that speak for the nation. At the global level, the media play a central role in this process by transforming the plurality of the public sphere (Habermas, 1974, 1987) into a public stage and de-differentiating the previously separate spheres of the public and the pri-vate (Cohen & Arato, 1992). Media images appear visibly staged and entail performances in which almost anything can be brought to the public stage. Examples include the Live Aid concert, the Olympic Games or the death and funeral of Princess Diana. These globally circulated and con-sumed images are central to the iconography of global citizenship as they both depict and speak to the globe through a complex *deixis* or point of reference that speaks to multiple and particular audiences that go beyond national borders. The depiction of 'banal globalism' (Billig, 1995) high-lights the way in which contemporary citizenship is intertwined with rep-resentations of the globe that simultaneously speak for the globe and are constitutive of contemporary culture which is itself bound up with questions of citizenship. This involves the implosion of the boundaries between 'public citizenship' and 'private consumerism': advertising and branding being a central component of contemporary citizenship owing to the implosion of the boundaries between education and entertain-ment. Consumer objects can provide a sense of vicarious 'network mem-bership' or consumer citizenship. This highlights the changing nature of 'membership' in the context of global complexity. In the modern period, conferred rights and duties were secured through the membership of organizations with a clear and formal hierarchy – as is the case with polit-ical parties or trade unions. Contemporary organizations are more net-worked and mediated, as is the case of Greenpeace which, in speaking for the world, has developed an iconic brand identity.

Liminal citizenships

The development of the 'cultural', 'global' and 'complexity' turns has resulted in the modern concept of citizenship becoming relativized, de-territorialized and hybridized. The 'modern' paradigm of political socio-logy articulated the universalism of Enlightenment thought and the 'ideal' of citizenship as a universal category of membership within a political community mostly defined through the notion of 'nation-hood'. Critics of classical liberalism, such as T.H. Marshall, highlighted the ways in which the realization of this 'ideal' were undermined by ongoing class inequalities resulting from the operation of the capitalist economy and the ways in which this problem had been resolved by the development of the KWS. The universalism of liberal citizenship was challenged by both Marxism and feminism and the latter provided an important dynamic to the subsequent development of the 'cultural turn'. The 'cultural turn' involved a rejection of liberal citizenship on the basis that it failed to recognize difference, diversity and 'otherness' and therefore denied the full rights of citizenship to those individuals and groups that deviated from the 'normal', white, male, heterosexual citizen. This resulted in claims for 'group-differentiated rights' or 'multi-cultural citizenship' in order to ensure that the voices of oppressed minorities were heard in the process of political decision-making. The 'global turn' has highlighted the ways in which citizenship rights have become increasingly de-territorialized owing to intense patterns of migration, the development of universal human rights and the ways in which rights have been institutionalized within transnational state agencies such as the European Union. Recognition of the global reach of environmental risks and hazards has also resulted in a concern to develop forms of 'environmental citizenship' which have served to decouple further the relationship between citizenship and the territorially bounded nation state. The 'complexity turn' has focused on the emergence of a new citizenship of 'flow' within a complex global system of interacting hybrids. In this context, the rights of citizenship are no longer attached to individuals but to hybridized flows in complex configurations of hazards, rights and duties in time and space. These are important insights but fail to address adequately the ambiguous nature of contemporary citizenship.

The ambiguity of contemporary citizenship is a product of the ways in which cultural and transnational forms of citizenship have developed within modernity. This has resulted in the development of complex and liminal forms of citizenship that embody both modern and postmodern forms and which find expression at all levels of the multi-level systems of governance that dominate the global system. As I demonstrated in Chapter 6, the global justice movement through its manifestation at 'events' such as the World Social Forum represents an emergent 'alternative, post-bourgeois conception of the public sphere' (Fraser, 1997: 72): a space that is 'placed but transnational, localized but characterized by expanding globality' (Conway, 2004: 376). In this context, the demand for democracy, rights and participation is transformed from an institutional practice into a cultural practice. Citizenship is increasingly about 'being political' and is enacted through engagement in conflicts over power and the recognition of the agnostic nature of citizenship (Isin, 2002). However, citizenship remains a 'conflictual practice related to power' (Jelin, 2000: 53). The main objects of contention are the policies and practices of organizations such as MNCs, the WTO, IMF, G8 and EU which remain underpinned by the institutional power of capital and the state. The struggle for cultural citizenship rights beyond the nation state is thus another example of postmodern politics within modern society (Heller & Fehér, 1988). The success of the global justice movement in achieving post-national citizenship rights remains dependent on its ability to develop concrete strategies for political change and engagement with state actors and traditional forms of institutional politics (Patomäki & Teivainen, 2004: 151).

The development of European citizenship also highlights the liminal nature of contemporary citizenship. During the 1990s, a network of activists emerged in Europe in opposition to the neo-liberal policies being pursued by the European Union. The creation of a single market and the convergence process being pursued in preparation for the introduction of the euro were widely perceived as threatening nationally determined citizenship rights, particularly rights to welfare and social protection. The resulting protests included strikes, protests, transnational mobilizations such as demonstrations at EU summit meetings and a transnational network of activists that combined radical trade unionists alongside groups representing the unemployed, migrants without papers, gay and lesbian activists, the homeless, students, anti-fascist groups and environmental campaigns (Taylor & Mathers, 2002a, 2002b). There were examples of direct action such as the occupation of Milan railway station leading to free train travel to the Amsterdam counter-summit in 1997 and occupations of job centres and employment agencies. These actions displayed a new form of internationalism, with activists sharing knowledge and tactics, and this provided a further impetus to ongoing nationally based struggles. These networks mobilized around a political engagement with transnational institutions and the demand for concrete, substantive rights at the European level. The same network campaigned against the introduction of a European constitution of fundamental rights on the grounds that such a constitution would undermine established citizenship rights at the national level (Taylor & Mathers, 2004). While the mobilizations of the mid-1990s were successful in precipitating the inclusion of an Employment Chapter into the 1999 Treaty of Amsterdam, the subsequent development of a European employment policy was marked by 'soft' forms of coordination at the European level underpinned by the Realpolitik of intergovernmentalism and the dynamic of subsidiarity which have ensured that any expansion of European employment rights is subject to national-level veto (Taylor, 2006). The struggles against neo-liberalism in Europe highlighted the emergence of new transnational political spaces at the European level where political struggle was transnational in form but international and ultimately national in focus. This complex and emergent space is marked by liminality: located between the global and the local and delivering transnational policy solutions through intergovernmental institutional forms. European rights of citizenship cannot escape the complex ambiguities of this institutional framework and European citizenship is 'lived' as an ambiguous social form.

Summary and conclusion

In this chapter, I have outlined and explored the development of modern citizenship and the ways in which the discourse and practice of citizenship have been transformed by the 'cultural', 'global' and 'complexity' turns. I began with a discussion of the work of T.H. Marshall and the forms of 'universal' citizenship associated with the development of the KWS. I demonstrated how the 'universalism' associated with the KWS was increasingly questioned both by sociologists associated with the 'cultural' turn and by the practical struggles of liberation movements against the liberal democratic state and the institutions of social welfare. I highlighted how the 'cultural turn' involved a shift in focus away from universalistic notions of citizenship towards group-differentiated citizenship that recognized and gave voice to 'difference'. The chapter then moved on to consider the ways in which the 'global turn' impacted on the discourse and practice of citizenship with a particular focus on the ways in which the dynamic of globalization has resulted in the development of new forms of post-national citizenship based on notions of universal personhood. I then explored how the application of the 'complexity' turn to the analysis of citizenship has resulted in a focus on the rights and obligations associated with hybrid 'flows' and 'networks' in a context of global complexity. Throughout this chapter, I have highlighted the genuine insights and also the important limitations provided by the 'cultural', 'global' and 'complexity' turns to the changing nature of citizenship as a discourse and practice. In the final section of the chapter, I argued that these 'turns' fail to grasp how citizenship has become increasingly ambiguous in the context of a society in transition and provided a series of examples which highlight the 'liminal' forms of citizenship that are emerging between the modern and the postmodern and between the local, national and transnational.

9
Global Civil Society? The Prospects for Cosmocracy

In recent decades, the concept of civil society has emerged as a dominant political discourse and practice. The increasing popularity of civil society can be located in the decreasing popularity and the generalized public disaffection with models of social and political coordination based on state and market mechanisms. State-centred models of public administration started to decline in the 1970s, and during the 1980s market-based models emerged as dominant. During the 1990s, however, the growing disparities of wealth and power, both within the developed societies and between developed and developing societies, undermined the popularity and legitimacy of market mechanisms. In the context of enduring distrust and dissatisfaction with state-based solutions to social and economic problems, a series of alternative or 'third way' solutions have emerged that combined 'state' and 'market' in an active partnership with the 'civic'. The crisis of Soviet-style socialism and the fall of the Berlin Wall in 1989 gave further impetus to the discrediting of centralized state planning and administration, while the dissident politics within state socialist societies provided a model of civil society politics that has subsequently proved influential in the West. The associational potential of civil society has thus become a central leitmotiv in political discourse and practice during the early twenty-first century. The precise meaning of civil society is, however, ambiguous and contested: alternative models and paradigms have presented civil society as *part* of society; a *kind* of society based on positive norms and values; and as the *public sphere* (Edwards, 2004: 3–10). Civil society has been presented both as a specific product of the nation state and capitalism and as a universal expression of the collective life of individuals that has existed in different forms in specific historical contexts. In some versions, civil society is presented as one of three 'sectors' alongside the state and the market, while others highlight the connections between these sectors. There is no consensus with regard to the organizations and institutions that comprise civil society. While some versions limit membership on the basis of normative criteria to specific institutions such as those that are democratic, modern and 'civil', other versions include 'uncivil' institutions such as those based on religion and ethnicity. Civil society is presented in different versions as both a bulwark against state power and an indispensable part of democratic government. This analytical and conceptual confusion suggests that associational spaces within contemporary societies are likely to be complex and ambiguous. Furthermore, this complexity and ambiguity are likely to be intensified as associational spaces develop beyond the boundaries of nation state societies.

In this chapter, I explore the development of global civil society and assess the potential for a global public sphere or *cosmocracy* to implement a new world order based on global justice and economic and environmental sustainability. I begin by exploring the historical origins of the concept of civil society and highlight the ambiguous and contested usages of the concept within modern political sociology. In the section 'Civil society and the cultural turn' I highlight the ways in which the 'cultural turn' has questioned the universal character of civil society and the public sphere and the forms of inequality and non-recognition that have marked the operation of these associational spaces. In particular, the work of feminist writers has been instrumental in the deconstruction of these concepts and the development of alternative models of social and political life based on the existence of a diversity of subaltern 'counter-publics' in opposition to and resistance to dominant or hegemonic public realms. The section 'The globalization of civil society?' explores in detail the 'global turn' in the analysis of civil society. There is an exploration of the debate on the development and form of global civil society that highlights the ways in which the meaning and usage of the concept have remained ambiguous and contested through the 'global turn' and a consideration of the principal axes of association and division that mark global civil society. This is followed, in 'The global public sphere', by a consideration of the democratizing potential of the global polity or 'cosmocracy' in the context of the undeveloped and conflict-ridden nature of global civil society. The chapter concludes with an examination of the complexity of global civil society and a critical evaluation of the ability of complexity to adequately capture the sociological origins and consequences of this complexity.

The origins and form of modern civil society

The precise meaning of the term 'civil society' and the related concept of the 'public sphere' has changed over time and remains open to competing interpretations. In classical thought, 'civil society' and the state were indistinguishable, as demonstrated by Aristotle's *polis* which amounted to an association of associations that enabled citizens to share the virtuous tasks of ruling and being ruled. The notion of civil society as an arena or set of institutions separate from the state was related to the processes of social and structural differentiation associated with the development of modernity. The development of a sovereign and constitutional nation state involved the differentiation of 'political' and 'civil' society. While the former was differentiated into administrative, judicial and representative functions, the latter became differentiated from the political realm as a sphere of legal or contractual relations, civil freedom, plurality and civility. In the work of early political philosophers such as Thomas Hobbes and John Locke, civil society was essentially an aspect of government, but in the work of Scottish Enlightenment thinker Adam Ferguson, civil society emerged as an autonomous sphere that was separate from the state. Ferguson argued that the development of civil society reflected the shift from a clan-based society to a complex commercial society: civil society referred to the morally guided, rule-following relations on which anonymous social exchanges are premised and through which the conflicts endemic to commercial society are overcome (Ray, 2004: 221). Advocates of this version of civil society included James Madison and, above all, Alexis de Tocqueville, who argued that civil society provided self-regulating spheres of voluntary associations that needed protection from the state in order to protect individual freedoms and rights from despotism.

The conflict inherent to civil society was explicitly elaborated in the work of Hegel for whom civil society was a process to overcome the tension between egotistical self-interest and ethical life (*Sittlichkeit*). In complex societies, the private life of the family is transcended through association in civil society which has regulatory institutions underpinned by morality that serve egotistical ends. For Hegel, the tension underpinning civil society would be overcome by the development and consolidation of the constitutional-legal state (*Rechtsstaat*). The state would synthesize ethical life with the public domain of civil society while transcending them and thereby dissolve differences of class, rank and religion in universal law and formal rights (Ray, 2004:

222). In his critique of Hegel, Marx dismissed as illusory the proposition that the development of formal legal equality associated with the development of the modern state overcame the deep class-based inequalities located within civil society. Indeed, the formal equality of the 'public sphere' obscured the perpetuation and intensification of inequality within the 'private sphere' of civil society. The project of communism involved abolishing the boundaries between the political and civil realms in order to establish a classless association of workers.

The concept of civil society fell increasingly into disuse during the twentieth century and the term only re-entered academic and political discourse from the 1970s onwards as a result of two related developments. First, the crisis of 'orthodox Marxism' in Western Europe and the development of a 'Euro-Communist' discourse and practice built explicitly on the work of Antonio Gramsci. Gramsci (1971) presented civil society as a 'cultural' sphere between the state and the economy where working-class political parties could engage in 'counter-hegemonic' struggles in trade unions and other social and educational institutions alongside 'organic intellectuals'. This reinstated civil society as a socio-cultural institutional arena differentiated from both state and economy. Second, the development of anti-communist and dissident movements in Eastern Europe resurrected the concept of civil society as a social sphere that facilitated public discussion and voluntary association that was autonomous from both market and the state. This version of civil society was premised on the importance of creating an active public sphere that combined radical civic republicanism and Habermasian discourse ethics. The linkages between the 'civil' and the 'political' are, however, complex and contested and it is important to differentiate between existing civil societies and normative models of future developments. In this context, there is often presumed to be a distinction between Civil Society I and Civil Society II (Foley & Edwards, 1996).

Civil Society I derives its lineage from Ferguson, de Tocqueville and Durkheim and contemporary commentators such as Robert Putnam, Michael Walzer and William Glaston (Putnam, 2001; Galston, 2001; Walzer, 1989; and more generally Post & Rosenblum, 2002; Chambers and Kymlicka, 2002) and is premised on the notion that a democratic polity is ensured by the existence of a dense network of civil associations to generate 'social capital'. The existence of the network preserves and extends democracy and protects the autonomy of civil society from incursions by the state. This model of civil society is premised on the assumption that complex modern societies generate highly differentiated social structures that are overlapping and multi-layered. Civil

Society I is not so much a definable social space as a complex web of processes and connections underpinned by a network of institutional and moral linkages (Ray, 2004: 224). In the work of Habermas (1987), the 'social' is premised upon both 'system integration' through power and money and 'social integration' through normative communication in the 'lifeworld'. The potential for the expansion of public spheres is provided by the actions of social movements, which form on the contested boundaries between 'system' and 'lifeworld'. There is, however, a question as to whether the existence of a public sphere of active citizens is consistent with the observation by Habermas that the public sphere is increasingly eroded by the technicization and mediatization of social life and the extent to which this renders the vision of a reconstructed public sphere of active citizens utopian and nostalgic (Ray, 2004: 224; 1993: 51–3). There is also the potential for a strong and vibrant civil society to undermine multinational and secular states and thereby intensify ethnic and religious solidarities and increase the risk of political violence (Mennell, 1995; Foley & Edwards, 1996). However, it is equally conceivable to conceptualize ethnic and religious nationalism as a failure of Civil Society I based on the political and juridical disengagement of religious and ethnic groups (Misztal, 1996: 197). This highlights the ways in which a vibrant and healthy civil society is premised upon a shared ethical commitment to the procedures of democratic politics rather than a substantive agreement on matters of identity and opinion (Cohen & Arato, 1992: 421).

In contrast, Civil Society II is a normative construction comprising an alternative public sphere of autonomous social groups that are deemed necessary in order to limit the power of the state. This conception of the state emerged as part of the anti-Soviet dissident politics in the context of the disintegration of state socialism during the 1970s and 1980s (Vajda, 1988; Konrad, 1984; Fehér & Heller, 1986; Havel, 1988). In this conception, civil society and the public realm were often conflated through the ways in which the private sphere of autonomous social groups was posited as an alternative and authentic public sphere in contrast to the state. The dissident movements that formed in the state socialist societies of Central-Eastern Europe, such as Solidarity in Poland, were explicitly *anti-political*: forms of anti-politics that aimed to limit or bypass the state rather than seize the state as part of a project of revolutionary social change (Pelczynski, 1988). The *podmiotowosc* or self-government programme of Solidarity presented an alternative to both state socialism and capitalist liberal democracy and involved proposals for the construction of a democratized economy regulated through professional self-government in ways that negated the distinction between the 'public' and 'private' spheres (Glasman, 1994). In this context, therefore, civil society emerged as a social space that facilitated dialogue between autonomous voluntary groups that was neither coterminous with the market nor an extension of the state. This model of civil society developed in a specific historical context and, while commentators have explored its potential to revitalize civil society in the West, it is acknowledged that Civil Society II overemphasizes the institutional unity of civil society *vis-à-vis* the state and may undermine the potential of social and political pluralism (Cohen & Arato, 1992: 67). Indeed, in the context of post-communist restructuring, many commentators have highlighted the essentially mythical nature of Civil Society II as a non-coercive political order of non-hierarchical contract (Tamás, 1994) and the ways in which early popular enthusiasm for the concept was appropriated by intellectual elites who subsequently demobilized society and failed to develop civil initiatives and popular participation (Lomax, 1997). In this context, the revolutions of 1989 amounted to an attack on the public sphere by the private sphere underpinned by a discourse of 'rational utopia' communism. Both Civil Society I and Civil Society II share a conception of civil society and the public sphere as unitary and universal associational spaces. This has been challenged by commentators associated with the 'cultural turn' who have attempted to deconstruct these concepts in order to highlight the exclusionary character of civil society and the existence of a plurality of alternative and competing public spheres.

Civil society and the cultural turn: deconstructing the public sphere

The feminist critique of civil society and the public sphere is an important contribution to the 'cultural turn' in the analysis of civil society. There has been a concern to deconstruct the universalism of civil society in order to highlight the ways in which the gender-neutral vocabulary of civil society and the public sphere conceals the colonization of the public sphere by men and the feminization of the private sphere (Pateman, 1988; Okin, 1991). The historical roots of this settlement are seen as being located historically in the relationship between citizenship and the capacity to bear arms, which reinforced male dominance in the public sphere in the form of a civil contract between brothers, while reinforcing the position of women in the privatized realm of the family (Fraser, 1989a). The Habermasian distinction between the public and private realms treats the family as a black box in which patriarchal power remains invisible: the male 'citizen-speaker' role links the state to the family while the 'worker-breadwinner' role integrates the family with the economy and the state thereby confirming the dependent status of women in each (Ray, 2004: 226). This raises the question as to whether these criticisms invalidate the concepts of civil society and the public sphere or whether more inclusive, non-gendered institutional forms may be possible.

According to Fraser (1997), the model of the public sphere developed by Habermas provides an unrealized basis for overcoming many of the weaknesses in both Marxist and feminist conceptualizations of the public sphere and a way of reconceptualizing the relationship between civil society and the public sphere(s). The Marxist paradigm tended to conflate the public sphere and the state and, translated into socialist practice, this resulted in the development of authoritarian state forms that undermined the idea of socialist democracy. Feminism tended to present the public sphere as everything outside the realm of the family which conflated the distinctive spheres of state, economy and public discourse. Habermas (1989) overcame these problems on the basis of a model of the public sphere as an arena of debate and deliberation that was distinct from both the state and the economy. However, the model of the public sphere developed by Habermas was the highly specific 'bourgeois public sphere' that existed in order to allow private persons to discuss matters of public concern in an arena where status was 'bracketed' and power excluded. According to Habermas, this model of the public sphere had become increasingly unfeasible in the age of the welfare state. Non-bourgeois groups had gained access to the public sphere resulting in class polarization and the fragmentation of the public sphere. In this context, the critical function of 'publicity' or the critical scrutiny of the state had given way to mediated public relations and the manipulation of public opinion. Fraser (1997: 71) argues that Habermas never satisfactorily carried out the task of setting out the contours of a 'post-bourgeois' public sphere capable of salvaging the critical democratic functions of the 'bourgeois public sphere'. The reason for this can be found in the serious weaknesses and exclusions underpinning the model of the bourgeois public sphere developed by Habermas.

According to Fraser (1997: 72–7), a range of historical studies have served to highlight the ways in which Habermas idealized the 'bourgeois public sphere' and ignored a number of serious exclusions from the sphere. In a study of France, for example, Landes (1988) highlighted how the republican public sphere was underpinned by a range of masculine-gender constructions that served to marginalize or exclude women. In a study of England, France and Germany, Eley (1992) highlighted how 'civil society' emerged as a training ground and power base for a stratum of bourgeois men who came to see themselves as a 'universal class' and, on this basis, elaborated a distinctive culture of civil society and its associated public sphere. This constituted the public sphere on a distinctive set of class and gender norms, including new gender norms of female domesticity premised on the distinction between the 'public' and 'private' spheres. There have also been studies that have highlighted the importance of competing non-liberal public spheres in bourgeois society such as those provided by women-only voluntary associations (Ryan, 1990) or the 'black' church in the USA (Brooks-Higginbottom, 1993). Hence, the 'bourgeois public' was never *the* public, and counter-publics developed simultaneously with the 'bourgeois public'. The bourgeois struggle against traditional authority addressed simultaneously the problem of public containment, and the public sphere was always constituted by conflict rather than as an unrealized utopian ideal.

On the basis of the above historical research, Fraser (1997: 76–7) calls into question four of the central assumptions on which the model of the 'bourgeois public sphere' developed by Habermas is premised. First, she questions the assumption that it is possible for interlocutors in the public sphere to 'bracket' status differentials and deliberate 'as if' they were social equals and, therefore, the assumption that social equality is not necessarily a precondition for political democracy. The bracketing of social inequalities works to the advantage of advantaged groups as their culture is inscribed within the form and practices of the public sphere. Social and political justice requires the elimination of systematic social inequalities rather than participatory parity in the public sphere. Second, she questions the assumption that a proliferation of competing publics is an obstacle rather than an important step towards greater democracy. Fraser argues that in both stratified and egalitarian societies, competing publics ensure participatory parity in a more effective way than a single overarching public. In stratified societies, it is not possible to insulate discursive deliberation from the effects of social inequality and, consequently, marginal groups have found it advantageous to constitute subaltern counter-publics in order to facilitate the generation and circulation of counter-discourses. In an egalitarian society, the public sphere would be an important site of identity formation and, in this context, a single overarching public sphere would force a plurality of divergent 'voices' to be filtered through a single overarching deliberative framework. Third, she questions the assumption that deliberation in the public sphere should be restricted to deliberation about the 'common good' and that the appearance of private interests and issues is always undesirable. This assumption militates against the principal aim of deliberation, which is to enable participants in a deliberative process to clarify their interests, even when, or especially when, their interests conflict with the interests of others. Furthermore, the 'public' and the 'private' are not straightforward designations of distinct social spheres, but cultural classifications and rhetorical labels through which the powerful may attempt to exclude some issues and interests from public debate. Examples of this include the 'personalization' of economic issues through the prerogative of 'private property' and the familialization of gender relations in the private or domestic sphere. Fourth, she questions the assumption that a functioning public sphere requires a sharp separation between civil society and the state. This proposition is based on a particular version of civil society as a network of 'secondary' associations that are neither economic nor administrative and which serve as a counterweight to the power of the state. This liberal formulation encourages 'weak publics' that facilitate opinion formation but not decision-making. However, parliamentary democracy blurs the line between civil society and the state owing to the status of parliament as a public sphere *within* the state. The liberal model is unable to consider the relationship of accountability between such strong publics and the weaker and hybrid publics to which they are accountable. Consequently, a conception of the public sphere based on a sharp separation between the state and civil society is unable to imagine forms of self-management, inter-public coordination and political accountability that are essential to the workings of a well-functioning democratic and egalitarian state. A post-bourgeois conception of the public sphere thus requires a consideration of the relationship between 'strong', 'weak' and 'hybrid' publics in order to open up democratic possibilities beyond actually existing democracy. This project has become particularly essential owing to the ways in which the processes associated with globalization have tended to undermine nationally bounded civil societies and public spheres and raised important questions with regard to the possible democratization of the social, political and economic spaces that are opening up beyond the nation state. In the following section, I consider how these issues and problems have become a key concern of the 'global turn' in political sociology.

The globalization of civil society?

The 'global turn' in political sociology has focused on the extent to which the dynamic processes of globalization have reconstituted civil society at the global or transnational level and the extent to which this is connected to the development of a public sphere at the global or transnational level. The focus has thus been on exploring the development and democratic possibilities of the related concepts of 'global civil society' and 'cosmocracy'. The notion of global civil society (GCS) emerged as a neologism in the 1990s in response to a number of changes which seemed to be transforming the global political system. These included the implosion and collapse of the Soviet Bloc and the important role played by civil society ideas and movements in the crisis and collapse of state socialist societies; the growing interconnectedness of the world through the development and proliferation of ICT; the growth and spread of neo-liberal economics and the dynamic and disruptive effects of the resulting 'turbo-capitalism'; the growing perception of the threat to the world system posed by ecological and nuclear risks; and the dangers of collapsing empires and states to world peace. The translation of the concept to the transnational level has not, however, increased the definitional clarity or agreement surrounding the concept of civil society. There is no clear or uncontested meaning of GCS and it has been used in a number of conflicting and contradictory ways. According to Keane (2003: 3–4), it has been used as both an analytical or descriptive term in an attempt to uncover the emerging complexities of global socio-political realities and as a strategic or political calculation in the form of a campaigning criterion. It is, therefore, important to separate normative accounts of the civilizing potential of global civil society from more empirical analyses that focus on the balance of global forces and the extent to which the global 'public sphere' has indeed been civilized. The former tendency is associated with analyses based on the notion that civil society became radicalized following the global turn and the fall of the Berlin Wall. The substantive content of this model of global civil society is relatively unambiguous and uncontroversial comprising a 'new form of global politics' where 'the array of organizations and groups through which individuals have a voice at the global level ... parallels and supplements formal democracy at the national level' (Kaldor, 2003: 197). This is somewhat contradictory, however, as the non-governmental institutions that have a global presence in the promotion of civility contribute to an inherent pluralism that generates potential conflict (Keane, 2003: 8–14). The origins of the global turn are, moreover, unclear and contested. Kaldor highlights the collapse of the Soviet Bloc and the way in which global civil society was constructed 'from below' as networks of activists from 'East' and 'West' exploited the spaces opened up by ICT and internationalizing markets to construct new institutions beyond the nation state and forms of contestation beyond class politics. There is a normative element to this type of account which presents the emergence of global civil society as benign and irreversible. This is often combined with a tendency to play down the importance of the labour movement in the struggle for democracy, particularly in places such as Latin America, Korea and South Africa (Colás, 2005: 181). Hence, it is important to recognize the extent to which 'turbo-capitalism' acts as a disruptive force within global civil society through the way it creates and maintains socio-economic and political inequalities (Keane, 2003: 88). Global civil society is not, therefore, a unified 'third subject' but an exploitative and antagonistic domain. In this sphere, competing forces compete for power through transnational mobilization (Meiksins Wood, 2003: 11) and the nation state system is transformed into a 'pluriverse' of nation states authored by the world's most powerful – the USA (Meiksins Wood, 2003: 141).

The conflation of the empirical and normative meanings of GCS has resulted in confused and misleading claims with regard to the size and importance of this emerging configuration. This has been compounded by the fact that it is difficult to chart the size and scope of GCS with any degree of accuracy. The twentieth century is widely regarded as having produced a tectonic shift in the size and scale of global civil society owing to the proliferation of international non-governmental organizations (INGOs). There are currently estimated to be 50,000 INGOs and 5000 world congresses annually (Keane, 2003: 5). The data is, however, distorted by conceptual nationalism and it is difficult to chart the size and scope of global civil society with any accuracy. This is exacerbated by the epistemological difficulty that GCS, as a set of overlapping and interlocking institutions, is linked to territory but not restricted to territory. The constellation is dynamic and marked by 'non-integration and multiplicity without unity', while its actors treat it as perceived or reflexive (Beck, 2000: 10). Keane (2003: 8) provides the following ideal-typical definition of global civil society:

> A dynamic non-governmental system of interconnected socio-economic institutions that straddle the whole earth, and have complex effects that are felt in its four corners. Global civil society is neither a static object nor a *fait accompli*. It is an unfinished project that consists of sometimes thick, sometimes thinly stretched networks, pyramids and hub-and-spoke clusters of socio-economic institutions and actors who organize themselves across borders, with the deliberate aim of drawing the world together in new ways. These non-governmental institutions and actors tend to pluralize power and

to problematize violence; consequently, their peaceful or 'civil' effects are felt everywhere, here and there, far and wide, to and from local areas, through wider regions, to the planetary level itself.

In this ideal-typical formulation, GCS has the following five characteristics. First, GCS is comprised of *non-governmental* structures and activities. It is constituted as a vast interconnected and multi-layered non-governmental space made up of hundreds and thousands of self-directing ways of life. This space is neither an appendage nor a puppet of government structures nor is it a simple alter ego of the state, but comprises one particular set of non-state institutions based on particular norms and practices. Second, GCS is a *society* comprising a dynamic ensemble of interlinked social processes. It is constituted as a sprawling, non-governmental constellation of many institutionalized structures, associations and networks within which individuals and groups are interrelated and functionally interdependent. It thus forms a 'society of societies' and has a durability and a life of its own. While this constellation is complex, it is a society and not an organism or mechanism and, therefore, complexity theory is of limited value in uncovering the interactive dynamics of this configuration. Third, GCS is *civil* and is premised on the values and norms of respect for others, politeness and acceptance of strangers. In a world constituted by intermingling rather than 'pure' civilizations, GCS is constituted as a space inhabited by overlapping norms of non-violent politeness, mutual respect, compromise and power-sharing, but is surrounded by pockets of incivility in the form of organized crime, violence and terrorism. Fourth, GCS is *pluralistic* and has a strong potential for conflict. Within GCS, many ways of life coexist and borders may function like bridges where diverse identities interact. However, constant skirmishes may also occur both within GCS and between GCS and state institutions. Fifth, GCS is *global* and is politically framed and circumscribed by social relations which stretch across state boundaries and other governmental forms. GCS constitutes a special form of 'unbounded' society marked by constant feedback from its component parts and consequently is the first planetary order to understand itself as precarious. While GCS could be described as 'nested systems within nested systems' (Keane, 2003: 19), complexity theory is of limited value in describing an emerging system that is naturally embedded but socially produced. Moreover, GCS is not the binary opposite of 'national' civil society where the latter represents a sphere of self-regarding national interests while the former represents the transnational public interest (Keane, 2003: 23–7; Wapner, 2000). Rather, the local and the global constantly interact and co-define one another and are interrelated recursively through power-ridden processes of entangled pasts and presents.

The main catalysts underpinning the emergence and development of GCS have deep and complex historical roots. These can be found in the world-views of religious civilizations and the globalizing tendencies of Western modernity – particularly in the half-century before World War I. The 'century of violence' which followed was marked by global imperialism, rabid nationalism, global war and nuclear proliferation. Ironically, this provided an important catalyst to the development of GCS owing to the ways in which it broke down the Hobbesian axiom of protection and obedience between government and governed. This resulted in increasing levels of civilian mistrust in political authorities and the emergence of forms of civic activism which celebrate the power of autonomous moral choice and moral action over government institutions and action. In this context, organizations such as Amnesty International have demonstrated the civilizing effects of good laws, and by acting in ways that assume the existence of a global framework of laws such organizations have played a key role in the development of international human rights norms. The 'anti-globalization' movement, which grew out of the demonstrations against the WTO in Seattle in 1999, demonstrated the ways in which civic action can develop into social movement organizations with world-transforming potential. Keane (2003: 66–91) has argued that the other important energizer of GCS is market forces or 'turbo-capitalism'. The crisis and decomposition of the KWS has resulted in markets becoming 'disembedded' from social obligations and the regulatory controls of territorially based governments. In the context of the collapse of the Soviet Bloc and the industrialization of China and India, transnational corporations (TNCs) have almost unlimited 'grazing rights' within the global economy, which has become deeply integrated through the development of global commodity chains. In contrast to the Gramscian tradition, which differentiates between 'civil society' and the 'market' (for example, Rupert, 1995), therefore, Keane (2003: 76–88) has argued that for a number of reasons market forces have contributed to the development of GCS. First, markets draw on endogenous sources of sociability as the activities of business are embedded within civil society interactions and are lubricated by norms such as punctuality, trust, honesty, reliability and non-violence. Second, turbo-capitalist firms cultivate social meaning through advertising and the social practice of consumption which contributes to the development of shared symbols, ideas and values on a global scale. Third, the operations and reach of TNCs have contributed to the thickening of communications networks and this has facilitated the emergence of networks of NGOs and civil society activists. This is not to deny, however, the gross inequalities generated by turbo-capitalism and the ways in which this threatens to destroy the structures of civil society within which it is embedded. The investment decisions of TNCs contribute to intense levels of overwork and unemployment and generate extraordinary deprivation and staggering inequality on a global scale (Sen, 2000).

Global civil society is best understood as a distinctive space of transnational activism that has been fostered, however contradictorily, by the development of capitalist imperialism (Keane, 2003: 35) and which illuminates the enduring connections between capitalism, nationalism and imperialism. Keane (2003: 125) has highlighted the tension between universalism and pluralism in the cosmopolitan vision of global civil society and the implausibility of the argument that the world is in the grip of a 'teleology of normative progress'. The institutions of global governance lack both the resources and the legitimacy to enforce stability and cooperation: a situation that is compounded by the enduring dominance of the USA (Keane, 2003: 98). Indeed, in the context of 9/11 and the war in Iraq, we seemingly face a war without aims and end (Meiksins Wood, 2003: 149). The latter has taken the form of an Anglo-American alliance that has trampled on global civil society in order to exercise global supremacy. The experience of the UK/US invasion of Iraq, however, highlights the limits of 'Empire' (cf. Hardt & Negri, 2001) and the control of territory and people in the post-colonial period. Despite the contradictions of global civil society, therefore, it represents a new transnational space to resist and contest the neo-imperialism of Empire. However, the reverse is also worth pondering. There are increasingly critical voices that doubt the transformative power of a 'global civil society' owing to the fact that it lacks an institutional counterpart in the form of a global state. In its national form, civil society always relied on the legal and institutional framework guaranteed by the state (Etzioni, 2004; Olesen, 2005). Thus, the claim that GCS is both a product of globalization and a sphere that can civilize it is a disputed one and raises questions about its capabilities and limits. Lipschutz (1996) asserts that global civil society can form a decentralized, democratic form of global governance, while Kaldor (2000) argues that it is a sphere in which alternative models of globalization from below can be developed and mobilized. A more sceptical perspective is offered by Colás (1997), who argues that global civil society contains reactionary as well as progressive elements, and Scholte (2000), who argues that the NGOs that form its mainstay are not necessarily democratic organizations. The 'Charter of Principles' of the WSF, for example, excludes right-wing religious fundamentalists from participation (Patomäki & Teivainen, 2004: 149). In this sense, it is best to think of global civil society as a contested arena, the form of which is dependent on the changing coalitions and cleavages of its constituent organizations and movements. According to Kaldor (2000: 109–11), these cleavages and coalitions are forming between organizations and movements that emphasize parochialism and cosmopolitanism and between those with neo-liberal and redistributionist objectives. The 'old left' and the 'new right' are fragmenting into 'parochial' and 'cosmopolitan' elements and this is resulting in an increasingly complex pattern of political cleavages, coalitions and identities (see Table 1). The future shape of global civil society and the extent to which it is able to civilize globalization is likely to be dependent on the forms of coalitions that develop between the constituent elements of global civil society. These elements are outlined in the Table.

The dominant coalition is currently between MNCs and national representatives of the New Right. This coalition provides the principal dynamic for the atomizing politics of neo-liberal globalism. This coalition has undermined the redistributionist Old Left which has been either excluded from workplace, state-level and global-level corporatism or reincorporated based on a negative and defensive neo-liberal agenda with few redistributionist concessions. In this context, there is an emerging

Table 1   Global political cleavages

	Parochial	Cosmopolitan
Neo-liberal	New Right. Religious identities and traditional values. Opposition to globalization through various forms of nationalism and fundamentalism.	MNCs, international liberalism. Supported by corporate executives, centrist politicians and economic experts. Globalization is a positive development and benefits developing nations.
Redistributionist	Old Left. Belief in strong nation state, welfare and full employment. Support de-globalization.	Global civic networks, i.e. NGOs, Aid Agencies, etc. Aspire to a global civilizing process. Globalization is uneven in nature and skewed to interests of rich nations.

Source: Adapted from Kaldor (2000: 109)

coalition between the global civil networks and sections of the labour movement committed to developing 'social movement unionism' or 'community unionism'. This coalition has successfully mobilized against neo-liberal globalism and in the process constructed new political spaces and a nascent political subject at the global level. There is an undeveloped coalition between cosmopolitan neo-liberals and the global civic networks currently dominated by Third Way social democrats and their attempts to build new forms of social dialogue at the global, regional (particularly European) and local levels. The emerging cleavage between the parochial and the cosmopolitan is encouraging the growth of nationalism and fundamentalism. The political configuration of contemporary global politics is thus a product of this complex of competing forces in global civil society and the changing multi-level cleavages and coalitions between these interests. The future shape of GCS is also likely to be affected by government or state action within the multi-levelled and overlapping networks of global governance. The development of 'cosmocracy' and its likely impact on the new world (dis)order is explored in detail in the following section.

The global public sphere: towards cosmocracy?

The importance of neo-liberal capitalism and civil initiatives in producing the main contours of GCS should not be allowed to downplay the importance of government action and inaction in framing and enabling the actions and activities of NGOs and other GCS actors. While the status and actions of many NGOs are premised on formal agreements to which nation states are signatories, this does not necessarily imply that GCS is dependent on nation states or the nation state system. GCS has emerged and developed in the absence of a global state, world empire or comprehensive regulatory structure. This is, however, disputed by advocates of the 'realist' school of international relations for whom the world remains dominated by territorially defined nation states that engage in international cooperation and agreements in purely self-interested ways (Hobsbawm, 2001): in the absence of a global state there can be no global civil society (Brown, 2000). The 'global governance' school of international relations points to the emergence of a post-national order marked by 'governance without government' (Rosenau & Czempiel, 1992) which also problematizes the existence of either an emergent world polity or the existence of global civil society. This approach has highlighted the emergence of a multiplicity of governance systems designed to solve collective action problems. The result is not a global political system but a 'disaggregated networked minimalism' (Nye & Donahue, 2000: 14) constituted as non-hierarchical arrays of governmental units, private firms and NGOs focused on specific policy problems. These rather extreme positions underplay the ambiguous and essentially *liminal* nature of the international political (dis)order as an emerging world polity between the Westphalian model of sovereign states and a single unitary world government. Keane (2003: 97) has described this 'cosmocracy' as a *sui generis* form of government that defies all previous typologies of government: a world polity constituted by a complex mélange of legal, governmental, military and police networks arranged over worldwide distances. Keane (2003: 98) has provided the following definition of cosmocracy:

> A conglomeration of interlocking and overlapping sub-state, state and suprastate institutions and multi-dimensional processes that interact, and have political and social effects, on a global scale.

The political landscape of cosmocracy is divided into a 'core' where webs of interdependence are thickest and a series of uneven outer zones where interdependence diminishes as one moves out from the 'core'. The 'core' is made up of North America, the EU and South East Asia where political interdependence is greatest and which are most marked by monitoring, surveillance and coordination mechanisms. The EU provides an excellent illustration of this type of political integration. The 'core' is surrounded by an array of large, populous, quasi-imperial territorial states such as China, India and the Russian Federation which guard jealously their territorial independence, but which are nevertheless interlinked with the structures of cosmocracy in more or less conflictual ways. Beyond this zone is an agglomeration of interrelated and territorially bound units which include potentially powerful state actors such as Brazil and less powerful smaller states such as Nigeria, Thailand and the Philippines. Interdependence is thinnest and most frayed with respect to failing states such as Zimbabwe and states hostile to cosmocracy such as Burma and North Korea. Beyond, there is an outer zone taking the form of 'landscapes of war' and marked by areas such as Somalia, Southern Sudan and the Congo. This landscape is arranged across a number of levels stretching from micro-government, through meso-government to macro-government. The micro-governmental level is sub-territorial and is constituted by local and regional government institutions and agencies whose decision-making powers have effects elsewhere. The meso-governmental level includes territorially defined states and proto-regional institutions which are interlinked and have effects at a distance. These include institutions such as the EU, NAFTA, ASEAN and CARICOM. The macro-governmental level has a global reach owing to its autonomous institutional logic. The three levels are linked through security communities, mechanisms of global governance, 'spill-over effects', 'arbitrage pressures' and the interdependence and internationalization of states on the basis of issues such as militarization, environmental protection, economic policy, immigration and extradition.

Cosmocracy is an emergent and dynamic polity whose institutions have the power to shape and reshape the lives of people across the terrain of the global system. The configuration has no single organizing principle, but is rather a hybrid with 'recombinant' structures which are constituted by the hybridization of existing structures and decisions (Keane, 2003: 103). Cosmocracy is thus a 'polity on the move' operating according to a multi-level and non-hierarchical logic with power distributed and dispersed across interlocking micro, meso and macro levels. In this context, the territorial state does not melt away, but retains its sovereignty within a multi-level polity. An important dynamic in the determination of the new polity has been the trend towards multilateral legal networks in areas such as global commons (Oceans, Antarctica), crime and the environment. These networks have grown and developed in an *ad hoc* way and, therefore, legal norms and jurisdictional boundaries have been constantly defined and redefined resulting in a complex process of legalization within global civil society. This is not a zero-sum relationship in favour of the state system, however, as non-state actors such as the ECJ or WTO are able to influence the legal parameters of the cosmocracy. The movements and institutions within GCS are also able to augment their position *vis-á-vis* the cosmocracy owing to the preponderance of 'clumsy' decision-making procedures within the latter. In this context, NGOs have been able to highlight the arbitrary excesses of government power, dissolve into the state apparatus or emerge as deliberate creations of state governments, as is the case with GRINGOs or GONGOs such as the International Air Transport Association. Others such as Oxfam or Greenpeace occupy a space between independence and state reliance.

There are, however, instabilities within cosmocracy determined by political entropy, unaccountability problems and the existence of a dominant power in the form of the USA (Keane, 2003: 112–20). The confusion and ineffectiveness of political institutions within the emergent cosmocracy result in a state of entropy as manifested in the inertness and self-degradation that result from formlessness. The cosmocracy is undermined by an under-concentration of power and the resulting lack of steering mechanisms. The steering mechanisms which exist are often impotent owing to a lack of resources, jurisdictional disputes and a lack of reputation. This is often compounded by the bureaucratic sclerosis that results from demarcation disputes and the opacity of the tangled and rhizomatic structure of decision-making. An example of this is the self-paralysis underlying the decision-making processes of the UN. The cosmocracy is also destabilized by the lack of public accountability underpinning many of its political institutions, and the configuration has a greater affinity with authoritarian rather than democratic and accountable political procedures. The cosmocracy tends to be dominated by obscure and secretive 'cliques' and 'cabals': networks of professions operating on the basis of a technocratic mindset and unresponsive to outside perceptions and demands. The cosmocracy is also destabilized by the existence of a dominant power or 'destabilizing antibody' within its networks in the form of the USA. The USA is unusual in historical terms as it constitutes a dominant power with a revolutionary world outlook: liberal democracy and free market capitalism. The USA creates instability through the bullish behaviour of 'outflanking' and through direct intervention in global problems such as the recent 'war on terror'. The USA also constitutes the dominant engine and the deficit-of-last-resort for the system of global capitalism.

There is no consensus on the question of how the unaccountable institutions of cosmocracy can be subjected to public accountability. This reflects the disproportionate power and strength of neo-liberal forces in GCS that champion neo-liberal capitalism and the tendency of opponents of neo-liberalism to argue against the injustices of 'globalization' in terms of a need to strengthen the nation state. In academic circles, there has been an appeal to the neo-Kantian notion of 'cosmopolitan democracy' based on a model in which citizens are able to gain a voice both within their own state and in the sites of power between states (Archibugi & Held, 1995). In this model of democracy, individuals have voice, input and political representation in international affairs in parallel with and independently of their own government. Keane (2003: 123) has argued that this is premised on a rather vague and tautological definition of democracy and implies the ultimate goal of a peaceful coexistence between clearly demarcated 'national' and 'international' levels of politics in a way that ignores the complex and contradictory determination of cosmocracy. More recently, Held (2002a, 2002b) has reformulated the concept of cosmopolitan democracy in terms of the universalization of regulatory principles that claim to be universal or which could become universal through open-ended interaction, uncoerced argument or the force of better argument. However, as Keane (2003: 124–5) has noted, the substance of these ethical principles is premised on the equal moral value of all individuals, reciprocal recognition and the notion that the claims of individuals should be impartially considered. This highlights the conceptual imperialism underpinning the notion of cosmopolitan democracy, which is ultimately analogous to Western liberal humanism and antithetical to many value systems in the developing societies of Asia. In the complex worlds of GCS and the emerging cosmocracy, the concept of democracy has become highly ambiguous and subject to contestation and reformulation in the liminal spaces that have emerged between the local and the global. I have already noted a series of limitations with regard to the application of complexity theory to the analysis of global civil society and will now explore in more detail the limitations of the 'complexity turn' to grasp adequately the sociological complexity of global civil society and the global public sphere.

The complexity of global civil society

The analysis of civil society on the basis of the theories and concepts associated with complexity and chaos theory is quite undeveloped and consists mainly of attempts to impute examples of complexity thinking from the work of authors and commentators which is most accurately associated with the 'cultural' and 'global' turns. The work of Castells on the 'networked society' has provided a particular source of inspiration for complexity theorists (Capra, 2003: 191–8; Urry, 2003: 10). In the work of Castells (1997), civil society assumes the form of a network or a network of networks that spreads across time and space and links people and things in ways that overcome the limits of space. According to Urry (2003: 10), the work of Castells is useful to the complexity approach owing to the ways in which it stresses the unfinished and ongoing nature of the globalization process and thus the importance of contingency, openness and unpredictability in the development of global systems and networks. This is a result of the way in which networks of power generate networks of resistance which, Urry suggests, can be understood in terms of a 'power-resistance attractor' and the ways in which networks are self-organizing and often short-term and non-hierarchical in nature. Hence, 'virtual communities' are replacing the formal institutions of civil society as the latter shrinks and is disarticulated as a result of the lack of continuity between the logic of power-making in global networks and the logic of association and representation in specific societies and cultures (Castells, 1997: 11). In contrast, virtual communities are formed through identifications constructed in the non-geographical spaces of activist discourse, cultural products and media images (Rose, 1996: 333). The 'new' civil society is thus an attempt to reshape globalization through the articulation of 'resistance identities' based on the social/political relationship between actors in two types of networks: local grassroots organizations (living human networks) and global communications technologies (electronic networks) (Capra, 2003: 192). The complexity turn thus attempts to highlight the hybrid nature of global civil society.

There has also been a focus on the extent to which global civil society is determined by a complex process of global emergence constituted by multiple iterations of the 'global' in the everyday life of social actors. In order to substantiate this position, Urry (2003: 98) imputes an underlying association between complexity theory and a study of global 'performivity' that draws on the work of the feminist theorist Judith Butler. In this study, Franklin *et al.* (2000) highlight the ways in which the transnational communities that emerge around the issues of science, the media and environmentalism emerge on the basis of a reflexive concern with the putative universalism of the global. This constituency has a tendency to be more female than male owing to the tendency for women to be more committed to issues of environmentalism, conservation and universal human rights. Thus the 'global' is constituted through its 'naming' and 'performance' in millions of iterations and is, therefore, 'auto-enabled' or 'auto-produced'. The global constitutes its own domain through material-semiotic practices (Franklin *et al.*, 2000: 5) and is 'performed, imagined and practised' across multiple domains, scales and levels. According to Urry (2003: 98), the performivity of the global highlights the self-organizing nature of global culture and the open nature of global systems and hence the relevance of complexity theory to the analysis of global civil society and global culture. The 'global' is a product of 'autopoesis'. It is determined by multiple iterations and is vulnerable to the disruptive effects of information flows and the constant threat of catastrophe and chaos.

The networks and systems that constitute global civil society and its emergent public sphere are clearly complex, but does the somewhat forced application of the theoretical constructs of complexity and chaos theory really add anything to our sociological understanding of this complexity? As I mentioned earlier, global civil society is a society and not an organism or a machine. GCS has developed on the basis of social interaction and the political opportunity structures and networks of obligation that increasingly stretch across multiple levels and scales. While GCS can be conceptualized in terms of 'nested systems within nested systems', these systems constitute an emergent system that is naturally embedded but socially produced. The complexity of GCS is a result of the complex interplay between the local and the global whereby the global and the local constantly interact and co-define one another and are interrelated recursively through power-ridden processes of entangled pasts and presents (Keane, 2003: 24). This is manifested in reciprocal relations of superiority and subordination on a planetary scale and a proliferation of integrative and oppositional networks that are increasingly manifest in postmodern forms of identity politics. In essence, GCS is an ambiguous or liminal space between the local and the global and this ambiguity or liminality is compounded by the preponderance of postmodern political identities and practices within the decomposing shell of the international nation state system. The global justice movement is often used to support complexity arguments. However, while the GJM may be constituted as a 'network of networks' and while these networks may behave 'as if' they were 'global fluids', ultimately these networks are not global fluids but flows of social actors and flows of information and communication between social actors. It is not the iteration of a global discourse in multiple localities that determines the globality of the world system but the ways in which global issues and problems are experienced and lived in multiple and diverse localities and the ways in which these lived experiences are projected back onto the transnational or global plane. Complexity theory may have a convenient and handy stock of metaphors for describing the contemporary world, but this is no replacement for rigorous social scientific analysis to explore and uncover emerging patterns of social interaction and social inequality in a complex global society.

Summary and conclusion

In this chapter, I have explored the development and globalization of civil society and the public sphere. The chapter began with an exploration of the ways in which civil society was conceptualized by modern political sociology. It was noted that the definition and scope of civil society have always been unclear and contested. This highlighted the extent to which civil society has always been much more than an object of academic enquiry and has formed an object of political struggle and contestation throughout the modern era. An important distinction was made between analytical and normative models of civil society which provide divergent models of the relationship between the 'civic' and the 'political' and the extent to which the boundaries of civil society and the state overlap and hence the nature and extent of the 'public sphere' in modern society. The 'cultural turn' in political sociology was then explored in order to demonstrate how, *inter alia*, feminist theorists have deconstructed the universalism of modern civil society in order to demonstrate the powerful exclusionary discourses and practices underpinning this form of social and political association. In the work of Nancy Fraser, there is a powerful critique of the model of the public sphere developed by Habermas and an alternative conceptualization based on the existence of a plurality of competing 'subaltern counter-publics' in opposition to dominant or hegemonic public spheres. The chapter then turned to an exploration of how the 'global turn' has impacted on the analysis of civil society and the public sphere and there was an extended exploration of the development and form of global civil society and the democratic potential of the emerging global polity or 'cosmocracy'. The distinction between analytical and normative models of civil society was again stressed, this time with regard to developments at the global level, and the inability of the latter model to capture the tensions and conflicts underpinning global civil society was highlighted. This was followed by a discussion of the main cleavages and divisions that mark global civil society along the axes of parochial–cosmopolitan and neo-liberal and redistributionist. The potential of cosmocracy to deliver cosmopolitan democracy was then evaluated and it was argued that this potential was seriously undermined by instabilities generated within the global public sphere by political entropy, unaccountability problems and the existence of a dominant power in the form of the USA. This was followed by a discussion of the complex nature of global civil society and the inability of complexity and chaos theory to grasp this complexity in an adequate way. It was argued that while complexity theory is able to provide a range of interesting and useful metaphors to describe global civil society, it is unable to analyse the complex networks of social interaction and patterns of social inequality that mark global civil society. The chapter concluded with the argument that global civil society and the global public sphere are ambiguous or liminal forms of association that can be adequately understood through an understanding of the ways in which transnational forms of association are lived and experienced by social actors.

10
Conclusion: Towards an 'Existential Turn' in Political Sociology

In this book, I have highlighted the ways in which complex, non-linear change has generated ambiguous and liminal social and political change between the modern and the postmodern and between the local and the global. As Best and Kellner (1997: 32–3) have argued, living in the borderland between the modern and the postmodern generates tensions, insecurity, confusion and panic alongside excitement and exhilaration as the vista of an open but troubling future opens up on the uneven horizon of social change. If we add to this the tensions, insecurity, confusion and panic that is generated by living between 'nation state' and 'global' society we can see just how complex and confusing the contemporary world is today. The complexity that defines the contemporary world is real and has been produced by several decades of intense social and political change that have decomposed and dissolved many of the defining features of social and political modernity. However, herein lies the problem of how we are to analyse and understand the complexity generated by these intense processes of social and political change. As I have demonstrated throughout this book, it is by no means clear that modern institutions and processes have totally decomposed and dissolved and been replaced by a global society based on postmodern institutions and processes. A defining feature of modernity was always its revolutionary dynamism and its ability to constantly destroy and renew its own social foundations through violent and often catastrophic processes of creative destruction and destructive creation (Berman, 1983). In the *Communist Manifesto*, Marx and Engels described this famously in terms of how, with the development of capitalism, 'all fixed fast-frozen relations are swept away, all new-formed ones become antiquated before they ossify ... all that is solid melts into air' (Marx and Engels, 1969: 475–6). When we gaze across the complexity of the contemporary social world what we see, therefore, is not simply the decomposition of modernity but the simultaneous recomposition of modernity on a more intensive and extensive scale. What we have witnessed is the decomposition of a particular form of modernity at a particular stage of modern development that was marked by the development and consolidation of the nation state. What we refer to as 'postmodern' are the recomposed forms in which the discontents generated by modernity are now increasingly manifest. These postmodern forms operate both within and beyond modernity and are responsible for the ambiguous and liminal forms that dominate the contemporary world. For example, as I demonstrated in Chapter 6, the global justice movement is a networked social form that constitutes a postmodern form of struggle within a globalized hypermodernity. This has a transformative effect and serves to push modernity beyond its own institutional and structural limits. This is an important example of how intense processes of social and political change push modernity beyond its own institutional coordinates towards a new social order that remains undefined and open to a myriad of possible futures.

The stage of modern development that has decomposed in recent decades is the phase of development which witnessed the development and consolidation of the science of modern society *qua* sociology. The crisis and decomposition of nationally defined modernity has also, therefore, had the effect of undermining and rendering problematic the theories and concepts of 'nation state' sociology. In the preceding chapters, I have explored how the theories and concepts associated with the sub-discipline of modern political sociology have been challenged and reformulated as a result of the 'cultural', 'global' and 'complexity' turns. I have constantly stressed both the analytical promise of these paradigms in illustrating key trajectories of social and political change, but I have also stressed the analytical limitations of these approaches. The 'cultural turn' has usefully deconstructed the universalism of modern institutions and demonstrated how the decomposition of the nation state has rendered social and political identities increasingly fluid and fragmented. The 'global turn' has usefully demonstrated how social and political power has become unbounded and escaped the territoriality of the nation state and the ways in which this has generated new 'global' forms of culture and identity. The 'complexity turn' has usefully demonstrated how the complex interplay between the global and the local has generated new complex forms of non-linear causality and new forms of asymmetric relationality. The limits and weaknesses of these approaches derive from the ways in which each of these turns represents a loss of faith in the core intellectual project of modern sociology: namely, to investigate and uncover the *social* relationships and *social* forms that constitute the *social* order. In the context of a loss of faith in modern sociology, each of these turns has appropriated tools and concepts from other disciplines: the 'cultural turn' from cultural and literary studies; the 'global turn' from geography; and the 'complexity turn' from physics and mathematics. The main problem with these developments is that the social world is not simply constituted by text, spatial units and inanimate objects, but continues to be constituted by conscious and reflexive human beings. The best that the more extreme manifestations of the 'cultural', 'global' and 'complexity' turns can offer is a series of interesting and illuminating metaphors to illustrate more fundamental processes of social, political and economic restructuring. The anti-humanism at the heart of these 'turns' limits severely their contribution to an understanding of what is truly *social* about complex and emergent forms of social power, social identities and social movements.

Throughout this book I have argued for the intellectual and analytical promise of an 'existential turn' in the analysis of global complexity and as a contribution to a reformulated political sociology for a complex age. I am, of course, aware that in many ways this is a rather speculative, undeveloped and unsubstantiated theoretical and conceptual position from which to argue. The dominance of the 'cultural', 'global' and 'complexity' turns has made phenomenological approaches to social and political life increasingly marginal and unpopular. As I have demonstrated throughout this book, however, these approaches have failed to capture adequately the *social* forms of interaction and association that underpin changing and increasingly complex forms of governance, identity, social movement organization, political violence, citizenship and civil society. I began my analysis with the insight from Simmel (1896: 169) regarding the extent to which relations of superiority and inferiority are manifested in every human association and constitute one of the forms in which 'society' comes into being. The task of sociology was, and I would argue remains, to interpret historical examples in order to demonstrate the material or formal conditions underpinning this form of society and to discover the material and formal consequences associated with the resulting social relations. This remains the largely unfulfilled promise of political sociology in the complex, globalized contemporary world. A research agenda for a renewed and revitalized political sociology needs to focus on the ways in which people 'feel', 'experience' and 'live' the complex contradictions of the social and political world. What do people do when they feel power escaping the territorial confines of the nation state? How does it make them feel? How does this translate into how people define themselves and their relationship with others? How does this impact on the ways in which people experience forms of political association and membership? This is a manifesto for a human-centred political sociology rather than a political sociology focused on discourse, space and systems. In problematizing the 'cultural', 'global' and 'complexity' turns in political sociology, I present this book as a contribution to an 'existential turn' that will hopefully refocus the sub-discipline on the phenomenology of social and political interaction and inequality.

Glossary

Citizenship   A status and identity defined by membership of a political community. While modern citizenship was defined in terms of a relationship or contract between the individual and the nation state, postmodern citizenship has tended to focus on group rights for marginalized minorities, and the dynamics associated with globalization have resulted in conceptions of post-national citizenship.

Civil society   The precise definition is contentious, but civil society can be defined as an arena of uncoerced collective association that is distinct from state, market and family, though in practice the boundaries are complex and negotiated.

Complexity theory   An approach overarching the natural, physical and social sciences focused on how the components of complex systems interact and the relationships between complex systems and their environment.

Cosmocracy   A conglomeration of interlocking and overlapping sub-state, state and suprastate institutions and multidimensional processes that interact, and have political and social effects, on a global scale.

Cosmopolitan democracy   A political project that aims to build a new world order based on the rule of law and democracy.

Global civil society   A dynamic non-governmental system of interconnected socio-economic institutions that straddle the whole earth, and have complex effects that are felt in its four corners. These non-governmental institutions and actors tend to pluralize power and to problematize violence and therefore have peaceful or 'civil' effects.

Globalism   A contestable political discourse that promotes a transnational worldview, a philosophy of governance and a particular set of institutional structures. In recent decades a neo-liberal version of globalism has been dominant or hegemonic.

Globality   An amalgam of forces, many of which are technological and irreversible, that are breaking down barriers of time, space and nation and fashioning the planet into a coherent global community.

Globalization   A range of processes through which sovereign nation states are criss-crossed and undermined by a range of transnational actors and networks with variable power capacities, ideological orientations and social and political identities.

Glocalization   A process that highlights the complex and often contradictory relationship between *globalization* and localization.

Governance   A decentred form of public administration that is process-oriented and collaborative and which involves networks of social actors from public, private and 'third' sectors.

Identity   Cultural-political identity relates to the linkages between the 'self' and a wider 'community of fate'. This relationship can be defined by the related concepts of 'being', 'belonging' and 'becoming'.

Ideology   A coherent set of ideas through which individuals come to terms with the world and develop the means to change it. There are four related aspects to ideology: ideas are part of a wider system of beliefs; systems of belief have internal consistency; ideologies contain views about the nature of humanity; and ideologies are related to a particular situation or a projected set of arrangements in the future.

Liminality   The threshold between existential planes marked by indeterminacy, openness and ambiguity. A period of transition or inbetweenness.

Nation state   A compulsory political association that claims a monopoly of the legitimate use of force in a given territory. The nation state is associated with the powerful ideology of nationalism and forms of identity associated with the national political community or nationhood.

Neo-liberalism   An ideology that emerged in the late twentieth century that attempts to revive and redefine the classical liberalism of the eighteenth and nineteenth centuries. It is linked to the revival of neoclassical economics and has a principal concern with the defence and development of private enterprise, free markets and free trade.

Power   The ability of individuals or groups to exercise their will or create intended consequences. In its specific sociological usage, there is also a concern with potential power and the unintended consequences of power. Power can be exercised in a variety of ways, including violence, force, knowledge, wealth, charisma and authority, and for both individual and collective ends.

Public sphere   A discursive arena where individuals meet in order to discuss matters of common interest and formulate conceptions of the 'common good'. The 'public sphere' mediates between the 'private sphere' of *civil society* and the public authority of the state.

Social movements   Groups or networks of social actors that can be either formally or informally organized which focus on specific political or social issues in order to achieve, resist or reverse social and political change.

Terrorism   The premeditated use of violence to achieve political ends. It tends to be a pejorative term and is used by both democracies and autocracies to delegitimize political enemies.

Bibliography

Abbinnett, R. (2000) 'Science, technology and modernity: Beck and Derrida on the politics of risk' *Cultural Values* vol. 4, no. 1, pp. 101–26.

Abrams, P. (1988) 'Notes on the difficulty of studying the state' *Journal of Historical Sociology* vol. 1, no. 1, pp. 58–89.

Aingers, K., Chesters, G., Credland, T., Jordan, J., Stern, A. & Whitney, J. (2003) *We are Everywhere: The Irresistible Rise of Global Anticapitalism* London: Verso.

Albrow, M. (1996) *The Global Age: State and Society beyond Modernity* Cambridge: Polity.

Alexander, J.C. (1991) 'Bringing democracy back in: Universalistic solidarity and the civil sphere' in C.C. Lemert (ed.) *Intellectuals and Politics: Social Theory in a Changing World* Newbury Park CA: Sage.

—— (2006) *The Civil Sphere* Oxford University Press.

Allen, J. (2000) 'Power: Its institutional guises' in G. Hughes and R. Fergusson (eds) *Ordering Lives: Family, Work and Welfare* London: Routledge.

Almond, G.A. & Verba, S. (1963) *The Civic Culture: Political Attitudes and Democracy in Five Nations* Princeton University Press.

Alter, P. (1994) *Nationalism* Second Edition London: Edward Arnold.

Althusser, L. (1971) *Lenin and Philosophy and Other Essays* London: New Left Books.

Anderson, B. (1991) *Imagined Communities: Reflections on the Origin and Spread of Nationalism* London: Verso.

Appadurai, A. (1990) 'Disjuncture and difference in the global cultural economy' in M. Featherstone (ed.) *Global Culture: Nationalism, Globalization and Modernity* London: Sage.

—— (1996) *Modernity at Large: Cultural Dimensions of Globalization* Minneapolis: University of Minnesota Press.

—— (1998a) 'Full attachment' *Public Culture* vol. 10, no. 2, pp. 443–9.

—— (1998b) 'Dead certainty: Ethnic violence in the era of globalization' *Public Culture* vol. 10, no. 2, pp. 225–47.

—— (2006) *Fear of Small Numbers: Essays on the Geography of Anger* Durham NC: Duke University Press.

Archibugi, D. & Held, D. (1995) *Cosmopolitan Democracy: An Agenda for a New World Order* Cambridge: Polity.

Arendt, H. (1958) *The Human Condition* University of Chicago Press.

—— (1970) *On Violence* London: Allen Lane.

—— (1973) *The Origins of Totalitarianism* San Diego: Harcourt Brace.

Aron, R. (1950) 'Social structure and the ruling class: Part 1' *British Journal of Sociology* vol. 1, no. 1, pp. 1–16.

Arquilla, J. & Ronfeldt, D. (2001) 'The advent of netwars (revisited)' in J. Arquilla & D. Ronfeldt (eds) *Networks and Netwars* Santa Monica CA: Rand.

Axford, B. (2000) 'Globalization' in G. Browning, A. Halcli & F. Webster (eds) *Understanding Contemporary Society: Theories of the Present* London: Sage.

Bachrach, P. & Baratz, M.S. (1963) 'Decisions and nondecisions' *American Political Science Review* vol. 57, no. 3, pp. 632–42.

—— (1970) *Power and Poverty: Theory and Practice* Oxford University Press.

Bagguley, P. (1995) 'Protest, poverty and power: A case study of the anti-poll tax movement' *Sociological Review* vol. 43, no. 4, pp. 693–719.

Baglioni, G. (1987) 'Constants and variants in political exchange' *Labour* no. 1, pp. 57–94.

Baker, P. (1993) 'Chaos, order and sociological theory' *Sociological Enquiry* vol. 63, no. 2, pp. 123–49.

Bakvis, H. (1997) 'Advising the executive: Think tanks, consultants, political staff and kitchen cabinets' in P. Weller, H. Bakvis & R.A.W. Rhodes (eds) *The Hollow Crown: Couterveiling Trends in Core Executives* London: Macmillan.

Barber, B. (1996) *Jihad Versus McWorld: Terrorism's Challenge to Democracy* New York: Ballantine.

Barrett, M. (1986) *Women's Oppression Today: Problems in Marxist Feminist Analysis* London: Verso.

Baruah, S. (1986) 'Immigration, ethnic conflict and political turmoil, Assam 1979–1985' *Asian Survey* vol. 26, no. 11, pp. 1184–1206.

Batty, H. & Gray, T. (1996) 'Environmental rights and national sovereignty' in S. Caney, D. George & P. Jones (eds) *National Rights, International Obligations* Boulder CO: Westview Press.

Baudrillard, J. (1983a) *In the Shadow of Silent Majorities* New York: Semiotext(e).

—— (1983b) *Simulations* New York: Semiotext(e).

—— (1994a) *Simulcra and Simulation*

—— (1994b) *The Transparency of Evil: Essays on Extreme Phenomena* London: Verso.

—— (1995) *The Gulf War did not Take Place* Bloomington: Indiana University Press.

—— (2001) 'L'Esprit du terrorisme' *Le Monde* 3 November: 11.

Bauman, Z. (1989) *Modernity and the Holocaust* Cambridge: Polity.

—— (1991) *Modernity and Ambivalence* Cambridge: Polity.

—— (1992) *Imitations of Postmodernity* London: Routledge.

—— (1996) 'From pilgrim to tourist – or a short history of identity' in S. Hall & P. Du Gay (eds) *Questions of Cultural Identity* London: Sage.

—— (1997) *Postmodernity and its Discontents* Cambridge: Polity.

—— (1998) *Work, Consumption and the New Poor* Cambridge: Polity.

—— (2000) *Liquid Modernity* Cambridge: Polity.

—— (2002) 'Reconnaissance wars of the planetary frontierland' *Theory, Culture and Society* vol. 19, no. 4, pp. 81–90.

Bauman, Z. & Tester, K. (2001) *Conversations with Zygmunt Bauman* Cambridge: Polity.

Beck, U. (1992) *Risk Society: Towards a New Modernity* London: Sage.

—— (1994) 'The reinvention of politics: Towards a theory of reflexive modernization' in U. Beck, A. Giddens and S. Lash (eds) *Reflexive Modernization: Politics, Tradition and Aesthetics in the Modern Social Order* Cambridge: Polity.

—— (1995) *Ecological Politics in an Age of Risk* Cambridge: Polity.

—— (1997) *The Reinvention of Politics: Rethinking Modernity in the Global Social Order* Cambridge: Polity.

—— (1998a) *Democracy without Enemies* Cambridge: Polity.

—— (1998b) 'Politics of risk society' in J. Franklin (ed.) *The Politics of Risk Society* Cambridge: Polity.

—— (1999) *World Risk Society* Cambridge: Polity.

—— (2000) *What is Globalization?* Cambridge: Polity.

—— (2002a) 'The cosmopolitan society and its enemies' *Theory, Culture and Society* vol. 19, nos 1–2, pp. 17–44.

—— (2002b) 'The terrorist threat: World risk society revisited' *Theory, Culture and Society* vol. 19, no. 4, pp. 39–55.

—— (2005) *Power in the Global Age* Cambridge: Polity.

Beck, U. & Beck-Gernsheim, E. (2002) *Individualization* London: Sage.

Beck, U., Lash, S. & Giddens, A. (1994) *Reflexive Modernization: Politics, Tradition and Aesthetics in the Modern Social Order* Cambridge: Polity.

Beck, U. & Willms, J. (2003) *Conversations with Ulrich Beck* Cambridge: Polity.

Benhabib, S. & Cornell, D. (eds) (1987) *Feminism as Critique: Essays on the Politics of Gender in Late Capitalist Societies* Cambridge: Polity.

Berking, H. (1996) 'Solidary individualism: The moral impact of cultural modernisation in late modernity' in S. Lash, B. Szerszynski and B. Wynne (eds) *Risk, Environment and Modernity* London: Sage

Berman, M. (1983) *All That is Solid Melts into Air: The Experience of Modernity* London: Verso.

Best, S. & Kellner, D. (1997) *The Postmodern Turn* New York and London: Guildford Press.

Bhabha, J. (1998) '"Get back to where you once belonged": Identity, citizenship and exclusion in Europe' *Human Rights Quarterly* vol. 20, pp. 592–627.

Billig, M. (1995) *Banal Nationalism* London: Sage.

Birnbaum, P. (1997) 'Citoyenneté et identité: De T.H. Marshall à Talcott Parsons' *Citizenship Studies* vol. 1, no. 1, pp. 133–51.

Blyth, M. (2002) *Great Transformations: Economic Ideas and Institutional Change in the Twentieth Century* Cambridge University Press.

Bonefeld, W. & Holloway, J. (1991) *Post-Fordism and Social Form: A Marxist Debate on the Post-Fordist State* London: Macmillan.

Bordo, S. & Jagger, A. (eds) (1990) *Gender/Body/Knowledge* New Brunswick: Rutgers University Press.

Bottomore, T. (1992) 'Citizenship and social class' in R. Moore (ed.) *Citizenship and Social Class* London: Pluto Press.

—— (1993) *Political Sociology* Second Edition London: Pluto Press.

Bourdieu, P. (1994) 'Rethinking the state: Genesis and structure of the bureaucratic field' *Sociological Theory* vol. 12, no. 1, pp. 1–18.

—— (1996) *The State Nobility; Elite Schools in the Field of Power* Cambridge: Polity.

Brooks-Higginbottom, E. (1993) *Righteous Discontent: The Women's Movement in the Black Baptist Church 1880–1920* Cambridge MA: Harvard University Press.

Brown, C. (2000) 'Cosmopolitanism, world citizenship and global civil society' *Critical Review of International Social and Political Philosophy* vol. 3, no. 1, pp. 7–26.

Brubaker, R. (ed.) (1989) *Immigration and the Politics of Citizenship in Europe and North America* Lanham MD: University Press of America.

—— (1990) 'Immigration, citizenship and the nation state in France and Germany' *International Sociology* vol. 5, no. 4, pp. 379–407.

Bruce, S. (2000) *Fundamentalism* Cambridge: Polity.

Buchanan, J. (1975) *The Limits of Liberty* Chicago University Press.

Buchanan, J.M. & Tullock, G. (1962) *The Calculus of Consent* Ann Arbor: University of Michigan Press.

Burstyn, V. (1983) 'Masculine dominance and the state' in R. Miliband & J. Saville (eds) *The Socialist Register 1983* London: Merlin Press.

Butler, J. (1997) *Excitable Speech: A Politics of the Performative* New York: Routledge.

Byrne, D. (1998) *Complexity Theory and the Social Sciences: An Introduction* London: Routledge.

Calhoon, C. (1995) '"New social movements" of the early nineteenth century' in M. Traugott (ed.) *Repertoires and Cycles of Collective Action* Durham NC: Duke University Press.

Caplan, P. (2000) *Risk Revisited* London: Pluto Press.

Capra, F. (1996) *The Web of Life* London: HarperCollins.

—— (2003) *The Hidden Connections: A Science for Sustainable Living* London: Flamingo.

Carruthers, B.G. (1994) 'When is the state autonomous? Culture, organization theory and the political sociology of the state' *Sociological Theory* vol. 12, no. 1, pp. 19–44.

Castel, R. (1991) 'From dangerousness to risk' in G. Burchell, C. Gorden & P. Miller (eds) *The Foucault Effect: Studies in Governmentability* London: Harvester Wheatsheaf.

Castells, M. (1997) *The Information Age: Economy, Society and Culture.* Vol. 2: *The Power of Identity* Oxford: Blackwell.

—— (2000a) *The Information Age: Economy, Society and Culture.* Vol. 1: *The Rise of the Network Society* Second Edition. Oxford: Blackwell.

—— (2000b) *The Information Age: Economy, Society and Culture.* Vol. 3: *The End of Millennium* Oxford: Blackwell.

—— (2001) *The Internet Galaxy* Oxford University Press.

Cawson, A. (1982) *Corporatism and Welfare: Social Policy and State Intervention in Britain* London: Heinemann.

Cerny, P.G. (1990) *The Changing Architecture of Politics: Structure, Agency and the Future of the State* London: Sage.

—— (1998) 'Neomedievalism, civil wars and the new security dilemma: Globalization as durable disorder' *Civil Wars* vol. 1, no. 1, pp. 36–64.

—— (2000) 'Globalization and the disarticulation of political power: Towards a new Middle Ages' in H. Goverde, P.G. Cerney, M. Haugaard & H. Lentner (eds) *Power in Contemporary Politics: Theories, Practices, Globalizations* London: Sage.

Chambers, S. & Kymlicka, W. (2002) (eds) *Alternative Conceptions of Civil Society* Princeton University Press.

Chandler, D. (2004) 'Building global civil society "from below"?' *Millennium* vol. 33, no. 2, pp. 313–39.

Chesters, G. (2004) 'Global civil society and global complexity' *Voluntas* vol. 15, no. 4, pp. 314–35.

Chesters, G. & Welsh, I. (2005) 'Complexity and social movements: Process and emergence in planetary action systems' *Theory, Culture and Society* vol. 22, no. 5, pp. 187–211.

—— (2006) *Complexity and Social Movements: Multitudes at the Edge of Chaos* London: Routledge.

Chomsky, N. (1997) *World Orders, Old and New* London: Verso.

Chua, A. (2002) 'A world on the edge' *The Wilson Quarterly* vol. 26, no. 4.

Clarke, S. (ed.) (1991) *The State Debate* London: Macmillan.

Cleaver, H.M. (1998) 'The Zapatistas effect: The internet and the rise of an alternative political fabric' *Journal of International Affairs* vol. 51, no. 2, pp. 621–40.

Clegg, S. (1989) *Frameworks of Power* London: Sage.

—— (2000) 'Power and authority, resistance and legitimacy' in H. Goverde, P.G. Cerney, M. Haugaard & H. Lentner (eds) *Power in Contemporary Politics: Theories, Practices, Globalizations* London: Sage.

Clift, B, (2002) 'Social democracy and globalization: The cases of Britain and France' *Government and Opposition* vol. 37, no. 4, pp. 466–500.

Cohen, J. (1985) 'Strategy or identity: New theoretical paradigms and contemporary social movements' *Social Research* vol. 52, no. 4, pp. 663–716.

Cohen, J. & Arato, A. (1992) *Civil Society and Political Theory* Cambridge MA: MIT Press.

Cohen, R. & Rai, S. (2000) (eds) *Global Social Movements* London: Athlone Press.

Colás, A. (1997) 'The promise of an international civil society' *Global Society* no. 3, pp. 261–77.

—— (2005) 'Imperious civility: Violence and the dilemmas of global civil society' *Contemporary Politics* vol. 11, nos 2/3, pp. 179–88.

Connell, R.W. (1990) 'The state, gender and sexual politics: Theory and appraisal' *Theory and Society* vol. 19, no. 5, pp. 507–44.

Conway, J. (2004) 'Citizenship in a time of empire: The World Social Forum as a new public space' *Citizenship Studies* vol. 8, no. 4, pp. 367–81.

—— (2005) 'Social forums, social movements and social change: A response to Peter Marcuse on the subject of the World Social Forum' *International Journal of Urban and Regional Research* vol. 29, no. 2, pp. 425–8.

Cooper, D. (1995) *Power in Struggle: Feminism, Sexuality and the State* Buckingham: Open University Press.

Corrigan, P. & Sayer, D. (1985) *The Great Arch: English State Formation as Cultural Revolution* Oxford: Blackwell.

Cox, R.W. (1999) 'Civil society at the turn of the millennium: Prospects for an alternative world order' *Review of International Studies* vol. 25, no. 1, pp. 3–28.

Cranford, C.J. (2003) 'Community unionism: Organizing for fair employment in Canada' *Just Labour* vol. 3, Fall, pp. 46–59.

Crenson, M. (1972) *The Un-Politics of Air Pollution: A Study of Non-Decisionmaking in the Cities* Baltimore MD: Johns Hopkins University Press.

Crook, S., Pakulski, J. & Waters, M. (1992) *Postmodernization: Change in Advanced Society* London: Sage.

Crouch, C. (1993) *Industrial Relations and European State Traditions* Oxford: Clarenden Press.

Culpitt, I. (1999) *Social Policy and Risk* London: Sage.

Cunninghame, P. & Ballesteros Corona, C. (1998) 'A rainbow at midnight: Zapatistas and autonomy' *Capital and Class* no. 66, pp. 12–22.

Dagnino, E. (1998) 'Culture, citizenship and democracy: Changing discourses and practices of the Latin American left' in S.E. Alvarez, E. Dagnino & A. Escobar (eds) *Cultures of Politics, Politics of Culture: Re-Visioning Latin American Social Movements* Boulder CO: Westview.

Dahl, R. (1956) *A Preface to Democratic Theory* University of Chicago Press.

—— (1961) *Who Governs? Democracy and Power in an American City* New Haven: Yale University Press.

—— (1971) *Polyarchy: Participation and Opposition* New Haven: Yale University Press.

—— (1985) *A Preface to Economic Democracy* Cambridge: Polity.

—— (1989) *Democracy and its Critics* New Haven: Yale University Press.

Daly, M. (1987) *Gyn/Ecology: The Metaethics of Radical Feminism* London: Women's Press.

Davies, J.C. (1971) *When Men Revolt and Why* New York: Free Press.

Davis, M. (2000) *Magical Urbanism:* London: Verso.

—— (2005) *The Monster at Our Door: The Global Threat of Avian Flu* New York: The New Press.

De Angelis, M. (2000) 'New internationalism and the Zapatistas' *Capital and Class* no. 70, pp. 9–35.

Dean, M. (1999) 'Risk, calculable and incalculable' in D. Lupton (ed.) *Risk and Sociocultural Theory: New Directions and Perspectives* Cambridge University Press.

Debord, G. (1995) *The Society of the Spectacle* Boston: MIT Press.

Delanty, G. (2000) *Citizenship in a Global Age* Buckingham: Open University Press.

Deleuze, G. & Guattari, F. (1983) *Anti-Oedipus: Capitalism and Schizophrenia* Minneapolis: University of Minnesota Press.

—— (1986) *Nomadology* New York: Semiotext(e).

—— (2002) *A Thousand Plateaus: Capitalism and Schizophrenia* London: Continuum.

Devji, F. (2005) *Landscapes of the Jihad: Militancy, Morality, Modernity* London: Hurst.

Dillon, M. (2000) 'Post-structuralism, complexity and poetics' *Theory, Culture and Society* vol. 17, no. 5, pp. 1–26.

DiMaggio, P. & Powell, W. (1983) 'The iron cage revisited: Institutional isomorphism and collective rationality in organizational fields' *American Sociological Review* vol. 48, no. 2, pp. 147–60.

—— (1991) 'Introduction' in W.W. Powell & P.J. DiMaggio (eds) *The New Institutionalism in Organizational Analysis* Chicago University Press.

Dürrschmidt, J. & Taylor, G. (2007) *Globalization, Modernity and Social Change: Hotspots of Transition* London: Palgrave Macmillan.

Eatwell, J. & Taylor, L. (2000) *Global Finance at Risk* New York: New Press.

Eatwell, R. (2000) 'The rebirth of the "extreme right" in Western Europe' *Parliamentary Affairs* vol. 53, pp. 407–25.

Edwards, M. (2004) *Civil Society* Cambridge: Polity.

Eisenstein, Z. (1979) 'Developing a theory of capitalist patriarchy and socialist feminism' in Z. Eisenstein (ed.) *Capitalist Patriarchy and the Case for Socialist Feminism* New York: Monthly Review Press.

Eley, G. (1992) 'Nations, publics and political cultures: Placing Habermas in the 19th century' in C. Calhoon (ed.) *Habermas and the Public Sphere* Cambridge MA: MIT Press.

Ellem, B. (2003) 'New unionism in the old economy: Community and collectivism in the Pilbara's mining town' *Journal of Industrial Relations* vol. 45, no. 4, pp. 423–41.

Elster, J. & Hylland, A. (eds) (1986) *Foundations of Social Choice Theory* Cambridge University Press.

Engels, F. (1987) 'Anti-Dühring' in *Collected Works*. Vol. 25. New York: International Publishers.

Esteva, G. (1999) 'The Zapatistas and people's power' *Capital and Class* no. 68, pp. 153–82.

Etzioni, A. (2004) 'The capabilities and limits of the global civil society' *Millennium* vol. 33, no. 2, pp. 341–53.

Evans, M. (2006) 'Elitism' in C. Hay, M. Lister & D. Marsh (eds) *The State: Theories and Issues* London: Palgrave Macmillan.

Falk , R. (1994) 'The making of global citizenship' in B. van Steenbergen (ed.) *The Condition of Citizenship* London: Sage.

Fantasia, R. & Voss, K. (2004) *Hard Work: Remaking the American Labor Movement* Berkeley: University of California Press.

Faulks, K. (1999) *Political Sociology: A Critical Introduction* Edinburgh University Press.

—— (2000) *Citizenship* London: Routledge.

Fehér, F. & Heller, A. (1986) *Eastern Left – Western Left* Cambridge: Polity.

Ferguson, J. (2002) 'Global disconnect: Abjection and the aftermath of modernism' in J.X. Inda & R. Rosado (eds) *The Anthropology of Globalization: A Reader* Oxford: Blackwell.

Fligstein, N. & Mara-Drita, I. (1996) 'How to make a market: Reflections on the attempt to create a single market in the European Union' *American Journal of Sociology* vol. 102, no. 1, pp. 1–32.

Flyvbjerg, B. (1998a) 'Habermas and Foucault: Thinkers for civil society' *British Journal of Sociology* vol. 49, no. 2, pp. 210–33.

—— (1998b) *Rationality and Power: Democracy in Practice* University of Chicago Press.

Foley, M. & Edwards, B. (1996) 'The paradox of civil society' *Journal of Democracy* vol. 7, no. 3, pp. 38–52.

Forrest, J.B. (ed.) (2003) *Subnationalism in Africa: Ethnicity, Alliances and Politics* Boulder, CO: Lynne Rienner.

Foucault, M. (1973) *The Order of Things: An Archaeology of the Human Sciences* New York: Vintage Books.

—— (1977a) *Madness and Civilization: A History of Insanity in the Age of Reason* London: Tavistock.

—— (1977b) *Discipline and Punish: The Birth of the Prison* London: Allen Lane.

—— (1979) *The History of Sexuality*. Vol. 1: *An Introduction* London: Allen Lane.

—— (1980) *Power/Knowledge: Selected Interviews and Other Writings 1972–1977* Brighton: Harvester Press.

—— (1984) 'Space, knowledge, power' in P. Rabinow (ed.) *The Foucault Reader* New York: Pantheon.

—— (1987) *The History of Sexuality*. Vol. 2: *The Use of Pleasure* Harmondsworth: Penguin.

—— (1988a) *The History of Sexuality*. Vol. 3: *The Care of the Self* London: Allen Lane.

—— (1988b) 'The ethic of care for the self as a practice of freedom' in J. Bernauer & D. Rasmussen (eds) *The Final Foucault* Cambridge MA: MIT Press.

Fowkes, B. (1996) *The Disintegration of the Soviet Union: A Study in the Rise and Triumph of Nationalism* London: Palgrave.

Frankel, B. (1982) 'On the state of the state: Marxist theories of the state after Lenin' in A. Giddens & D. Held (eds) *Classes, Power and Conflict: Classical and Contemporary Debates* London: Macmillan.

Franklin, S. Lury, C. & Stacey, J. (2000) *Global Nature, Global Culture* London: Sage.

Franzway, S., Court, D. & Connell, R.W. (1989) *Staking a Claim: Feminism, Bureaucracy and the State* Sydney: Allen & Unwin.

Fraser, N. (1989a) *Unruly Practices: Power, Discourse and Gender in Contemporary Social Theory* Cambridge: Polity.

—— (1989b) 'Women, welfare and the politics of need interpretation' in P. Lassmann (ed.) *Politics and Social Theory* London: Routledge.

—— (1997) *Justice Interruptus: Reflections on the Postsocialist Condition* London: Routledge.

Friedman, T. (2000) *The Lexus and the Olive Tree: Understanding Globalization* London: HarperCollins.

Furedi, F. (1997) *Culture of Fear: Risk Taking and the Morality of Low Expectations* London: Cassell.

Galston, W. (2001) 'Political knowledge, political engagement and civic education' *Annual Review of Political Science* vol. 4, pp. 217–34.

Geertz, C. (1980) *Negara: The Theatre State in Nineteenth Century Bali* Princeton University Press.

—— (1993) *The Interpretation of Cultures* New York: Basic Books.

Gellner, E.(1983) *Nations and Nationalism* Oxford: Blackwell.

Geyer, M.H. & Paulmann, J. (2001) 'Introduction: The mechanics of internationalism' in M.H. Geyer & J. Paulmann (eds) *The Mechanics of Internationalism: Culture, Society and Politics from the 1830s to the First World War* Oxford University Press.

Giddens, A. (1976) *New Rules of Sociological Method: A Positive Critique of Interpretive Sociologies* London: Hutchinson.

—— (1982) 'Class divisions, class conflict and citizenship rights' *Profiles and Critiques and Social Theory* London: Macmillan.

—— (1985) *The Nation State and Violence* Berkeley: University of California Press.

—— (1990) *The Consequences of Modernity* Cambridge: Polity.

—— (1991) *Modernity and Self-Identity: Self and Society in Late Modern Age* Cambridge: Polity.

—— (1994) *Beyond Left and Right: The Future of Radical Politics* Cambridge: Polity.

—— (1998) *The Third Way: The Renewal of Social Democracy* Cambridge: Polity.

Gilbert, L. & Philips, C. (2003) 'Practices of urban environmental citizenship: Rights to the city and rights to nature in Toronto' *Citizenship Studies* vol. 7, no. 3, pp. 313–30.

Gill, S. (2000) 'Towards a postmodern prince? The battle of Seattle as a moment in the new politics of globalization' *Millennium: Journal of International Studies* vol. 29, no. 1, pp. 131–40.

Glasman, M. (1994) 'The great deformation: Polanyi, Poland and the terrors of planned spontaneity' *New Left Review* vol. 204, pp. 59–86.

Goehler, G. (2000) 'Constitution and use of power' in H. Goverde, P.G. Cerney, M. Haugaard & H. Lentner (eds) *Power in Contemporary Politics: Theories, Practices, Globalizations* London: Sage.

Goetz, K.H. & Margetts, H.Z. (1999) 'The solitary center: The core executive in Central and Eastern Europe' *Governance* vol. 12, no. 4, pp. 425–53.

Goldblatt, D. (1997) 'Liberal democracy and the globalization of environmental risks' in A. McGrew (ed.) *The Transformation of Democracy? Globalization and Territorial Democracy* Cambridge: Polity.

Gordon, L. (1990) 'The new feminist scholarship on the welfare state' in L. Gordon (ed.) *Women, the State and Welfare* Madison: University of Wisconsin Press.

Gramsci, A. (1971) *Selections from Prison Notebooks* London: Lawrence & Wishart.

Granovetter, M.S. (1973) 'The strength of weak ties' *American Journal of Sociology* vol. 78, no. 6, pp. 1360–80.

Gray, J. (2001) 'The era of globalization is over' *New Statesman*, 24 September.

Gurr, T.R. (1971) *Why Men Rebel* Princeton University Press.

Haas, E.B. (1991) *When Knowledge is Power: Three Models of Change in International Organizations* Berkeley: University of California Press.

Haas, P.M. (1992) 'Introduction: Epistemic communities and international policy coordination' *International Organization* vol. 46, no. 1, pp. 1–35.

Habermas, J. (1974) 'The public sphere' *New German Critique* vol. 3, pp. 49–55.

—— (1976) *Legitimation Crisis* London: Heinemann.

—— (1979) *Communication and the Evolution of Society* London: Heinemann.

—— (1983) *The Theory of Communicative Action.* Vol. 1. Cambridge MA: MIT Press.

—— (1987) *The Theory of Communicative Action.* Vol. 2: *System and Lifeworld: A Critique of Functionalist Reason* Boston: Beacon Press.

—— (1989) *The Structural Transformation of the Public Sphere: An Inquiry into a Category of Bourgeois Society* Cambridge MA: MIT Press.

—— (1990) *Moral Consciousness and Communicative Action* Cambridge MA: MIT Press.

—— (2001) *The Postnational Constellation* Cambridge: Polity.

Hajer, M. & Kesselring, S. (1999) 'Democracy in the risk society? Learning from the new politics of mobility in Munich' *Environmental Politics* vol. 8, no. 3, pp. 1–23.

Hall, P.A. (1986) *Governing the Economy: The Politics of State Intervention in Britain and France* Cambridge: Polity.

Hall, P. & Soskice, D. (2001) 'Introduction' in P. Hall & D. Soskice (eds) *Varieties of Capitalism: The Institutional Foundations of Comparative Advantage* Oxford University Press.

Hall, P. & Taylor, R. (1996) 'Political science and the three new institutionalisms' *Political Studies* vol. 44, no. 4, pp. 936–57.

Hall, S., Critcher, C., Jefferson, T., Clarke, J. & Roberts, B. (1978) *Policing the Crisis: Mugging, the State and Law and Order* London: Macmillan.

Hanf, K. (1978) 'Introduction' in K. Hanf & F.W. Scharpf (eds) *Interorganizational Policy Making: Limits to Coordination and Central Control* London: Sage.

Hannerz, U. (1998) *Transnational Connections: Culture, People, Places* London: Routledge.

Hardt, M. & Negri, A. (2001) *Empire* Cambridge MA: Harvard University Press.

Harvey, D. (1989) *The Condition of Postmodernity* Oxford: Blackwell.

—— (2005) *A Brief History of Neo-Liberalism* Oxford University Press.

Harvey, P. (1996) *Hybrids of Modernity* London: Routledge.

Haugaard, M. (2002) *Power: A Reader* Manchester University Press.

Havel, V. (1988) 'Anti-political politics' in J. Keane (ed.) *Civil Society and the State* London: Verso.

Hay, C. (1996) *Re-Stating Social and Political Change* Buckingham: Open University Press.
—— (2006) 'What's Marxist about Marxist state theory' in C. Hay, M. Lister & D. Marsh (eds) *The State: Theories and Issues* London: Palgrave Macmillan.
Hay, C., Lister, M. & Marsh, D. (eds) (2006) *The State: Theories and Issues* London: Palgrave Macmillan.
Hay, C. & Marsh, D. (2000) 'Introduction' in C. Hay & D. Marsh (eds) *Demystifying Globalization* London: Palgrave Macmillan.
Hay, C. & Richards, D. (2000) 'The tangled webs of Westminster and Whitehall: The discourse, strategy and practice of networking within the British core executive' *Public Administration* vol. 78, no. 1, pp. 1–28.
Hearnes, H.M. (1987) 'Women and the welfare state: The transition from private to public dependence' in A. Showstack-Sassoon (ed.) *Women and the State* London: Routledge.
Heater, D. (1990) *Citizenship* London: Longman.
Held, D. (1995) *Democracy and the Global Order: From the Modern State to Cosmopolitan Governance* Cambridge: Polity.
—— (2000) 'Regulating globalization? The reinvention of politics' *International Sociology* vol. 15, no. 2, pp. 394–408.
—— (2002a) *Cosmopolitanism: A Defence* Cambridge: Polity.
—— (2002b) 'Globalization, corporate practice and cosmopolitan social standards' *Contemporary Political Theory* vol. 1, no. 1, pp. 59–78.
Held, D. & McGrew, A. (2002) *Globalization/Antiglobalization* Cambridge: Polity.
—— (2003) 'The great globalization debate' in D. Held & A. McGrew (eds) *The Global Transformations Reader* Cambridge: Polity.
Held, D., McGrew, A., Goldblatt, D. & Perraton, J. (1999) *Global Transformations* Cambridge: Polity.
Heller, A. & Fehér, F. (1988) *The Postmodern Political Condition* New York: Columbia University Press.
Hernes, H.M. (1987) *Welfare State and Woman Power: Essays in State Feminism* Oslo: Norwegian University Press.
Hindess, B. (1996) *Discourses of Power: From Hobbes to Foucault* Oxford: Blackwell.
Hirst, P. & Thompson, G. (1999) *Globalization in Question* Second Edition Cambridge: Polity.
Hobsbawm, E. (1992) *Nations and Nationalism since 1780: Programme, Myth, Reality* Second Edition Cambridge University Press.
—— (2001) *On the Edge of the New Century* New York: New Press.
—— (2007) *Globalization, Democracy and Terrorism* London: Abacus.
Hochschild, A.R. (2003) *The Managed Heart: The Commercialization of Feeling* Twentieth Anniversary Edition Berkeley: University of California Press.
Hoffer, E. (1951) *Thoughts on the Nature of Mass Movements* New York: Harper & Row.
Hoffman, J. (1998) *Sovereignty* Buckingham: Open University Press.
—— (2001) *Gender and Sovereignty: Feminism, the State and International Relations* London: Macmillan.
Holliday, I. (2000) 'Is the British state hollowing out?' *Political Quarterly* vol. 71, no. 2, pp. 167–76.

Holloway, J. (2002) *Change the World Without Taking Power: The Meaning of Revolution Today* London: Pluto Press.

Holloway, J. & Peláez, E. (1998) (eds) *Zapatista! Reinventing Revolution in Mexico* London: Pluto Press.

Holton, R.J. (2005) *Making Globalization* London: Palgrave Macmillan.

Hood, C. (2000) *The Art of the State: Culture, Rhetoric and Public Management* Oxford: Clarendon Press.

Hopkins, D.N. (ed.) (2001) *Regions/Globalizations: Theories and Cases* Durham NC: Duke University Press.

Hunter, F. (1953) *Community Power Structure: A Study of Decision Makers* Chapel Hill: North Carolina Press.

Huntington, S.P. (1968) *Political Order in Changing Societies* New Haven: Yale University Press.

—— (1998) *The Clash of Civilizations and the Remaking of the World Order* London: Touchstone.

Inglehart, R. (1990) *Culture Shift in Advanced Industrial Society* Princeton University Press.

Isin, E.F. (2002) 'Citizenship after Orientalism' in E.F. Isin & B.S. Turner (eds) *Handbook of Citizenship Studies* London: Sage.

Isin, E.F. & Turner, B. (2002) 'Citizenship studies: An introduction' in E.F. Isin & B.S. Turner (eds) *Handbook of Citizenship Studies* London: Sage.

Isin, E.F. & Wood, P.K. (1999) *Citizenship and Identity* London: Sage.

Jasper, J. (1997) *The Art of Moral Protest: Culture, Biography and Creativity in Social Movements* University of Chicago Press.

Jelin, E. (2000) 'Towards a global environmental citizenship' *Citizenship Studies* vol. 4, no. 1, pp. 47–63.

Jessop, B. (1990) *State Theory: Putting Capitalist States in their Place* Cambridge: Polity.

—— (1997) 'Capitalism and its future: Remarks on regulation, government and governance' *Review of International Political Economy* vol. 4, no. 3, pp. 561–81.

—— (2001a) 'Bringing the state back in (yet again): Reviews, revisions, rejections and redirections' *International Review of Sociology* vol. 11, no. 2, pp. 149–73.

—— (2001b) *The Gender Selectivities of the State* http://www.lancs.ac.uk/fass/sociology/papers/jessop-gender-selectivities.pdf. Accessed on 5 August 2009.

—— (2002) *The Future of the Capitalist State* Cambridge: Polity.

—— (2008) *State Power: A Strategic Relational Approach* Cambridge: Polity.

Johnston, P. (2000) 'The resurgence of labor as a citizenship movement in the New Labour relations environment' *Critical Sociology* vol. 26, nos 1/2, pp. 109–38.

—— (2002) 'Citizen movement unionism: For the defense of local communities in the global age' in B. Nissen (ed.) *Unions in a Globalized Environment: Changing Borders, Organizational Boundaries and Social Roles* New York: M.E. Sharpe.

Jordon, J. (1998) 'The art of necessity: The subversive imagination of anti-road protest and Reclaim the Streets' in G. McKay (ed.) *DiY Culture: Party and Protest in the Nineties* London: Verso.

Jowers, P., Dürrschmidt, J., O'Doherty, R. & Purdue, D. (1999) 'Affective and aesthetic dimensions of contemporary social movements in south west England' *Innovation* vol. 12, no. 1, pp. 99–118.

Kaldor, M. (2000) 'Civilising globalisation? The implications of the "battle of Seattle"' *Millennium: Journal of International Studies* vol. 29, no. 1, pp. 105–14.
—— (2003) *Global Civil Society: An Answer to War* Cambridge: Polity.
Katzenstein, P. (ed.) (1978) *Between Power and Plenty* Maddison: University of Wisconsin Press.
Keane, J. (2003) *Global Civil Society?* Cambridge University Press.
Keating, M. (1988) *State and Regional Nationalism: Territorial Politics and the European State* Hemel Hempstead: Harvester Wheatsheaf.
Keck, M.E. & Sikkink, K. (1998) *Activists Beyond Borders: Advocacy Networks in Global Politics* Ithaca NY: Cornell University Press.
Kimmel. M.S. (1990) *Revolution: A Sociological Interpretation* Cambridge: Polity.
King, A. (1975) 'Overload: The problems of governing in the 1970s' *Political Studies* vol. 23, no. 2, pp. 284–96.
Klein, N. (2002) *No Logo: No Space, No Choice, No Jobs* New York: Picador.
Konrad, G. (1984) *Antipolitics* London: Harcourt Brace Jovanovich.
Kwa, C. (2002) 'Romantic and baroque conceptions of complex wholes in the sciences' in J. Law & A. Mol (eds) *Complexities: Social Studies of Knowledge Practices* Durham NC: Duke University Press.
Kymlicka, W. (1995) *Multi-cultural Citizenship: A Liberal Theory of Minority Rights* Oxford University Press.
Laclau, E. & Mouffe, C. (1985) *Hegemony and Socialist Strategy* London: Verso.
Lake, D.A. (1999) 'Global governance: A relational contracting approach' in A. Prakash & J.A. Hart (eds) *Globalization and Governance* London: Routledge.
Landes, J. (1988) *Women in the Public Sphere in the Age of the French Revolution* Ithaca NY: Cornell University Press.
Lash, S. (2000) 'Risk culture' in B. Adam, U. Beck & J. van Loon (eds) *The Risk Society and Beyond: Critical Issues for Social Theory* London: Sage.
Lash, S. & Urry, J. (1994) *Economies of Signs and Space* London: Sage.
Laski, H.J. (1967) *A Grammar of Politics* Fifth Edition London: George Allen & Unwin.
Latour, B. (1999) 'On recalling ANT' in J. Law & J. Hassard (eds) *Actor Network Theory and After* Oxford: Blackwell.
Law, J. (1994) *Organizing Modernity* Oxford: Blackwell.
Lawrence, B.B. & Karim, A. (eds) (2007) *On Violence* Durham NC: Duke University Press.
Lee, J. (2004) *The European Social Forum at 3: Facing Old Challenges to go Forward* Geneva: Centre for Applied Studies in International Negotiations (CASIN).
Lentner, H.H. (2000) 'Politics, power and states in globalization' in H. Goverde, P.G. Cerney, M. Haugaard & H. Lentner (eds) *Power in Contemporary Politics: Theories, Practices, Globalizations* London: Sage.
Lia, B. (2005) *Globalization and the Future of Terrorism: Patterns and Predictions* London and New York: Routledge.
Lindblom, C. (1977) *Politics and Markets: The World's Political-Economic Systems* New York: Basic Books.
Lipovetsky, G. (2005) *Hypermodern Times* Cambridge: Polity.
Lipschutz, R.D. (1992) 'Reconstructing world politics: The emergence of global civil society' *Millenium* vol. 21, no. 3, pp. 389–420.

—— (1996) *Global Civil Society and Global Environmental Governance* Albany NY: SUNY Press.

Lister, R. (1993) 'Tracing the contours of women's citizenship' *Policy and Politics* vol. 21, no. 1, pp. 3–16.

—— (1997) *Citizenship: Feminist Perspectives* London: Macmillan.

Lomax, B. (1997) 'The strange death of civil society in Hungary' *Journal of Communist Studies and Transition Studies* vol. 13, no. 1, pp. 14–63.

Lowe, R. & Rollings, N. (2000) 'Modernizing Britain 1957–64: A classic case of centralization and fragmentation?' in R.A.W. Rhodes (ed.) *Transforming British Government*. Vol. 1: *Changing Institutions* London: Macmillan.

Lukes, S. (2004) *Power: A Radical View* Second Edition London: Palgrave Macmillan.

Lupton, D. (ed.) (1999) *Risk and Sociocultural Theory: New Directions and Perspectives* Cambridge University Press.

Lyotard, J.-F. (1984) *The Postmodern Condition: A Report on Knowledge* Manchester University Press.

McAdam, D., McCarthy, J. & Zald, M. (eds) (1996) *Comparative Perspectives on Social Movements: Political Opportunities, Mobilizing Structures and Cultural Framings* Cambridge University Press.

McAdam, D., Tarrow, S. & Tilly, C. (2001) *Dynamics of Contention* Cambridge University Press.

McAllister-Groves, J. (1995) 'Learning to feel: The neglected sociology of social movements' *Sociology Review* vol. 43, no. 3, pp. 435–61.

McCrone, D. (1998) *The Sociology of Nationalism* London: Routledge.

McCubbins, M.D. & Sullivan, T. (1987) *Congress: Structure and Policy* Cambridge University Press.

McDonald, K. (2002) 'From solidarity to fluidarity: Social movements beyond "collective identity"' *Social Movement Studies* vol. 1, no. 2, pp. 109–28.

McGrew, A. (1997) 'Democracy beyond borders' in A. McGrew (ed.) *The Transformation of Democracy? Globalization and Territorial Democracy* Cambridge: Polity.

—— (2002) 'From global governance to good governance: Theories and prospects of democratizing the global polity' in M. Ougaard & R. Higgott (eds) *Towards a Global Polity* London: Routledge.

McKay, G. (1996) *Senseless Acts of Beauty: Cultures of Resistance since the Sixties* London: Verso.

—— (1998) *DIY Culture: Party and Protest in Nineties Britain* London: Verso.

Mackinnon, C.A. (1989) *Towards a Feminist Theory of the State* Cambridge MA: Harvard University Press.

McLellan, D. (1980) *The Thought of Karl Marx* Second Edition London: Macmillan.

McLennan, G. (2003) 'Sociology's complexity' *Sociology* vol. 37, no. 3, pp. 547–64.

McNaughton, C. (2008) 'A critique of John Holloway's *Change the World Without Taking Power*' *Capital and Class* no. 95, Summer, pp. 3–28.

McNay, L. (1992) *Foucault and Feminism: Power, Gender and the Self* Boston: Northeastern University Press.

Maffesoli, M. (1996) *The Time of the Tribes* London: Sage.

Maier, C. (1994) 'A surfeit of memory? Reflections of history, melancholy and denial' *History and Memory* vol. 5, no. 2, pp. 136–52.

Malik, K. (1996) *The Meaning of Race* London: Macmillan.

Mann, M. (1993) *The Sources of Social Power: Rise of Classes and Nation States, 1760–1914*. Vol. 2. Cambridge University Press.

—— (1996) 'Ruling class strategies and citizenship' in M. Bulmer & A. Rees (eds) *Citizenship Today: The Contemporary Relevance of T.H. Marshall* London: UCL Press.

—— (2001) 'Globalization and September 11' *New Left Review* no. 12, pp. 51–72.

March, J.G. & Olsen, J.P (1989) *Rediscovering Institutions: The Organizational Basis of Politics* New York: Free Press.

Marcuse, H. (1972) *One Dimensional Man* London: Abacus.

Marcuse, P. (2005) 'Are social forums the future of social movements?' *International Journal of Urban and Regional Research* vol. 29, no. 2, pp. 417–24.

Marinetto, M. (2007) *Social Theory, the State and Modern Society: The State in Contemporary Social Thought* Maidenhead: Open University Press.

Marks, G., Hooghe, L. & Blank, K. (1996) 'European integration from the 1980s: State centric vs multi-level governance' *Journal of Common Market Studies* vol. 34, no. 3, pp. 341–78.

Marshall, T.H. (1981) *The Right to Welfare and Other Essays* London: Heinemann.

—— (1992) 'Citizenship and social class' in T.H. Marshall & T. Bottomore *Citizenship and Social Class* London: Pluto Press.

Marx, K. (1976) *Capital*. Vol. 1: *A Critique of Political Economy* Harmondsworth: Penguin.

Marx, K. & Engels, F. (1969) 'The Manifesto of the Communist Party' in *Collected Works*. Vol. 1. Moscow: Progress.

Mathers, A. (1999) 'Euromarch: The struggle for a social Europe' *Capital and Class* no. 69, pp. 15–19.

Mazarr, M. (2007) *Unmodern Men in the Modern World: Radical Islam, Terrorism and the War on Modernity* Cambridge University Press.

Mazur, A.G. & Stetson, D.M. (1995) 'Conclusion: The case for state feminism' in D.M. Stetson & A.G. Mazur (eds) *Comparative State Feminism* Thousand Oaks CA: Sage.

Meiksins Wood, E. (2003) *Empire of Capital* London: Verso.

Melucci, A. (1989) *Nomads of the Present* London: Hutchinson.

—— (1996) *Challenging Codes: Collective Action in the Information Age* Cambridge University Press.

Mennell, S. (1995) 'Civilization and de-civilization, civil society and violence' *Irish Journal of Sociology* vol. 5, pp. 1–21.

Meyer, J.W. (1997) 'The changing cultural content of the nation state: A world society perspective' in G. Steinmetz (ed.) *New Approaches to the State in the Social Sciences* Ithaca NY: Cornell University Press.

—— (2000) 'Globalization: Sources and effects on national states and societies' *International Sociology* vol. 15, no. 2, pp. 233–48.

Meyer, J., Boli, J., Thomas, G. & Ramirez, F. (1997a) 'World society and the nation state' *American Journal of Sociology* vol. 103, no. 1, pp. 144–81.

Meyer, J.W., Frank, D.J., Hironaka, A., Schofer, E. & Tuma, N.B. (1997b) 'The structuring of a world environmental regime 1870–1990' *International Organization* vol. 51, no. 4, pp. 623–51.

Michels, R. (1962) *Political Parties* New York: Free Press.

Miliband, R. (1969) *The State in Capitalist Society* London: Weidenfeld & Nicholson.

Miller, D. (1995) 'Citizenship and pluralism' *Political Studies* vol. 43, pp. 432–50.

Mills, C. (2003) 'Contesting the political: Butler and Foucault on power and resistance' *Journal of Political Philosophy* vol. 11, no. 3, pp. 253–72.

Mills, C.W. (1956) *The Power Elite* Oxford University Press.

Milward, H.B. & Francisco, R.A. (1983) 'Subsystem politics and corporatism in the United States' *Policy and Politics* vol. 11, no. 3, pp. 273–93.

Misztal, B. (1996) *Trust in Modern Societies: The Search for the Bases of Social Order* Cambridge: Polity.

Mitchell, T. (1999) 'Society, economy and the state effect' in G. Steinmetz (ed.) *State/Culture: State Formation after the Cultural Turn* Ithaca NY: Cornell University Press.

Moravcsik, A. (1998) *The Choice for Europe: Social Purpose and State Power from Messina to Maastricht* Ithaca NY: Cornell University Press.

Morgan, K., Rees, G. & Garmise, S. (1999) 'Networking for local economic development' in G. Stoker (ed.) *The New Management of British Local Governance* London: Macmillan.

Mosca, G. (1939) *The Ruling Class* New York: McGraw-Hill.

Mouffe, C. (1993) *The Return of the Political* London: Verso.

Müller, W.C. & Wright, V. (1994) 'Reshaping the state in Western Europe: The limits to retreat' *West European Politics* vol. 17, no. 3, pp. 1–11.

Munck, R. (2004) *Labour and Globalization: Results and Prospects* Liverpool University Press.

Munck, R. & Waterman, P. (1998) *Labour Worldwide in the Era of Globalization: Alternative Union Models in the New World Order* London: Macmillan.

Murdoch, J. (1995) 'Actor-networks and the evolution of economic forms: Combining description and explanation in theories of regulation, flexible specialization and networks' *Environment and Planning A* no. 27, pp. 731–57.

Mythen, G. (2004) *Ulrich Beck: A Critical Introduction* London: Polity.

Nairn, T (1988) *The Enchanted Glass: Britain and its Monarchy* London: Radius.

—— (2005) 'Global trajectories: America and the unchosen' in T. Nairn & P. James (eds) *Global Matrix: Nationalism, Globalism and State Terrorism* London: Pluto Press.

Nairn, T. & James, P. (eds) (2005) *Global Matrix: Globalization, Politics and Power* Oxford: Blackwell.

Nash, K. (2000) *Contemporary Political Sociology: Globalization, Politics and Power* Oxford: Blackwell.

Ness, I. & Eimer, S. (2001) (eds) *Central Labor Councils and the Revival of American Unionism: Organising for Justice in our Communities* Armonk NY: M.E. Sharpe.

Newby, H. (1996) 'Citizenship in a green world: Global commons and human stewardship' in M. Bulmer & A. Rees (eds) *Citizenship Today* London: UCL Press.

Notes from Nowhere (2003) *We are Everywhere: The Irresistible Rise of Global Anti-Capitalism* London: Verso.

Nugent, S. (2000) 'Good risk, bad risk: Reflexive modernization and Amazonia' in P. Caplan (ed.) *Risk Revisited* London: Pluto Press.

Nye, J.S. & Donahue, J.D. (eds) (2000) *Governance in a Globalizing World* Washington DC: Brookings Institution Press.

Oberschall, A. (1973) *Social Conflict and Social Movements* Englewood Cliffs NJ: Prentice Hall.

O'Brian, M. (1999) 'Theorizing modernity: Reflexivity, identity and evironment in Giddens' social theory' in M. O'Brian, S. Pena & C. Hay (eds) *Theorising Modernity: Reflexivity, Environment and Identity in Giddens' Social Theory* London and New York: Longman.

Offe, C. (1984) *The Contradictions of the Welfare State* Boston: MIT Press.

—— (1985a) *Disorganized Capitalism* Cambridge: Polity Press.

—— (1985b) 'The new social movements: Challenging the boundaries of institutional politics' *Social Research* vol. 52, pp. 817–68.

—— (1987) 'Challenging the boundaries of institutional politics: Social movements since the 1960s' in C.S. Maier (ed.) *Changing Boundaries of the Political: Essays on the Evolving Balance between State and Society, Public and Private in Europe* Cambridge University Press.

Offe, C. & Wiesenthal, H. (1985) 'Two logics of collective action' in C. Offe *Disorganized Capitalism* Cambridge: Polity.

Ohmae, K. (1995) *The End of the Nation State: The Rise of Regional Economics* London: HarperCollins.

Okin, S.M. (1991) 'Gender, the public and the private' in D. Held (ed.) *Political Theory Today* Cambridge: Polity.

O'Leary, S. (1998) 'The options for the reform of European Union citizenship' in S. O'Leary & T. Tiilikainen (eds) *Citizenship and Nationality Status in the New Europe* London: IPPR.

Olesen, T. (2005) 'Transnational publics: New spaces of social movement activism and the problem of global long-sightedness' *Current Sociology* vol. 53, no. 3, pp. 419–40.

Olson, M. (1965) *The Logic of Collective Action* New York: Schoken Books.

Ostrom, E. (1990) *Governing the Commons* Cambridge University Press.

Ougaard, M. (2004) *Political Globalization: State, Power and Social Forces* London: Palgrave Macmillan.

Pakulski, J. (1995) 'Social movements and class: The decline of the Marxist paradigm' in L. Maheu (ed.) *Social Movements and Social Classes: The Future of Collective Action* London: Sage.

Pareto, V. (1963) *Treatise on General Sociology* New York: Dover Publications.

Parsons, T. (1951) *The Social System* New York: Free Press.

—— (1969) *Politics and Social Structure* New York: Free Press.

—— (1986) 'On the concept of political power' in S. Lukes (ed.) *Power* New York University Press.

Pateman, C. (1979) *The Problem of Political Obligation: A Critical Analysis of Liberal Theory* Chichester: Wiley.

—— (1988) *The Sexual Contract* Cambridge: Polity.

—— (1989) *The Disorder of Women* Cambridge: Polity.

Patomäki, H. (2000) 'The Tobin Tax: A new phase in the politics of globalization' *Theory, Culture & Society* vol. 17, no. 4, pp. 77–91.

Patomäki, H. & Teivainen, T. (2004) 'The World Social Forum: An open space or a movement of movements' *Theory, Culture and Society* vol. 21, no. 6, pp. 145–54.

Patterson, A. & Pinch, P.L. (1995) 'Hollowing out the local state: Compulsory competitive tendering and the restructuring of British public sector services' *Environment and Planning A* vol. 27, pp. 1437–61.

Payne, S. (1999) *Fascism: Theory and Practice* London: Pluto Press.

Pelczynski, Z.A. (1988) 'Solidarity and the re-birth of civil society in Poland 1976–81' in J. Keane (ed.) *Civil Society and the State* London: Verso.

Penttinen, E. (2000) 'Capitalism as a system of global power' in H. Goverde, P.G. Cerney, M. Haugaard & H. Lentner (eds) *Power in Contemporary Politics: Theories, Practices, Globalizations* London: Sage.

Peters, B.G. (1993) 'Managing the hollow state' in K.A. Eliassen & J. Kooiman (eds) *Managing Public Organizations: Lessons from Contemporary European Experience* Second Edition London: Sage.

Pfaff-Czainecka, J. (2005) *Ethnic Futures: The State and Identity Politics in Asia* London: Sage.

Pierson, C. (1996) *The Modern State* London and New York: Routledge.

Plant, S. (1997) *Zeros and Ones* London: Fourth Estate.

—— (1992) *The Most Radical Gesture: The Situationist International in a Postmodern Age* London: Routledge.

Poggi, G. (1978) *The Development of the Modern State: A Sociological Introduction* London: Hutchinson.

Pollack, M. (1997) 'Delegation, agency and agenda setting in the European Community' *International Organization* vol. 51, no. 1, pp. 99–134.

Post, R. & Rosenblum, N. (2002) (eds) *Civil Society and Government* Princeton University Press.

Poulantzas, N. (1978) *State, Power, Socialism* London: New Left Books.

Preston, P.W. (1997) *Political/Cultural Identity: Citizens and Nations in a Global Era* London: Sage.

Prigogine, I. (1997) *The End of Certainty* New York: Free Press.

Pringle, R. & Watson, S. (1992) 'Women's interests and the post-structuralist state' in M. Barrett & A. Philips (eds) *Destabilizing Theory: Contemporary Feminist Debates* Cambridge: Polity.

Protevi, J. (2001) *Political Physics* London: Athlone Press.

Putnam, R.D. (2001) *Bowling Alone: The Collapse and Revival of American Community* New York: Simon and Schuster.

Ray, L. (1993) *Re-thinking Critical Theory: Emancipation in an Age of Global Social Movements* London: Sage.

—— (2004) 'Civil society and the public sphere' in K. Nash & A. Scott (eds) *The Blackwell Companion to Political Sociology* Oxford: Blackwell.

Reinharz, J. & Mosse, G.L. (1992) (eds) *The Impact of Western Nationalisms* London: Sage.

Rhodes, R.A.W. (1994) 'The hollowing out of the state: The changing nature of public service in Britain' *Political Quarterly* vol. 65, no. 2, pp. 138–51.

—— (1996) 'The new governance: Governing without government' *Political Studies* vol. 44, no. 4, pp. 652–67.

—— (1997) *Understanding Governance: Policy Networks, Governance, Reflexivity and Accountability* Buckingham: Open University Press.

Rieger, E. & Leibfried, S. (2003) *Limits to Globalization* Cambridge: Polity.

Ritzer, G. (2004) *The Globalization of Nothing* Thousand Oaks CA: Pine Forge.

Robertson, R. (1992) *Globalization: Social Theory and Global Culture* London: Sage.

Robinson, I. (2000) 'Neo-liberal restructuring and US unions: Towards social movement unions' *Critical Sociology* vol. 26, nos 1/2, pp. 109–38.

—— (2002) 'Does neo-liberal restructuring promote social movement unionism? Developments in comparative perspective' in B. Nissen (ed.) *Unions in a*

Globalized Environment: Changing Borders, Organizational Boundaries and Social Roles New York, M.E. Sharpe.

Rose, N. (1996) 'Refiguring the territory of government' *Economy and Society* vol. 25, no. 3, pp. 327–56.

Rosenau, J.N. (1990) *Turbulence in World Politics: A Theory of Change and Continuity* London: Harvester Wheatsheaf.

—— (1997) *Along the Domestic–Foreign Frontier: Exploring Governance in a Turbulent World* Cambridge University Press.

—— (1999) 'Toward an ontology for global governance' in M. Hewson & T.J. Sinclair (eds) *Approaches to Global Governance Theory* University of New York Press.

Rosenau, J.N. & Czempiel, E.-O. (eds) (1992) *Governance without Government: Order and Change in World Politics* Cambridge University Press.

Rumford, C. (2003) 'European civil society or transnational social space? Conceptions of society in discourses of EU citizenship, governance and the democratic deficit: An emerging agenda' *European Journal of Social Theory* vol. 6, no. 1, pp. 25–43.

Rupert, M. (1995) *Producing Hegemony: The Politics of Mass Production and American Global Power* Cambridge University Press.

Rush, M. (1992) *Politics and Society: An Introduction to Political Sociology* London: Prentice Hall.

Rustin, M. (1994) 'Incomplete modernity: Ulrich Beck's risk society' *Radical Philosophy* vol. 67, pp. 3–11.

Ryan, M.P. (1990) *Women in Public: Between the Banners and the Ballots 1825–1880* Baltimore: Johns Hopkins University Press.

—— (1992) 'Gender and public access: Women's politics in nineteenth century America' in C. Calhoon (ed.) *Habermas and the Public Sphere* Cambridge MA: MIT Press.

Sabatier, P. & Jenkins-Smith, H.C. (eds) (1993) *Policy Change and Learning: An Advocacy Coalition Approach* Boulder CO: Westview Press.

Sarup, M. (1993) *An Introductory Guide to Postmodernism and Poststructuralism* Second Edition London: Harvester Wheatsheaf.

Scharpf, F.W. (1978) 'Interorganizational policy studies: Issues, concepts and perspectives' in K. Hanf & F.W. Scharpf (eds) *Interorganizational Policy Making: Limits to Coordination and Central Control* London: Sage.

Scharpf, F.W., Reissert, B. & Schabel, F. (1978) 'Policy effectiveness and conflict avoidance in intergovernmental policy formation' in K. Hanf & F.W. Scharpf (eds) *Interorganizational Policy Making: Limits to Coordination and Central Control* London: Sage.

Schmidt, V. (2002) *The Futures of European Capitalism* Oxford University Press.

—— (2006) 'Institutionalism 'in C. Hay, M. Lister & D. Marsh (eds) *The State: Theories and Issues* London: Palgrave Macmillan.

Scholte, J.A. (2000) 'Cautionary reflections on Seattle' *Millennium: Journal of International Studies* vol. 29, no. 1, pp. 115–21.

Schuck, P. (1998) 'The re-evaluation of American citizenship' in C. Joppke (ed.) *Challenges to the Nation State: Immigration in Western Europe and the United States* Oxford University Press.

Schumpeter, J. (1943) *Capitalism, Socialism and Democracy* London: Unwin.

Scott, A. (1997) (ed.) *The Limits of Globalization* London: Routledge.

Scott, J. (2001) *Power* Cambridge: Polity.

Scott, J.C. (1998) *Seeing Like a State: How Certain Schemes to Improve the Human Condition have Failed* New Haven: Yale University Press.

Sen, A. (2000) 'Work and rights' *International Labour Review* vol. 139, no. 2, pp. 119–28.

Sennett, R. (1998) *The Corrosion of Character: The Personal Consequences of Work in the New Capitalism* New York: W.W. Norton.

Sheller, M. (2001) *The Mechanisms of Mobility and Liquidity: Re-thinking the Movement in Social Movements* http://www.lancs.ac.uk/fass/sociology/papers/sheller-mechanisms-of-mobility-and-liquidity.pdf. Accessed on 6 August 2009.

Simmel, G. (1896) 'Superiority and subordination as subject-matter of sociology' *American Journal of Sociology* vol. 2, pp. 167–89.

—— (1978) *The Philosophy of Money* London: Routledge.

Simon, R. (1982) *Gramsci's Political Thought: An Introduction* London: Lawrence & Wishart.

Skelcher, C. (2000) 'Changing images of the state: Overloaded, hollowed-out, congested' *Public Policy and Administration* vol. 15, no. 3, pp. 3–19.

Sklair, L. (2001) *The Transnational Capitalist Class* New York: Harvester Wheatsheaf.

Skocpol, T. (1979) *States and Social Revolutions: A Comparative Analysis of France, Russia and China* Cambridge University Press.

—— (1993) *Diminished Democracy: From Membership to Management in American Civil Life* Norman: University of Oklahoma Press.

Smelser, N. (1959) *Social Change and the Industrial Revolution* London: Routledge and Kegan Paul.

—— (1962) *A Theory of Collective Behaviour* New York: Free Press.

Smith, A.D. (1986) *The Ethnic Origins of Nations* Oxford: Blackwell.

—— (1990) 'Towards a global culture' in M. Featherstone (ed.) *Global Culture: Nationalism, Globalization and Modernity* London: Sage.

Smith, M. (1998) *Ecologism* Buckingham: Open University Press.

Smith, M.J. (1999) *The Core Executive in Britain* London: Macmillan.

—— (2006) 'Pluralism' in C. Hay, M. Lister & D. Marsh (eds) *The State: Theories and Issues* London: Palgrave Macmillan.

Snow, D. & Benford, R. (1988) 'Ideology, frame resonance and participant mobilization' in B. Klandermans, H. Kriesi & S. Tarrow (eds) *From Structure to Action: Social Movement Research across Different Cultures* Greenwich CT: JAI Press.

—— (1992) 'Master frames and cycles of protest' in A. Morris & C. Mueller (eds) *Frontiers in Social Movement Theory* New Haven: Yale University Press.

Snow, D., Rocheford, E., Worden, S. & Benford, R. (1986) 'Frame alignment processes, micromobilization and movement participation' *American Sociological Review* vol. 51, no. 4, pp. 464–81.

Snow, D., Zurchner, L. & Ekland-Olson, S. (1980) 'Social networks and social movements' *American Sociological Review* vol. 51, no. 5, pp. 787–801.

Snyder, S.L. & Mitchell, D.T. (2006) *Cultural Locations of Disability* Chicago University Press.

Sørensen, G. (2004) *The Transformation of the State: Beyond the Myth of Retreat* London: Palgrave Macmillan.

—— (2006) 'The transformation of the state' in C. Hay, M. Lister & D. Marsh (eds) *The State: Theories and Issues* London: Palgrave Macmillan.

Soysal, Y. (1994) *Limits of Citizenship* University of Chicago Press.

Steiger, M.B. (2005) *Globalism: Market Ideology Meets Terrorism* Lanham MD: Rowman and Littlefield.

Steinmetz, G. (1999) 'Introduction: Culture and the state' in G. Steinmetz (ed.) *State/Culture: State Formation after the Cultural Turn* Ithaca NY: Cornell University Press.

Stevenson, N. (1997) 'Globalization, national cultures and cultural citizenship' *The Sociological Quarterly* vol. 38, no. 1, pp. 41–66.

Steward, F. (1991) 'Citizens of planet earth' in G. Andrews (ed.) *Citizenship* London: Lawrence and Wishart.

Stewart, P. (2001) 'Complexity theories, social theory and the question of social complexity' *Philosophy of the Social Sciences* vol. 31, no. 3, pp. 323–60.

Strange, S. (1996) *The Retreat of the State: The Diffusion of Power in the World Economy* Cambridge University Press.

Sullivan, R.R. (2000) *Liberalism and Crime: The British Experience* Lanham MD: Lexington Books.

Swyngedouw, E. (1992) 'Territorial organization and the space technology nexus' *Transactions, Institute of British Geographers* vol. 17, pp. 417–33.

Tamás, G.M. (1994) 'A disquisition on civil society' *Social Research* vol. 61, no. 2, pp. 205–22.

Tarrow, S. (1998) *Power in Movement: Social Movements and Contentious Politics* Cambridge University Press.

Tattersall, A. (2005) 'There is power in coalition: A framework for assessing how and when union–community coalitions are effective and enhance union power' *Labour and Industry* vol. 16, no. 2, pp. 97–112.

Taussig, M. (1996) *Shamanism, Colonialism and the Wild Man: A Study in Terror and Healing* Chicago University Press.

Taylor, A. (1997) '"Arm's length but hands on": Mapping the new governance: The Department of National Heritage and cultural politics in Britain' *Public Administration* vol. 75, no. 3, pp. 441–66.

Taylor, G. (2006) 'European employment policy: Governance as regulation' in G.P.E. Walzenbach (ed.) *European Governance: Policy Making Between Politicization and Control* Aldershot: Ashgate.

—— (2008) 'Europe: The double-edged sword of justice? New Labour, trade unions and the politics of Social Europe' in G. Daniels and J. McIlroy (eds) *Trade Unions in a Neo-Liberal World: British Trade Unions under New Labour* London: Routledge.

Taylor, G. & Mathers, A. (2002a) 'The politics of European integration: A European labour movement in the making?' *Capital and Class* no. 77, pp. 37–78.

—— (2002b) 'Social partner or social movement? European integration and trade union renewal in Europe' *Labor Studies Journal* vol. 27, no. 1, pp. 93–108.

—— (2004) 'The European Trade Union Confederation at the crossroads of change? Traversing the variable geometry of European trade unionism' *European Journal of Industrial Relations* vol. 10, no. 3, pp. 267–85.

Therborn, G. (1978) *What Does the Ruling Class Do when it Rules?* London: Verso.

—— (1992) 'Lessons from "corporatist" theorizations' in J. Pekkarinen, M. Pohjola and B. Rowthorn (eds) *Social Corporatism: A Superior Economic System* Oxford: Clarendon Press.

—— (1995) 'Routes to/through modernity' in M. Featherstone, S. Lash & R. Robertson (eds) *Global Modernities* London: Sage.

Tilly, C. (1978) *From Mobilization to Revolution* Reading MA: Addison Wesley.

—— (1984) 'Social movements and national politics' in C. Bright & S. Harding (eds) *Statemaking and Social Movements* Ann Arbor: University of Michigan Press.

Tocqueville, A. de (1945) *Democracy in America* 2 vols New York: Alfred Knopf.

Tormey, S. (2001) *Agnes Heller: Socialism, Autonomy and the Postmodern* Manchester University Press.

Touraine, A. (1971) *The Post-industrial Society: Tomorrow's Social History: Classes, Conflicts and Culture in the Programmed Society* London: Wildwood House.

—— (1981) *The Voice and the Eye: An Analysis of Social Movements* Cambridge University Press.

—— (1997) *What is Democracy?* Boulder CO: Westview Press.

Tremain, S. (2005) (ed.) *Foucault and the Government of Disability* Chicago University Press.

Trimberger, E.K. (1978) *Revolution from Above: Military Bureaucrats and Development in Japan, Egypt, Turkey and Peru* New Brunswick NJ: Transaction Books.

Truman, D.B. (1981) *The Governmental Process: Political Interests and Public Opinion* Westport CT: Greenwood Press.

Turner, B.S. (1986) *Citizenship and Capitalism: The Debate over Reformism* London: Allen & Unwin.

—— (1993) 'Outline of a theory of human rights' in B. Turner (ed.) *Citizenship and Social Theory* London: Sage.

Urry, J. (2000) *Sociology Beyond Societies: Mobilities for the Twenty-First Century* London: Routledge.

—— (2002) 'The global complexities of September 11th' *Theory, Culture and Society* vol. 19, no. 4, pp. 57–69.

—— (2003) *Global Complexity* Cambridge: Polity.

—— (2005) 'The complexity of the global' *Theory, Culture and Society* vol. 22, no. 5, pp. 235–54.

—— (2006) 'Complexity' *Theory, Culture and Society* vol. 23, nos 2–3, pp. 111–17.

Vajda, M. (1988) 'East-Central European perspectives' in J. Keane (ed.) *Civil Society and the State* London: Verso.

Van Krieken, R. (1996) 'Proto-governmentalization and the historical formation of organizational subjectivity' *Economy and Society* vol. 25, no. 2, pp. 195–221.

Van Steenbergen, B. (1994) 'Towards a global ecological citizen' in B. van Steenbergen (ed.) *The Condition of Citizenship* London: Sage.

Veugelers, J.W.P. (1999) 'The challenge for political sociology: The rise of far-right parties in contemporary Western Europe' *Current Sociology* vol. 47, no. 4, pp. 78–100.

Vogel, U. (1991) 'Is citizenship gender specific?' in U. Vogel & M. Mann (eds) *The Frontiers of Citizenship* London: Macmillan.

Wagner, P. (1994) *A Sociology of Modernity: Liberty and Discipline* London: Routledge.

Walby, S. (1990) *Theorizing Patriarchy* Oxford: Blackwell.

—— (1999) 'The new regulatory state: The social powers of the European Union' *British Journal of Sociology* vol. 50, no. 1, pp. 118–40.

Walton, J. & Seddon, D. (1994) *Free Markets and Food Riots: The Politics of Global Adjustment* Oxford: Blackwell.

Walzer, M. (1989) 'Citizenship' in T. Ball, J. Farr & R.L. Hanson (eds) *Political Innovation and Conceptual Change* Cambridge University Press.
—— (1998) 'The idea of civil society: A path to social reconstruction' in E.J. Dionne (ed.) *Community Works: The Revival of Civil Society in America* Washington DC: Brookings Institution Press.
Wanna, J. (1997) 'Managing budgets' in P. Weller, H. Bakvis & R.A.W. Rhodes (eds) *The Hollow Crown: Counterveiling Trends in Core Executives* London: Macmillan.
Wapner, P. (2000) 'The normative promise of nonstate actors: A theoretical account of global civil society' in P. Wapner & L.E.J. Ruiz (eds) *Principled World Politics: The Challenge of Normative International Relations* Lanham MD: Rowman and Littlefield.
Wark, M. (2004) *Hacker Manifesto* Cambridge MA: Harvard University Press.
Waterman, P. (2000) 'Social movements, local places and globalized spaces: Implications for "globalization from below"' in B. Gills (ed.) *Globalization and the Politics of Resistance* London: Palgrave.
Weber, M. (1948) *From Max Weber: Essays in Sociology* London: Routledge.
—— (1978) *Economy and Society* ed. G. Roth & C. Wittich. Los Angeles: University of California Press.
Weeks, J. (1991) *Against Nature: Essays on History, Sexuality and Identity* London and New York: Rivers Oram Press.
Weiss, L. (1998) *The Myth of the Powerless State: Governing the Economy in a Global Era* Cambridge: Polity Press.
White, H. (1995) 'Network switchings and Bayesian forks: Reconstructing the social and behavioural sciences' *Social Research* vol. 62, pp. 1035–63.
White, S. (1991) *Political Theory and Postmodernism* Cambridge University Press.
Wills, J. (2001) 'Community unionism and trade union renewal in the UK: Moving beyond the fragments at last?' *Transactions of the Institute of British Geographers* vol. 26, pp. 465–83.
Wills, J. & Simms, M. (2004) 'Building reciprocal community unionism in the UK' *Capital and Class* no. 82, 59–84.
Wilson, E. (1977) *Women and the Welfare State* London: Tavistock.
Winch, P. (1958) *The Idea of a Social Science and its Relation to Philosophy* London: Routledge and Kegan Paul.
Young, I. (1989) 'Polity and group difference: A critique of the ideal of universal citizenship' *Ethics* vol. 99, pp. 250–74.
—— (1990) *Justice and the Politics of Difference* Princeton University Press.
Zald, M. & McCarthy, J. (1987) *Social Movements in an Organizational Society: Collected Essays* New Brunswick NJ: Transaction Books.
Zisserman-Brodsky, D. (ed.) (2003) *Constructing Ethnopolitics in the Soviet Union: Samizdat, Deprivation and the Rise of Ethnic Nationalism* London: Palgrave.
Žižek, S. (2004) *Organs without Bodies: On Deleuze and Consequences* London: Routledge.

Index